Perverts by Official Order: The Campaign Against Homosexuals by the United States Navy

Other books by Lawrence R. Murphy

Indian Agent in New Mexico (Santa Fe, 1967)
Out in God's Country: A History of Colfax County, New Mexico
 (Springer, N.M., 1969)
Philmont: A History of New Mexico's Cimarron Country
 (Albuquerque, 1972)
Frontier Crusader: William F. M. Arny (Tucson, 1973)
The Slave Narratives of Texas (with Ron C. Tyler) (Austin, 1974)
Anti-Slavery in the Southwest (El Paso, 1978)
The World of John Muir (with Dan Collins) (Stockton, 1981)
Lucien Bonaparte Maxwell: The Napoleon of the Southwest
 (Norman, OK, 1983)
The American University in Cairo: 1919-1987 (Cairo, Egypt,
 1987)

Perverts by
Official Order:
The Campaign Against
Homosexuals
by the
United States Navy

Lawrence R. Murphy

The Haworth Press
New York • London

Perverts by Official Order: The Campaign Against Homosexuals by the United States Navy is monographic supplement #1 to *Journal of Homosexuality*. It is not supplied as part of the subscription to the journal, but is available at an additional charge.

The Haworth Press, Inc., 12 West 32 Street, New York, NY 10001
EUROSPAN/Haworth, 3 Henrietta Street, London WC2E 8LU England

Library of Congress Cataloging-in-Publication Data

Murphy, Lawrence R., 1942-
    Perverts by official order.

    Bibliography: p.
    Includes index.
    1. United States. Navy—Gays. 2. Trials (Sodomy)—Rhode Island—Newport—History.
3. Gays—United States—History—20th century. 4. Newport (R.I.)—History. I. Title.
VB32.4.G38M87   1988b   359'.008806642   87-33914
ISBN 0-86656-708-9

FOR RUSSELL

without whose love, support, and assistance
this book could not have been completed

CONTENTS

ILLUSTRATIONS

Lawrence R. Murphy
1942-1987

A Personal Message

Unhappily, I have been asked to write a personal message for *Perverts By Official Order: The Campaign Against Homosexuals by the United States Navy*. I wish I did not have to do so. I have been associated with this book from the beginning. I saw the first cursory inquiry into this long-forgotten scandal. I assisted with the research, witnessed the writing, and finally helped ready the manuscript for publication.

The manuscript was finished in 1983, but Larry could not find a publisher willing or able to accept it. Finally in 1986, The Haworth Press, and its imprint, Harrington Park Press, directed by publisher Bill Cohen, accepted the work for publication. It was and is a courageous act.

What emerges from this book is a sordid story. Not sordid because of the vivid descriptions of men together, nor the lifestyles of many in this book, it is sordid because of the actions of the United States Government. Here is the whole range of civil rights violations: mail covers and interceptions, eavesdropping, wiretapping, illegal searches and seizures, entrapment, and "third degree" coercion. Added to this must be the duplicity of United States governmental officials at the highest levels, including a future President of the United States. However, worst of all was the needless and cruel destruction of many lives. If no one remembers what happened in Newport in 1919 it could happen again.

Larry did not live to see the final act of publication. On September 26, 1987, a condition he had since his youth ended his life. After thirteen glorious and happy years our life together was over. In those first dark hours, days, and weeks I came to the realization that this book was his testament for freedom; his personal statement that all people must be free to live without shame or fear and that gays must not be denied their rights. It is in this spirit that I hope the book will be read.

Russell Len Griffin

Preface

Persecution is as old as civilization itself. People have been attacked, discriminated against, imprisoned and even killed by other humans because of religion, race, sex, ethnic background, or political belief. Toleration may be the exception rather than the rule. Even more grievous, nearly every government has been guilty of oppressing or at least tolerating the maltreatment of some group of its citizens. The powers of police, armies, courts, and civil officials have all too often been utilized to rid society of unwanted persons or to assure their relegation to second-class status.

Subjective considerations arise because what is clearly victimization to some people (especially those being attacked) becomes legitimate law enforcement or societal purification to others. The leaders of colonial America had no difficulty justifying the execution of Quakers, Catholics, or alleged "witches" for unacceptable beliefs or activities. Some Nazi Germans doubtless believed that the extermination of Jews, Gypsies, or homosexuals was necessary to preserve and strengthen their society. In the American West, the destruction of Native Americans was defended as progressive and civilizing. Even today, the incarceration or execution of individuals with unpopular political, religious, or social beliefs finds supporters in many nations of the world.

Only recently has the widespread persecution of individuals because of their personal sexual preference been openly discussed. For too long, gays considered themselves as the guilty and sometimes even justified persecution as morally or socially desirable. Few homosexuals were sufficiently self-confident or assertive to defend their sexual orientation and to denounce their persecutors' malevolence. Reticence has slowly diminished as gays have developed more positive self-images, become proud of themselves and their communities, and begun to explore their history. Gay "roots" differ from those of blacks, Native Americans, or Jews, but discovering and understanding them is no less important in enhancing gay identity and teaching about their heritage.

1

The United States government's systematic entrapment of homosexuals after World War I constitutes a significant but largely forgotten chapter in the long story of persecution. The government employed sailors to entrap military men and civilians, employing deceit and feigning sexual endearment to collect evidence. Sailors charged with being gay faced months of solitary confinement and trials in which they were denied fundamental constitutional rights. Many were convicted on the flimsiest circumstantial evidence. Only the refusal of civilian judges and juries to accept spurious government testimony saved dozens of non-sailors from similar fates. Even for them, notoriety stemming from the scandal undoubtedly ruined the lives of numerous victims. When publicity about the navy's anti-gay crusade threatened the careers of senior officials, especially Franklin Delano Roosevelt, the government manipulated the military "justice" system to spare its leaders and embarrass its critics. Never was adequate punishment meted out to those who perpetrated the campaign. To this day the stain of court-martial, a prison record, and dishonorable discharges remains on the records of the victims of government persecution.

The story of these injustices — no less than descriptions of German concentration camps, the Holy Inquisition, or the torture of political prisoners — is ugly. Descriptions of sexual encounters between federal detectives and their victims are vivid and occasionally sordid. Gays may find them strikingly familiar. No less disturbing are the heart-rending pleas for mercy by sailors about to have their lives devastated by their own government or of men hauled before court and forced to describe their most intimate sexual activities. No one can enjoy discovering how men lied to obtain evidence or how their detective work led them to open mail, read telegrams, or eavesdrop on telephone calls. These are, however, accurate portrayals of what was said and done over half a century ago; every quotation comes from a contemporary source. Such revelations can be valuable in strengthening our determination to see that we are never again the target for such treatment, and in stimulating vigilance against those who would like to see persecution revived.

Some explanation regarding the use of the terms "homosexual" and "gay" is required. Like such other historians as John Boswell and Johnathan Katz, I recognize that the terms such as these carry contemporary connotations that may not be applicable to the past — even to a period less than a century distant from our own. None of the sailors and civilians whom I have characterized as "gay" would have used that term; few would have termed themselves as "homosexuals." That term itself occurs only occasionally in contemporary records, and then the court stenographer was so unfamiliar with it that the spelling "homosectual" appears. Nevertheless, I have, for the contemporary reader, tended to use the terms "gay" and "homosexual" interchangeably to refer to those individuals whose sexual preferences were allegedly directed toward other men. In some cases, charges of physical sexual relations may have been untrue, in which case George Chauncey, Jr.'s term "homosocial" could be more appropriate. Application of the term to a particular individual does not, therefore, carry the necessary implication of a self-conscious same-sex orientation implied by today's use of the term "gay," or prove that the individual ever engaged in physical sexual activities with other men as implied by application of the word "homosexual."

In the course of completing this study, I have accumulated the usual debts of a researcher. The National Archives and Library of Congress helped locate material and arrange for duplication. Despite an initial defensive attitude toward Franklin Roosevelt and unhelpful correspondence, the staff of the Roosevelt Library at Hyde Park ultimately proved helpful during a week-long visit to that depository. Evelyn Cherpak at the Naval Historical Collection, Naval War College, Newport, and Stanley Kalkus, Naval Historical Center, Washington, were extremely helpful, although not wholly aware of the focus of my research. Library staffs at the University of the Pacific, Central Michigan University, and Wayne State University rendered important assistance.

Many individuals and organizations in Rhode Island aided me by mail and during a research trip there. Garrett Byrnes of the *Providence Journal* shared his knowledge. Librarians and staff at the Rhode Island Historical Society, Providence, and the Newport Historical Society did all they could to locate pertinent materials, as did the Episcopal Diocese of Rhode Island. In Newport, I benefited from tours or historical discussions at the Y.M.C.A., Emmanuel Church, Trinity Episcopal Church, the Newport Red Cross, and the Newport County Clerk's office. Newport gays frequenting 28 Prospect Hill reflected changes over sixty years. Elsewhere, assistance came from the Rev. John F. Maher, Jr. of St. Mary's Episcopal Church, Warwick (Elverson P.O.), Pennsylvania, the English Speaking Union in New York, the Lehigh University Library, the University of Michigan Library, the Detroit Public Library, and the Archives of the Episcopal Church in Austin, Texas.

Growing interest in gay history has stimulated helpful, informal networking among researchers and writers. I am grateful for the advice, encouragement, and inspiration of Alan Berube, whose study of gay life during World War II is warmly anticipated, and Eric Garber of the San Francisco Gay and Lesbian History Project as well as former colleagues A. G. Belles and Rick Hargrove from Western Illinois University. Many of the ideas propounded in this study had their origins in fruitful discussions and correspondence with Gregory Sprague, whose pioneering study of the growth and development of gay urban communities is a landmark of insight and research. His untimely death early in 1987 deprived the academic world of a promising young scholar and many gay historians (myself included) of a friend and colleague. Roger Austen shared his insights into the scandal at an early stage in my research; his death preceded completion of a fictionalized account of the Newport scandal. My own insight into American gay history has been enriched by Barry Adam, John D'Emilio, George Chauncey, Jr., and Walter Williams and by the pioneering collections and bibliographical work of Johnathan Katz.

Journal editors and book publishers have been less than enthusiastic about publishing gay historical studies, especially those like this that include explicit sexual references and may seem to have limited market appeal. I am particularly grateful to Ray Browne and Russel Nye whose acceptance of an essay on the Newport scandal for the *Journal of American Culture* encouraged me to persevere in completing and publishing this longer study; the article subsequently received the Carl Bode award from the American Culture Association. Senior editor John De Cecco and publisher Bill Cohen from The Haworth Press not only accepted the risk inherent in publishing a book of this kind, but assisted me in preparing the manuscript for publication.

Completion of this project has been facilitated by my appointment as a professor and dean at Wayne State University. President David W. Adamany has created an atmosphere that encourages scholarly work by faculty and administrators and study in areas that might seem controversial at less enlightened institutions.

Above all I am thankful to Russell Griffin, who over the past thirteen years has patiently provided encouragement, helped me understand myself, and at every stage has been a full partner in this project.

Lawrence R. Murphy

CHAPTER 1

"Half the World Is Queer"

I

Few New England towns rival the attractiveness of Newport, Rhode Island. Founded in 1639 on an island in Narragansett Bay, the town developed a prosperous fishing industry, cosmopolitan populace, and cultural sophistication that dominated the region until after the American Revolution. Its public buildings reflected the latest British styles; streets were paved long before those in most other cities; and wealthy citizens maintained a luxurious lifestyle which contrasted with New England's prevailing asceticism. Newport was also famed for its religious tolerance. In addition to the dominant Baptist church, it welcomed Episcopal, Congregational, Quaker, and Moravian churches, besides a Jewish synagogue.

Industrialization during the nineteenth century largely bypassed Newport in favor of such inland places as Fall River or Providence. Following the Civil War, however, the nation's wealthy discovered the town's quiet, unspoiled beauty. "Newport was the most palatial, extravagant, and expensive summer resort the world had seen since the days of the Roman Empire," exclaims one state historian with pardonable exaggeration. Led by New Yorker Samuel Ward McAllister, such Eastern moguls as the Astors, Vanderbilts, and Van Rensselaers erected fabulous mansions along Belleview Avenue, Ochre Point Road, and Ocean Drive. From late spring through early fall, the grandest, most elegant Americans enjoyed Newport's cool, balmy weather, its magnificent ocean views, and each other's company. Charming lawn parties, intimate teas, elegant banquets, cotillions, weddings, musicales, and picnics followed endlessly one after another. By the beginning of the twentieth century, Newport had earned a reputation as one of the United States' premier showplaces, the epitome of everything that made a Christian and capitalist society great.[1]

The U.S. Navy also discovered Newport. Expansion of American naval power necessitated added training facilities. Newport seemed an ideal location for its available land, and for the genteel atmosphere it provided to high ranking officers. The establishment of a major base became certain in late August of 1882 when the town transferred title to Coasters Harbor Island on its west edge to the federal government. The following June the Naval Training Station opened. After 1884 Newport was the home of the Naval War College, that provided advanced training to supplement what was taught at the Annapolis Naval Academy.[2]

As the principal East Coast training facility for young men preparing for service aboard the nation's coal-powered fleet, the Training Station became the foremost "school for tars." "From all over the country they arrive by the dozens daily," a 1911 article reported, "chiefly from the smaller towns: sons and grandsons of farmers, though with a sprinkling of city boys." Trainees began the day at 5 a.m. with cocoa and a shower, followed by a clean-up, breakfast, drill, and classes in signalling, compass use, and numerous specialized seafaring trades. Ample opportunity for shore liberty was built into the schedule. "In white uniforms, or for a Sunday afternoon in their 'blues,'" a reporter observed, "they swarm old Newport's streets." Most walked in pairs to a show or the beach. "'My buddie,'" noted the article, "one calls the other."[3] The size of the station increased slowly until, by 1917, 2,000 sailors could be accommodated.

II

Mobilization preceding American entry into World War I dramatically increased the military presence at Newport. The number of sailors expanded almost overnight to 25,000. Apprentice seamen, yeomen, firemen, and medical corpsmen lived on Coasters Harbor Island in temporary frame barracks sleeping 80 men each. At nearby Cloyne Field, naval reserve forces put up in similar, hastily constructed buildings. Sufficient housing was never available, however, so many sailors rented quarters in Newport. Growth at Fort Adams, southwest of the city, and at other small army installations nearby further added to Newport's military importance.[4]

The town accommodated remarkably well to the sudden influx.

Churches established special social, educational, cultural, and religious programs for servicemen. The Rev. C. W. Forster's Emmanuel Church, for example, focused its energies on the needs of army men from nearby Fort Adams; the parish hall of the United Congregational Church opened to sailors. Touro Synagogue's activities appealed mostly to Jewish youngsters, although anyone was welcome. The Catholic parish designed programs for "men of their own faith, of every faith, and [of] no faith. . . ." Voluntary organizations such as the Art Association also welcomed men in uniform. The War Camp Community Service opened a large building on Mill Street; and by the fall of 1918 the Red Cross field department opened an office on Church Street.[5]

Of all the Newport organizations serving sailors and soldiers, the Army and Navy Y.M.C.A. had the most impressive edifice. Located on Washington Square adjacent to the historic county courthouse, the handsome, five-storied building had been erected in 1911 with a $315,000 gift from Mrs. Thomas Emery of Cincinnati. The first floor featured a large, comfortably-furnished lobby where men relaxed, wrote letters, viewed films, attended concerts, or participated in ecumenical religious services. Nearby were a billiard room, restaurant, barber shop, a large gymnasium, locker room, and swimming pool. Upstairs, volunteers taught subjects of interest to servicemen. One man, for example, gave French lessons to young men headed for Europe. Other floors contained small, simple rooms which could be rented by the night. The Y.M.C.A. proved extremely popular among the young men assigned to Newport; during one day alone, 5,753 soldiers and sailors crossed its thresholds.[6]

Navy activities frequently contributed to the Newport social scene. Wealthy visitors attended exhibition drills at the Training Station or accepted luncheon invitations to the home of Commander Edward H. Campbell. Dignitaries visiting Newport could expect to be feted by the town's leading citizens. When Assistant Secretary of the Navy Franklin Delano Roosevelt visited during the summer of 1919, for instance, Captain Campbell showed him about town in company with Rhode Island Governor R. Livingston Beeckman.[7] In addition, numerous families took soldiers or sailors into their homes, and many residents invited boys to join them for a Sunday dinner or an evening of informal entertainment. "The good people of Newport," concluded the chaplain at the Station, "have practically without exception, and in a generous and hospitable manner, not only opened their homes to our men but have provided common centers where they can meet and be entertained."[8]

The arrival of so many sailors inevitably tested Newport's traditional open-mindedness. At the beginning of the war, liquor became so readily available that many youngsters fresh from home and farm learned to drink in Newport. The use of drugs, including cocaine, also increased, and men seeking female company found that a night — or at least a few hours — could readily be purchased. Investigators sent to the town discovered an "increasing number of houses of ill-fame, openly conducted illegal liquor traffic, drug selling, and the like. . . ."[9]

Rhode Islanders even seemed tolerant of men who dressed as women or otherwise displayed feminine characteristics. Among the many dramatic performances in Newport, the most popular featured sailors in female roles. "It is a corker," exclaimed Admiral William H. Sims after seeing a performance of "Jack and the Beanstalk." "I have never in my life seen a prettier 'girl' than 'Princess Mary.' She is the daintiest little thing I ever laid eyes on." A reviewer from the *Providence Journal* agreed. "She had the sweetest little face and tender, trusting blue eyes and that delightful elusive smile," he noted after seeing a Providence performance. "Oh, any man Jack would have climbed the beanstalk after such as she."[10]

Such openness collided, however, with the prudishness of Josephus Daniels, the North Carolina journalist whom President Woodrow Wilson named to head the Navy Department. "The authorities are not giving a wholesome atmosphere for young men in training for the navy," he observed in condemning Newport's "bad" conditions in 1917, ". . . failure of any community to safeguard young men who are to fight the nation's battles," he added, "cannot be tolerated." Late in June, Daniels wrote Governor Beeckman to demand that "the situation be immediately improved." News of immorality at Newport also came to the attention of *Providence Journal* editor John R. Rathom who instigated his own investigation. As reported to Daniels, he not only proved the secretary's charges correct but demonstrated "that house of prostitution of the lowest type have been maintained under the patronage of city officials. . . ." Police had been ordered "to keep visitors in orderly line," and houses had occasionally been closed "in order that others in which certain officials have been interested should become more prosperous." "The people of Rhode Island,"

Rathom concluded, "owe you a debt of gratitude for your timely exposure."[11]

Although immorality received little publicity, reports such as these stimulated prompt action. In March of 1918, the navy exercised expanded wartime powers to prohibit the sale or possession of alcohol within five miles of the station. "The barrooms are closed," lamented a local sailors' paper; "nothing may come in, and prohibition is master."[12] Soon after, a new police chief, John S. Tobin, closed down all the houses of prostitution and expelled their inmates. The only subsequent trouble occurred in late in April of 1919 when several hundred marines attempting to rescue a colleague who had been arrested created what the press termed "a small Bolshevist riot." Ultimately nine servicemen and five police were left "in a more or less battered condition."[13]

Subsequent complaints were limited to sailors who lamented the difficulty of meeting Newport girls. "We have long since learned," Frederick E. Corey announced in a letter to the *Providence Journal*, "that the girls of Newport not only ignored and kept clear of soldiers but sailors as well. . . ." As an experiment, he and five companions had gone to a Thames Street dance hall, approached a girl after each dance, and asked for the next. "We were met with the reply that she was engaged for the next dance," he complained, "when in reality she was not." Furthermore, the "main purpose" of local businessmen seemed to be "profiting by us or soaking us for anything we choose to buy."

A "Newport girl" defended the town's treatment of sailors. "When you consider the number of people who were able to give their time and their homes up to the recreation and entertainment of these boys and the number of boys that came to Newport," she argued, ". . . some could have been left out." She urged Corey and his friends to attend one of the dances regularly scheduled at St. Mary's Hall, the Community House, the Y.M.C.A., or the Knights of Columbus Hall. Many of the businessmen he complained of, she added, were not Newporters at all, but people "from out of town" whose only goal was "to take money." She hoped that before the sailors left the service they would discover the truth about Newport and "leave . . . with a better feeling."[14]

Town officials were equally determined to maintain Newport's good name. "My orders," explained Mayor Jeremiah P. Mahoney, "were that the city should be kept clean, and I prided myself that Newport was as clean as any city in the United States — north, east, south or west." No "disorderly houses" operated, and an army officer had praised Newport as the "cleanest city in the vicinity of one of the training camps." The town's reputation, concluded Police Chief Tobin, was as "good as any in America."[15]

III

Such was not, however, the opinion of Chief Machinist's Mate Ervin Arnold. A fourteen-year navy veteran, Arnold arrived at the Training Station in February 1919 from San Francisco. He suffered from such severe rheumatism that instead of taking up duties, doctors ordered him to Ward B of the Naval Training Station Hospital for treatment.

There Arnold revealed an intense hatred of homosexuals. Exactly how his antipathy developed or what motivated him remains a mystery. He traced his interest in the subject to nine years as a Connecticut state detective before entering the military. He had heard that there were homosexuals at Newport while in San Francisco. More important, Arnold claimed the ability to identify so-called perverts by appearance. Such characteristics as "feminine speech," a "peculiar" walk, or the use of cosmetics enabled him to tell if a person were "a degenerate of a nameless type." "I can take you up on Riverside Drive [in New York City] at night," he later told an investigating panel, "and show them [homosexuals] to you and if you follow them up nine times out of ten you will find it is true." "There are some now," he once told the Newport police chief. "I can tell them a mile off. . . . They are laying for the sailors coming up from the beach." During a visit with Episcopal Bishop James D. Perry, he claimed the power to identify a man as gay by "meeting . . . [him] on the street and by his bearing."[16]

This unique talent enabled Arnold to uncover a world of sex and drugs at Newport that naval officials or local residents could never have imagined. Beginning about February 20, 1919, and continuing through mid-March, sailors revealed graphic details about their sexual activities, their girlish nicknames, the preference of several for women's clothes, rouge, and powder, and orgiastic parties they held, and their use of alcohol and cocaine. Within a few minutes after each conversation, Arnold prepared notes for later reference.

According to these reports, Arnold first sensed that many sailors were gay as he observed a patient named Samuel Rogers use powder puffs, eyebrow and lip pencils, and perfumed powders. A week later another patient, Thomas Brunelle, told him about a "gang of perverts" numbering fifteen to twenty. Rogers, he learned, was known as a "pogue," who in Arnold's language, loved to be "screwed in the rectum." Later Rogers himself confessed to being "in the business because he liked it." What did that mean? asked Arnold. "By going to bed, going to bed with a man who had a large penis and was very passionate, and could give him all he wanted," replied the sailor.

In this and subsequent conversations with Arnold, Brunelle provided a directory of acquaintances who enjoyed sex with other men. Harrison Rideout, commonly called "Galli Gurci," was a "two-way artist," who "could be screwed in the rectum and also took it in the mouth." He took cocaine, as did Fred Hoage (better known as "Theda Bara") and John Gianelloni ("Ruth"), both "cocksuckers." A hospitalized baker, Albert Kirk, was another "two-way artist." Brunelle referred to Billy Hughes (called "Salome") as his wife, claimed he was "screwing him" nearly every night, and boasted that Billy gave him money whenever he needed any. Frank Dye, whom everyone knew as "Speedy," had a reputation as a "hard man." Arnold was told that a man he fellated felt as though someone was "draw[ing] his brains down through his penis." Jay Goldstein, "Beckie" to friends, was "still a harder one" who had "a nice chin to rest a pair of balls on."

Not all those whom Arnold claimed to have discovered were sailors. Arnold Reed, a former hospital apprentice who now worked in a Providence drug store, was a "cocksucker and cocaine fiend." So was John "Ella" Temple, who had moved to Massachusetts after leaving the navy. Reportedly, the "wildest of the bunch," he often kept a room at the Y.M.C.A. and celebrated his discharge by fellating fifteen or twenty recruits in a single night.

Among other allegedly gay civilians were a waiter at the Tokio Restaurant, a librarian from the navy Torpedo Station, several older men who "hung out" at the Newport Art Association, and a salesman from Providence who spent weekends with Newport friends. But no place harbored more immoral men, Arnold learned, than the Army and Navy Y.M.C.A. The black named Gus who ran the lunch counter there dispensed cocaine; the "short, chicken-breasted nigger" operating the elevator provided liquor and directed "business" to "girls' rooms." Especially infamous, however, were volunteer Arthur Green and, as Arnold listed him, "Samuel Neal Kent, Reverend." Both were "cocksucker[s]" who "would take the boys off and give them good times in their rooms."

The more Arnold heard, the more determined he became to dig up every tidbit of titillating gossip. He heard about a room at 15 Whitfield Court where two men kept corsets, dresses, gowns, women's shoes, vaseline, cosmetics, and incriminating photographs of one another. Gatherings there often included "booze" and cocaine; frequently they became "rough houses." Sometimes "a party would go in the bathroom to get sucked off . . . while the other party would be using the bed." "Beckie" Goldstein was famous for "sixty-nine" parties in which pairs of men ministered to one another. After one such episode, three different men boasted of having had sex with him the same night. Another party at the end of February honored a female impersonator appearing at the opera house. Several men promised Arnold liquor, cocaine, and a good time if he attended a party on Whitfield Court. Next morning Brunelle admitted to engaging in sex with two of the others in the bathroom and characterized the place as "the rottenest joint of its kind that he had ever seen or heard of." Rogers portrayed the event as a "beautiful time."

Men often gathered in John Gianelloni's apartment on Golden Hill Street. One party in early March included a crowd from the U.S.S. *Baltimore*. By the time Rogers arrived, "Beckie" Goldstein and George Richard were in full drag of ball gowns, ladies' lingerie, and wigs; much singing and dancing followed. "Every once in a while," Rogers told Arnold, "'Beckie' would go out of the room with a fellow and then they would come back . . . , some buttoning up their pants." Next day, it was reported he "had eight that night." One man from the *Baltimore* became so drunk that "cocksuckers . . . put him in the street and rolled him of all the money he had." So much furniture had been broken that Gianelloni had been afraid to face his landlord for several days.

Those in the group who "solicited trade" offered to pay sailors who professed to be heterosexual for the privilege of enjoying their genitals. Several spent nearly every evening in the lobby of the Y.M.C.A. openly proclaiming their interests. A few rented rooms upstairs were "customers" could be entertained. Others enhanced their meager navy pay by collecting money from those with whom they had sex. "They published the fact that they were prostitutes," reported one informant, adding that these men's talk was "cheaper

. . . than you would hear in a red light district.'' Boys asked why they engaged in such activities frequently answered: "us girls need our pennies,'' playing on the similarity of the words "penny'' and "penis.'' One night Arnold watched Goldstein strike up conversations with several men; his hand moved suggestively across one sailor's pants, and soon the pair headed for a room. Not surprisingly, one man concluded from such observations that "half the world is queer, and the other half trade.''[17]

IV

By early March Arnold's collection of gossip had been transformed into a major sleuthing effort. The nucleus of what became a squad of sailor "operators,'' began to help keep track of alleged gays. When Samuel Rogers announced that he had a date to go to Providence with a Chief Gunner's Mate, for example, Arnold's team went into operation. "On March 5, 1919,'' he noted, "Rogers checked out on liberty at 4:15 p.m., I having instructed Charles Zipf and [Gregory] Cunningham to watch out at the back of the hospital to see Chief Brugs appear with a motorcycle.'' Arnold requested Dr. Erastus M. Hudson, a thirty-three-year-old physician on the hospital staff, to "go out and take a good look at the men.'' Hudson observed as Arnold watched from the galley door. Zipf claimed to have read the chief's lips as he asked Rogers: "Are you all set for a good time?'' "Yes,'' the sailor nodded as the two sped off. When Rogers returned eight hours late on Monday morning, he reportedly told Arnold that they had gone to the Majestic Theatre in Providence, eaten supper together, and afterward found a room where they had "intercourse . . . a number of times.'' "He certainly gave . . . [me] a good time,'' the sailor boasted, "rolling his eyes in lady fashion.'' Later he added that the sensation had been "wonderful,'' for his partner had a "wonderful tool and was a wonderful man at the game.'' How many times did the chief do it to him that night'' asked Arnold. "As many times as he could get a hard on,'' came the reply.[18]

Arnold and his assistants also initiated nightly forays to the Army and Navy Y.M.C.A. to observe suspects. March 4, for example, nine men ate together in the dining room before they moved to the lobby to begin "soliciting trade.'' "I was solicited at different times by Dye and Goldstein,'' noted Arnold, without revealing what his response had been. Two nights later, nearly the same group appeared. Next evening, Dye was missing. Arnold learned the others considered him "too dirty a bitch' to hang out" with. Later that night Harrison Rideout (who presumed that Arnold shared his sexual orientation) asked whether a chief pharmacist's mate Arnold had been talking to was "any good." Arnold replied evasively that "he was a good sport," at which point Rideout pulled a tube of vaseline from his coat and announced: "we girls are ready for business."[19]

Exactly when and how Arnold first informed his superiors of what his sleuthing had uncovered is uncertain. An investigating committee later concluded that he reported his findings to Dr. E. M. Hudson as early as February 27.[20] By March 5 Hudson had begun participating in Arnold's observations; the beginning of the following week, Arnold and Hudson passed information to Ensign Leo Isaacson, Aide for Information in the Second Naval District. Isaacson recognized that "conditions affecting the morale of the men were not what they should be" and reported his concerns to Second District Commander Admiral Oman. Since his command was about to be incorporated into Boston's First District, however, Oman ordered Isaacson to see its commander, Admiral Spencer S. Wood. Wood concluded that "a thorough investigation" was justified and ordered that Arnold's charges be brought to the attention of the Secretary of the Navy.[21]

The case moved rapidly ahead. Isaacson arrived in Washington Monday the 11th of March and proceeded immediately to the Navy Department, where an appointment had been arranged with Secretary of the Navy Daniels. Some sailors admitted to having engaged in immoral practices, he had concluded from Arnold's observations, and "bad conditions" appeared to exist among a certain "clique of men" in Newport. He suspected that similar homosexual activities had occurred in Providence, Fall River, and elsewhere.

Coincidentally, the commander of the Newport Training Station, Captain Edward H. Campbell, had come to the capital on the same train as Isaacson and was waiting outside Daniels' office. The secretary summoned in Campbell, informed him of what he had been told, ordered him to rectify conditions, and gave him "any authority necessary" to conduct "a thorough housecleaning." As a first step Admiral Wood should convene a Court of Inquiry.[22]

Four days later Wood created a court headed by Lt. Commander Murphy J. Foster and including Lt. Commander Nelson W. Hibbs and Dr. Hudson, hardly a disinterested party by this time. Collecting and presenting evidence would be the task of Judge Advocate William H. Drury, Wood's Aide for Information. Time being critical, Wood ordered the inquiry to convene the following Tuesday, March 18, or as soon after as possible. Its charge: inquire "into the use of cocaine and other drugs, and immoral conditions believed to exist to some extent among Naval personnel and others in and around Newport." A "full statement of the facts" was needed as well as recommendations for further proceedings or ways to "better any conditions." Captain Campbell received notice of the forthcoming hearing and instructions to provide quarters and clerical assistance.[23]

The Foster Court of Inquiry convened at 10:00 a.m. the morning of March 19, 1919. No transcript exists, and none was probably prepared, even though a stenographer was present for the afternoon session. Presumably the principal witness was Arnold, although others could also have testified. The session lasted till 11:30 the first morning and continued over three hours that afternoon. No hearings occurred Wednesday, but after an hour and a half meeting Thursday morning, Foster and his associates drafted their report.[24]

The officers found the evidence less than fully convincing. It was "meager in quantity," had been collected by "inexperienced investigators . . . handicapped by insufficient authority and jurisdiction," and was largely based on hearsay. The officers concluded that insufficient evidence existed to convict anyone or, at least, to convict them of crimes as grave as might be possible after fuller investigation. Civilians as well as navy personnel were involved. The court lacked the power to "collect the evidence needed in order to effect the results demanded by the best interests of the service." It recommended, therefore, that the government devote "any expense and time necessary" to conducting a "most thorough and searching investigation. . . . made by a corps of highly experienced investigators." Exactly who would direct such an inquiry seemed uncertain; choices included dissolving this court and turning the investigation over to some other body, adjourning it temporarily "pending the collection of further and more conclusive evidence," or granting it the needed authority and facilities to investigate.[25]

What occurred immediately after the inquiry adjourned later generated major controversy. Foster and Hibbs presented the court's report to Admiral Wood the next day, March 21. Apparently, because civilians were involved, he preferred that the investigation be turned over to the Department of Justice. The next day Hibbs met with Judge Advocate General Clark. He expressed "surprise and dissatisfaction," since similar reports had been received from the large naval training stations at Norfolk, Virginia, and Great Lakes, Illinois. "My God," he exclaimed, "Now it's Newport." Because of the "far-reaching possibilities of the matter," Clark favored bringing the court's recommendations before the Assistant Secretary of the Navy (acting as Secretary during Daniels' absence from Washington), Franklin Delano Roosevelt. In advance of the meeting, Clark and Hibbs visited the Bureau of Navigation where Commander Albert Mayo helped draft a letter for Roosevelt's approval.[26]

Prior to his departure for Europe, Daniels had informed Roosevelt of his discussion with Isaacson and Campbell, characterized conditions in Newport as "serious," and asked him to "keep in touch with the situation." Thus when he received the draft letter to Attorney General A. Mitchell Palmer, Roosevelt signed it immediately and ordered it transmitted to the Justice Department. "Through the restricted investigation" already undertaken by local authorities, the letter began, the Navy Department had become convinced that "conditions of vice and depravity" existed in Newport. "A most searching and rigid investigation" was needed to prosecute and clean "out those people responsible for it." Local naval officers could identify army, navy, and marine corps personnel as well as civilians engaged in drug trafficking and "fostering dens where . . . perverted practices are carried on." Jurisdictional restrictions and participation by civilians limited the navy's ability to "handle the situation." "The combination" extended to Providence, New York, and Boston, so state authorities were constrained in what they could do. "Eager for the protection of . . . young men from such contaminating influences," Roosevelt asked Palmer to put his "most skilled investigators at work with a view of ultimately cleaning the whole matter up." Needed assistance would be provided by Admiral Wood in Boston or Captain Campbell at Newport.[27]

Roosevelt's request reached Palmer at a moment when the Justice Department was embarked on a crusade it deemed infinitely more important than pursuing homosexuals. A few months earlier, Palmer had launched a major effort to rid the United States of leftist influences. The following February "Red Scare" raids throughout the country resulted in the arrest of hundreds of American citizens and immigrants on charges of political subversion.[28]

Palmer's campaign against reds left so few resources that the kind of extensive probe Roosevelt requested never occurred. Within a few days after receiving the Acting Secretary's letter, Palmer ordered a lone investigator, John J. Daly, to Newport. He met with Campbell and interviewed the town's mayor, police chief, and a probation officer. Everyone seemed cooperative until he met Hudson and Arnold. "Lieut. Hudson," Daly recalled, "seemed to have suspicions that there was, or would be a leak." Whereas Arnold claimed to have evidence against eight individuals, charges against only two sailors had any apparent basis in fact. The evidence Daly saw was "insufficient, considerably exaggerated, and largely from hearsay." Arnold and Hudson withheld evidence from Daly on grounds that only the Judge Advocate for the Foster Court, Ensign Drury, could release it. Conferences with the U.S. District Attorney and Justice Department officials produced a consensus that the "whole matter was one for the Navy Department to handle," whereupon Daly's brief, superficial investigation ended.[29]

What no one at the time realized was that during the very weeks while these official activities had been underway, two members of the Foster Court of Inquiry—Dr. Hudson and Ensign Drury—were cooperating with Captain Campbell to initiate their own investigation. The methods these men utilized in endeavoring to "clean up Newport" ultimately led to the arrest of more than a dozen sailors, two trials for an accused civilian, and the emergence of a major national scandal which included not only the participants themselves but ultimately Secretary Daniels and Assistant Secretary Roosevelt as well.

Newport, Rhode Island, by World War I, the most luxurious resort town in America.
Credit: Author's collection.

The Newport Army and Navy Y.M.C.A. Built in 1911, it became the favorite gathering place for Newport sailors during World War I.
Credit: *Newport Recruit*, U.S. Naval Historical Center.

The Breakers: The Vanderbilt "summer cottage" at Newport.
Credit: Photo by the author.

Dressing Up at Newport. Sailors frequently dressed as "girls" to perform plays such as "Pinafore," the cast of which is shown here. Senior Navy Officials saw no harm in such activities, but others suspected that cross-dressing sailors were homosexual. Credit: *Newport Recruit*, U.S. Naval Historical Center.

CHAPTER 2

Cleaning Up the Navy

Despite the failure of government officials to pursue gays in Newport, in mid-March of 1919 Chief Machinist's Mate Ervin Arnold expanded his own investigation. Evidence collected during the next month seemed to demonstrate the truth of earlier suspicions, resulting in more than a dozen arrests from the Newport Naval Training Station. Ultimately, the extension of the search to civilians, the methods used to entrap suspects, and the approval of the investigation by senior government officials precipitated the most important homosexual scandal in United States history.

I

Details of Arnold's scheme to collect evidence against alleged gays emerged while the Foster Court of Inquiry — which had recommended that trained investigators be assigned to the case — was meeting. On March 18, Arnold conferred with Dr. Erastus M. Hudson and Ensign William Drury to outline his plan. Arnold urged that reliable undercover investigators be sent "out and would allow the pervert[s] to solicit them." During nine years as a detective, he and men working for him "never took the leading party" but "always had the other party do all the leading and commit all the acts." Starting required only the services of volunteer detectives, an off-base office, and modest funds to pay miscellaneous expenses. The cooperation of local police officials would assure that investigators who were arrested could be easily freed.[1] Drury and Hudson acquiesced to the plan, and Arnold began implementation.

Recruiting operators was critical to the success of the investigation. "In the selecting of men in the capacity of detectives," Arnold later explained, "we generally inquired among our friends

as to the character, honesty, and reliability of the men to be selected." Above all they must be "absolutely reliable and faithful."
Youth and good looks were also important: "in my experience, in
handling this class of work, with reference to perverts," Arnold
went on in his ungrammatical way, "a good looking man from the
average of 19 to 24 will be the best people." "Once a man passed
30 and lost his good looks," he explained, "they [homosexuals]
usually will not solicit or bother them." No training was necessary;
indeed, men "with no previous experience in this particular type of
work" would be more reliable and "get better results" than professionals. Of course, participation had to be voluntary.[2]

Arnold actually identified many of those with whom he would
work long before his plan had been approved. His first recruit was
Millard C. Haynes, another patient in Ward B at the hospital.
Arnold portrayed him as an "honest and reliable young man
. . . whom I could depend on to keep his mouth shut and keep things
quiet." He could also type. Arnold and Haynes spent half a day
closeted in Dr. Hudson's residence typing Arnold's hearsay reports
prior to his appearance before the Foster inquiry. Haynes also identified additional sex sleuths: "I asked Haynes," recalled Arnold,
"if he know of any good men who were honest and reliable and of
good character." The names and records of prospects were obtained from the pay office.[3]

Additional operators were soon identified. Charles B. Zipf, a
twenty-one year old native of Freeport, Illinois, had been a medical
student at the University of Michigan before entering the navy. Service at the Philadelphia Navy Yard and aboard the battleship *Massachusetts* preceded his assignment as a Pharmacist's Mate Second
Class in the operating room at the Newport hospital.[4] Gregory A.
Cunningham of East Malden, Massachusetts, was a Chief Pharmacist's Mate in the hospital; Pittsfield native John E. McCormick was
a Hospital's Apprentice First Class.[5]

Arnold's freshmen detectives began to demonstrate their sleuthing skills before their formal induction. On March 12 McCormick
visited the Y.M.C.A. to eavesdrop on suspected homosexuals.
Next morning he filed a detailed report with Arnold.[6] Three nights
later, Arnold, Haynes, and Cunningham joined McCormick at the
YMCA and observed a seventeen-year-old sailor chatting with a
volunteer worker named Green and then accompany him upstairs on
the elevator. No one had the slightest evidence of what transpired,
yet Cunningham's report implied sexual transgression. "The boy's

face was flushed when he left," wrote Cunningham, "and he acted very suspicious and did not walk with a very deliberate step. Green acting nervous."[7]

That night suspect Thomas Brunelle told Haynes and Arnold about Harrison Rideout's sex life. One he had stripped naked in the middle of a Newport cemetery, bent over a gravestone, and allowed a "strange person . . . to inject his penis into his rectum." Later Rideout predicted before departing for New York that he would be a "well-fucked hombre and that his ass hole would be hanging out all over his ears" by the time he returned.[8]

The night of March 17th the amateur detectives engaged in sex with Newport gays for the first time. McCormick, Zipf, and Haynes arrived at the Y that evening and began talking with suspects. After a few minutes, Brunelle invited McCormick to join him, "Salome" Hughes, and George Richard at an apartment. McCormick stepped away long enough to whisper where he was going. Zipf shadowed them. Inside the boarding house at 15 Whitfield Court, McCormick found two cots, a table, and a dresser. No women's clothing was visible, but face powder, a mirror, pin cushions, and several cheap lady's rings were spotted on a dresser. As soon as the sailors arrived, Brunelle and Hughes began to pat their faces, necks, and cheeks with powder puffs. Shortly they started carrying on with each other "as lovers would, putting their arms around each other and kissing as a man would a woman, also taking their tongues in each other's mouths." Half a hour later Richard invited McCormick into the bathroom. "I did," the operator reported, "and Richard followed me at once." Inside, continued the report, "he turned out the light and had me sit on the toilet seat while he felt my privates, even opening my trousers and kissing my penis . . ." McCormick's obvious nervousness produced a natural result: "He was very much put out," the operator explained candidly, "because I could not get a hard on." After ten minutes the novice detective suggested that they "give it up and try again some other time." Back in the bedroom, Hughes and Richard remarked: "If that head could only talk, what a story it could tell."[9]

The reports that McCormick, Zipf, and Haynes submitted to Arnold the next morning raised questions about the incipient investigation. How far, Arnold wondered, should the men be encouraged to go in the pursuit of evidence? What would happen if local police arrested an operator? Were detectives engaged in illegal acts as guilty as their partners? How could the secrecy of the investigation be preserved? Who would reimburse operators for expenses in carrying out their work? How could the men get off base when necessary or explain their absence from assigned duties? To secure answers to these questions, Arnold conferred with Ensign William Drury at his office in the Naval War College about how the investigation should proceed. The two agreed that Arnold and whatever other sailors he wished should be assigned to temporary duty under Drury. Captain Edward H. Campbell, the Training Station commander, agreed to the plan and issued the necessary orders on March 18.[10]

"You are hereby ordered to special recruiting duty" read the order addressed to Arnold, "said Recruiting Duty to be Temporary Duty, under the officer in charge, Naval Information Service, Newport, R.I." The only specified tasks were to "inquire into the use of cocaine and other drugs and immoral practices and conditions believed to exist to some extent both among the Naval personnel and others in and around Newport, Rhode Island." To assist him, Arnold was assigned thirteen men. In addition to Haynes, Zipf, McCormick, and Cunningham, the list included Clyde Rudy, Malcolm Crawford, Harry Smith, William McCoy, Paul Blacksheare, John Feiselman, Claude J. McQuillan, Floyd Brittain, and W. I. Crawford. Not all had apparently yet been told of their selection, for Drury emphasized that each participant must have "volunteered of his own accord."[11]

The first formal meeting of Arnold's squad occurred that evening when the four original men — Haynes, Zipf, McCormick, and Cunningham — gathered in the basement X-ray room of the Newport Naval Hospital. As if it were necessary, Arnold explained the nature of the work and gave each man an opportunity to withdraw. Dr. Hudson then administered an oath of secrecy to each: "I will not converse upon or in any manner whatsoever communicate any information concerning the business, files, policy or routine of the Office of Naval Intelligence," they promised, "with any persons outside of said office, or to any person whatsoever, without authority from the Director of Naval Intelligence."[12] Not surprisingly, such wording led several "operators" to conclude that the investigation had been authorized by and was part of the navy's official intelligence service.

Arnold distributed copies of a fourteen-point document describing duties and prescribing the rules under which operators were to work. It outlined three distinct goals: Gathering evidence about "cocaine joints" and "booze" came first. Second, the men would "obtain information and evidence pertaining to cocksuckers and rectum receivers and the ring leaders of this gang arranging from time to time meetings whereas to catch them in the act. . . ." Whenever new men were "mentioned" by "said 'fairies,'" their "full names, rates, and where they live and where they are stationed" must be ascertained. Third, squad members might collect information about "women that are in the same business," presumably referring to prostitutes rather than lesbians. Absolute secrecy, the duty sheet continued, was required. Anyone who gave "any information" or even "let his own family know what work is being carried on *will be convicted of perjury*."

A paragraph labeled "Advice" provided more detailed instructions to operators. "Men attached to and serving on this staff," it began,

> must keep their eyes wide open, observing everything and ears open for all conversation and make himself free with this class of men, being jolly and good natured, being careful as he pumps these men for information, making him believe that he is what is termed in the Navy as a "boy humper," making dates with them and so forth. Be careful not to arouse suspicion.

The remainder of the document spelled out procedures to be used in the investigation. Reports, for example, must be turned in by ten in the morning with four copies if typed, one if in long hand. Used carbon paper must be destroyed. All reports were to be headed uniformly; the initials of suspects should be used in the body; and the nicknames of "fairies" would appear in parentheses. Money must be spent prudently and be carefully accounted for. Each man received a general pass allowing him to leave the station any time. "Headquarters telephone number," continued the instructions, "will be given you, and you must memorize the same." Calls should be avoided wherever possible, and the "strictest precautions" must be taken during conversations "so that no one will be able to detect who you are, to whom you are talking or whom you are talking about." Motorcycles were available if needed, and operators could wear civilian clothes "when absolutely necessary to shadow a man or to aid yourself better." Last, Arnold advised his men that if they got "into trouble" or were arrested, "immediately call the number" you have memorized, "and aid will be given at once." Each man signed the order sheet, had it witnessed by Hudson and Arnold, and returned it to the files.[13]

The next day, additional men nominated for special duty in the anti-gay squad appeared in the basement X-ray room. By the time Hudson arrived, the room was "blue with smoke." Those inducted the night before returned, together with eight other sailors: Paul Blacksheare, Harry Smith, Claude McQuillan, Clyde Rudy, Floyd Brittain, John Feiselman, William McCoy, and W. I. Crawford. Each signed identical oaths administered by Hudson and witnessed by Arnold and received a copy of the duty sheet to read, sign, and return. Later, three additional men — Malcolm Crawford, Preston Paul, and Henry Dostalik — joined the team.[14]

Organization proceeded quickly. To insure secrecy, each operator received a code number. Arnold, for example, became number 2842, while Haynes was 4057, and Zipf was number 9. The duties of operator W. I. Crawford (5684) were limited to collecting hearsay about the Training Station. Floyd Brittain (66-4) prepared reports but also did "outside work." Malcolm Crawford (2141-0), a mail clerk in the Training Station, watched for letters to suspects and copied the postmarks and return addresses from envelopes. From the base pay office, Harry Smith (98 1/2) located suspects' full names, rates, and stations. Henry Dostalik (78), a Bohemian immigrant, hoped to use his knowledge of four languages and expertise in fingerprinting to good advantage. Those primarily responsible to tracking down and enticing gays into illegal activities were McCormick, Zipf, Haynes, Feiselman (26-4), Brittain (66-4), McCoy (7284-9), and Rudy (8092-1).[15]

II

No sooner had the second group of operators taken their oaths than several headed toward the Y.M.C.A. in pursuit of sin. They intermingled with the crowd and began picking up gossip. When Chaplain Samuel Kent and Arthur Green attended the evening movie with a marine and a hospital corpsmen, everyone drew sexual inferences from their companionship.[16] George Richard claimed Kent and Green paid "well for their pleasure," having given enlisted men up to five dollars "to let him go down and suck them off." Kent had been overheard saying: "there are two nice little sailor boys over there."[17]

McCormick began his evening by telling Richard he needed to take medicine for a cold before returning to the hospital. "I added that a little cocaine would not be bad, he reported, "and asked him if he had any." Richard offered one of four tablets from a vial and instructed McCormick on how to crush and sniff it. After leaving the Y, McCormick spotted a suspicious woman whom he followed into the Opera House. "She left the theater just before the last picture," he reported, "and I followed her, meeting her on Church Street." The woman told him that since her boyfriend's discharge from the service, she had been living alone and volunteered to find a room if McCormick would live with her. The sailor promised an answer by Friday. Meanwhile, he reported matter-of-factly, "she sucked me off while I leaned against a tree."[18]

Arnold was ecstatic about his men's success. Next morning he wrote Ensign Drury that it would be impossible to have the previous day's reports typed until late afternoon. Meanwhile, he provided a "synopsos" [*sic*] of the report. The tablet from Richard was being examined "to determine what kind of dope it is." The report about Kent was "of importance." "Other information," he continued, "was received which has not reached this office yet. . . . No suspicions aroused so far."[19]

The next evening was still more productive. Brittain arrived at the Y.M.C.A. with several others by seven o'clock, "to bring into line," as reported, "all the data we could pertaining to cocaine joints and cock suckers." Soon Maurice Kreisberg suggested going to a movie. Instead of hurrying to the early show, however, the pair walked down Belleview Avenue toward Cliff Walk. Brittain recalled that almost immediately Kreisberg began "to mush me up" and carry on "as if I were a girl." A few minutes later along the Cliff Walk, "he started this again and I let him get all worked up." "Then," continued the report, "we sat down on the grass beside some concrete steps and he sucked me off right away." Returning to town too late for the last movie, the men agreed to meet again the following week.[20]

During dinner at the station, William Crawford asked Thomas Brunelle if he was going to town that evening to attend a dance. "No," the sailor replied, "I am going down and throw a fuck into something." "You know the boys down there," he added. Later at the Y.M.C.A., Crawford's comment that he was seeking "a piece of tale" [*sic*] provoked Brunelle's suggestion that he get together with one of the "pipe blowers." Crawford confessed he had not "tried that" and was assured that arrangements could easily be made. Brunelle himself had been out so much lately that he was not interested. Jay Goldstein, who arrived shortly after, had been stood up by another date and sought a substitute. He invited Crawford to his place.

The couple headed for Goldstein's Golden Hill Street room and quickly fell into bed together. "Let's love it [up]," exclaimed Goldstein as he threw his arm over Crawford and kissed him. Crawford's third person report described what followed: "After loving a few minutes, Goldstein asked WC how he wanted it," began the narrative

> WC told him to suit himself. Goldstein asked if he wanted it French style, WC said any old way is good, then Goldstein said all right I'll suck it, then went down and sucked WC off. When he got through he torned [*sic*] over and spit in the chamber. Then threw his arm over WC and said "I like you."

Could he put some vaseline on his "cock and get some?" asked Goldstein. "'No,'" came the response, "he would not do that." Assurance that "it would slip in easily" and "not hurt" failed to reduce the operator's resistance. Soon Goldstein turned over, saying "let's go to sleep and we'll get some more in the morning." Next day the two parted without further sex. "Goldstein caught the 7:15 car for the Training Station," concluded the report, "and told WC that he would see him again and to be good."[21]

Zipf turned his attention to Duke Hawkins, the counter waiter at the Y.M.C.A. lunch room. "Hawkins is a good looking negro," the operator reported, "and appears to be above the ordinary type of negroes. He is twenty years old, five feet ten inches tall, and well proportioned." Zipf learned that Hawkins played the piano and asked to meet him on the second floor of the Y for a private recital. Moving onto a piano bench next to Duke, Zipf discussed "various subjects" while the waiter "stroked my leg in a most suggestive manner." The arrival of a second black, Gus, introduced the subject of cocaine. "Duke was greatly interested," Zipf wrote, "and wanted to know how it made one feel and act." "I described the effect," he added without noting the source of his own information, and "said that I used a little when on a booze party as I did not drink." Duke named a pharmacist in New Bedford who sold cocaine and proposed finding a "dark place" so that he would "take my tool and play with it." "Some other time," responded the sailor.[22]

Millard Haynes soon added detective work to his typing. By the time he arrived at the Y.M.C.A. about 1:00 a.m. on the 23rd of March, most lights were out, although Frank Dye, "Ruth" Gianelloni, and another "blue jacket" were still there. After a few minutes' conversation, "Ruth" and the sailor departed, leaving Dye and Haynes together. To questions about his date with Kreisberg that evening, Haynes replied that they had merely walked home and "nothing had happened." Dye said he was glad "you saved it for me," according to Haynes; "then he started to feel my penis." Dye sought a "dark place where he could pull a job off," so they walked down Farwell Street to Van Zandt Avenue. "As that was a dark place," the operator reported, "he wanted to get to business, so I stood against a fence while he sucked me off."[23]

III

As sleuthing continued, Arnold attempted to resolve remaining logistical and legal questions. The need for a room in which to work had been evident from the start. Having so many men use quarters at the hospital without drawing attention to their activities was impossible; remodeling at the War College prevented obtaining rooms there. As an alternative, Dr. Hudson approached Charles F. Hall, field director for the Red Cross in Newport. In obvious contrast to officials at the Y.M.C.A., Hall was portrayed as "a very honest and reliable man." In fact, long-standing antagonism between the leaders of the town's two largest social service agencies no doubt encouraged Hall's cooperation. "I said it was a confidential matter," recalled Hudson, "and that the whereabouts of the office was to be kept secret." Hall was led to think that the work had the full sanction of the navy. "I gave him to understand in so many words," Hudson admitted, "that it was to be used by Navy Intelligence, but I did not exactly tell him so." Hall responded that he had a back room available and would seek permission from his superior in Boston to let Hudson use it.

The necessary approval having been received, Arnold and his operators moved into a room behind the Red Cross office at 42 Church Street. Desks, chairs, a telephone, and a safe were already there. Typewriters came from Ensign Drury's office and the Naval Hospital. "At a meeting of the operators," explained Arnold, "I showed him how to get in [and] gave them certain signals" used in identifying themselves at the door. Black paint on the windows prevented outsiders from peering inside.[24]

Hall also resolved the bothersome problem of reimbursing operators' out-of-pocket expenses. Drury had no money in his office, and Captain Campbell refused to authorize cash from the post welfare fund. As hospital welfare officer, Hudson had previously arranged with the Red Cross to loan small sums of money to sailors who presented a note attesting to their honesty and reliability. Why not use the same procedure for operators? Hall agreed, and thereafter any operator who needed money for meals, transportation, room rent, or other activities associated with the investigation showed a paper from Hudson. Eventually, however, the navy would reimburse the Red Cross.[25]

Arnold also sought official assurance of his men's legal status. The night of the move into the Red Cross rooms, Drury visited the office to discuss this question. Arnold argued that civilians operating under state statutes or common law would be protected, but he was uncertain how military law or procedure applied. "I must have instructions and a decision in regard to these operators," he argued, ". . . before I can instruct them or tell them what to do." Drury ruled that military law protected detectives "if an act was committed upon them and they did not take any leading part." Arnold summoned the operators to inform them of their status. "You people will be on the field of operations," he remembered having told them. "You will have to use your judgment whether or not a full act is completed." "You have got," he concluded, "to form that judgment at the time you are on that field with that party."[26]

IV

Relative inactivity caused by moving in to new quarters and working out administrative details gave way to still more energetic sleuthing toward month's end. Zipf continued trying to get information about cocaine from Duke Hawkins, while Crawford interrogated a man named Vern Shortsleeve.[27] Dostalik focused on waiter Eddy Harrington at the Tokio Restaurant, a "chop shop" on Thames Street. "What will you have, dear?" were the man's welcoming words; in the course of taking orders and serving meals, he managed to squeeze the operator's hands and "feel all over. . . . [his] breast." Returning to the Tokio several days later, Dostalik received a welcoming kiss from Harrington. A date between the pair never transpired, however, because, as Dostalik reported, the waiter "got so drunk that he had to go home in a taxi."[28] McCormick, Feiselman, and Crawford spent nearly every evening picking up gossip and watching Kent and Green at the Y. One night when a marine toting a handbag went upstairs, Richard alleged that Green "sucked this man off every night." If he did not stop, he would soon "dry" the youngster up. Another night a sailor who had spoken to Green was overheard telling a buddy: "the bastard will be sucking my cock before morning."[29]

Sex was delayed until Thursday night, March 28. A suspect named Harold Trubshaw was at the Y soliciting trade when operator John Feiselman arrived. After a brief talk, the detective invited Trubshaw to share his upstairs room. "We talked for about an hour," reported the operator, discussing visits to New York, drinking sprees, and Trubshaw's "big time" the previous Tuesday. "He said he went on with four fellows," noted the operator. "One couldn't throw a load" though, so "he made it up by sucking one of the others three times." "Such a night,' he lamented; "it was terrible; I'll never do it again."

Deciding it was "time . . . to get busy," Trubshaw began tickling and "feeling up" Feiselman. "I knew if I'd let him have it early in the evening, he would kill me off," recalled the operator, who had been told that Trubshaw was "a rotten one and would go the limit." So he avoided sex that night. Both men slept until 6:00 the next morning, when the operator awoke to find Trubshaw "feeling me up." "I decided to let him take it then," he reported, "for I could get up immediately afterwards, so he would not have a chance to pester me and love me for he had an awful smelling breath." "I worked up a hard on," he continued, "and he hopped to it. I gave him a load and he ate it nicely." Trubshaw wanted more, but Feiselman feigned illness; by 6:45 both were en route back to the station.[30]

That evening Rudy acquired what he presumed to be cocaine. For some time he and other operators had coerced George Richard to provide them with drugs, but when the pair met at the Y in late afternoon, Richard still had no "coke." He promised to keep trying, however, and by 7:00 returned with an envelope labeled "U.S.N. Medical Department" that he claimed came from a hospital apprentice. Rudy hurried to the office with his evidence. Arnold carefully removed the white powder so fingerprints could be taken.

McCormick, Zipf, Brittain, Smith, Haynes, and Arnold attested to the procedures.[31]

That same night Rudy and McCormick concocted an elaborate scheme to entrap Maurice Kreisberg, with whom Rudy had a date. Early in the evening, the pair went to Rudy's room, where McCormick hid back of a curtain behind the bed. Rudy met the sailor in front of St. Joseph's Church and returned with him to the room. "Kreisberg wanted to kiss and love me," he recalled, "but I stood him off by saying I did not like that sort of game. He insisted and begged for it, but I insisted that he do his work below my chest." McCormick observed from only a few feet away: "Kreisberg then opened Rudy's trousers, and felt of his penis and private parts." "He tried to excite my passion," was Rudy's version, "but failed." The pair remained together until 9 o'clock, when Rudy left on the pretext of having another engagement.[32]

The 29th produced even more lurid evidence. Operator Zipf and suspect Trubshaw were busiest. Arriving at the Y about 7 o'clock, Zipf immediately began talking with Trubshaw, who invited him to room 406. "I entered the room with Trubshaw," Zipf reported, "took off my pants and jumper and got under the covers." Trubshaw soon joined him and "after a few minutes took my penis in his mouth and sucked it until I had an emission of semen."

The night had just begun for both sailors. As soon as Zipf returned to the lobby, he spotted Reverend Kent behind the desk. Zipf confessed loneliness since a friend had left the service whereupon the chaplain presented a card and invited the sailor to his apartment. "Come tonight, if you want to," he said, "and spend the night with me." Zipf agreed, passing the room key to Trubshaw, whom he told to use it with anyone he met.

Before long Trubshaw had identified another potential bed mate: operator William McCoy, out on his first major assignment. The suspect went upstairs and was already undressed in bed by the time the operator knocked at room 406. "As son as I got in bed," McCoy reported the next day, "he began feeling me up and wanted to know which way I wanted it, from behind or French. I said French," he continued, "and he did not wait for it to get hard but put his head under the cover and went to it. It took time," explained the freshman detective, "for I was trying to hold back." The two talked for a time, after which Trubshaw proposed that McCoy "do it from behind." Unlike Feiselman, who had anticipated and avoided such a request, McCoy agreed. "He put cold cream on my penis," the operator explained, "and said that would make it go in with ease. After he had put it in, he was talking all the time about how good it was." McCoy had gone too far, however. "His actions and the thought of what I was doing," he admitted in his formal account, "caused it to go dead." Despite Trubshaw's protests, the detective withdrew, dressed, and prepared to leave. "You won't speak to me after this," the sailor lamented as they separated, "but I thank you for this." Thereafter, McCoy limited his detection to eavesdropping.[33]

Meanwhile, Zipf and Kent left the Y for the cleric's quarters at the Emmanuel Church parish house. According to Zipf's report, Kent made up a bed and provided pajamas and slippers for his guest. Kent was tired but invited Zipf into his room to talk. "I sat down in a chair," reported the operator. "This did not appeal to Kent who threw the covers back and invited me to crawl in." The sailor complied, removing his bath robe and joining the chaplain in bed. Kent recalled Zipf's departed friend and suggested "bodily contact" before going to sleep. "Kent threw his arms around men," wrote Zipf, "and kissed me about the face. Repeatedly he tried to put his tongue in my mouth. His hand strayed and he felt of my penis, commenting on size, shape, etc. After a while Kent said, 'I am all yours.'" Zipf asked if the older man would like to take him, to which the response was, "any way." "French," replied the operator. "Kent acquiesced," continued the report, "so I shoved Kent's head under the covers." There must have been a misunderstanding, however, for the chaplain retorted: "Oh, no, I don't take it. I thought you did." Zipf refused so the two played with each other. "I went off," reported Zipf, "and Kent also." Near midnight the operator moved to the guest room until morning. "Kent made me promise not to say anything to the gang down at the Y.M.C.A.," recalled Zipf; "I promised faithfully."[34]

Apparent success in substantiating suspicions about Kent accelerated the attention paid to others at the Y.M.C.A. The night of April 1, no fewer than four operators "shadowed" waiter Duke Hawkins. Reaching the Y at 5:00 p.m., Zipf went directly to the lunch room where Duke told him that "the stuff" (presumably cocaine) had not yet arrived from Boston. Later Brittain overheard Dostalik make a date with Hawkins. "I walked around the Y.M.C.A.," he reported, "and passed the time away until that time which was only a few minutes." He followed Hawkins upstairs to a classroom. "While I was walking around seemingly not paying attention to anything," the operator continued, "Dostalik came in and went in this room. . . ." McCormick, too, watched outside. While Hawkins played the piano, two other blacks stood by watching. "I passed into the gymnasium and stood in the door for a few minutes. When I looked back they were gone." The door was sufficiently ajar for McCormick to see a negro wearing a grey sweater seated at the piano. A sailor's hat and coat lay nearby. "I could hear the sailor's voice," he concluded, "and it sounded like the voice of Dostalik."[35]

In truth, Hawkins had fallen for Dostalik. "He said he liked me," the operator put it, "and would do anything in the world to make me happy . . . I would have to be true to him and give all myself only to him and not go out with anyone else," he reported. Rather than return the man's affection, Dostalik manipulated it to entrap him. "I suggested that to make me happy, he would have to get some cocaine," he confided. Hawkins seemed doubtful that drugs could be obtained but would try regardless of risk or cost. The two agreed to meet next for a secluded date in a locked room.

Next night Dostalik used the fictitious name "Dill" to engage room 325 at the Y. Operators Haynes and McQuillan were stationed outside the door to watch. About 8:30 Duke knocked at the door and entered. The pair talked for a few minutes before moving to the bed. "Duke layed on me," Dostalik reported, "and played with my penis, unbuttoned my trousers, pulled it out, and worked his fist up and down to work it up." Meanwhile, Duke pleaded with the sailor to become "his steady and not go out with anyone else." Later he dropped to his knees at the side of the bed: "You will not tell anyone, and will not go out with anybody else, will you?" Dostalik pledged fidelity, although irritated that Duke kept a wad of gum in his mouth while he did "the job." "He sucked me off," Dostalik continued, "and took out a handkerchief from his pocket and wiped off my penis, then wiped off his mouth." Apparently Duke feared discovery, for he once again solicited promises that Dostalik would not tell anyone about their relationship. For his part, Hawkins offered to do anything the sailor wanted, including giving him money. "He said that he could learn to love me, but I had to be true for him." To questions about cocaine, Duke responded that it was "mighty hard to get." By 10:30 the pair left the Y.M.C.A. headed home.[36]

Zipf turned his attention to suspect Frank Dye, whom he met at the Y the afternoon of April 1. After lunch at the Ideal Sea Grill, they returned to the base hospital for aspirin. Next stop was the room Dye shared with another sailor. "Dye told me his room mate was a rube from Iowa," recalled the operator, "and not to make any cracks in front of him. . . ." A woman named Kitty also roomed in the building. "Dye said she only fucks her friends," the report continued, "and she has no enemies." They moved on to 6 Clarke Street, where Dye rented a room for the night. "After a few minutes in bed," Zipf recalled with unusual brevity, "Dye went down on me and sucked me off." Afterward, the operator's probe for information about cocaine produced a confession of occasional use but professed ignorance about where to buy drugs in Newport or Providence. Dye got his from George Richard who obtained it from a corpsman in the naval hospital. "We both slept until the next morning," he concluded. "No further conversation."[37]

Preston Paul, a new recruit, turned his attention to Seaman Second Class Samuel Rogers. During a conversation in the Ward B head the afternoon of April 1, Rogers invited Paul to a movie that evening. The operator explained that he was going to a dance with his girl friend but agreed to meet afterward at the Y.M.C.A. The two met as prescribed, but since the Y was "too public" a place, they walked together to a house at 118 Spring Street to rent a room. Both undressed and got into bed. "Rogers at once started to love and kiss me and put his hand on my penis and fingered my balls," reported Paul; once he had achieved a "state of rigidity," Rogers suggested applying cold cream so they could "go to it." "I consented," he continued, "and after using the cold cream he rolled over on his belly and opened his legs like a woman and assisted me to enter by way of the rectum. We stalled along for about twenty minutes," he concluded, "and then I went off." "He kissed me," closed the report, "when I left."[38]

Zipf's next conquest was Jay "Beckie" Goldstein, the cook with whom Crawford had previously enjoyed sex. They met at the Y cigar counter the night of April 3. "Goldstein asked me if I wanted to have some fun," confided the operator, "and I said yes." They considered renting a room at the Y but—in the first hint that anyone suspected an investigation—Goldstein said he was "afraid" and suggested a rooming house. Before they left, Goldstein warned George Richard "to be careful" in the Y.M.C.A. because of chiefs spying on every floor. Zipf paid $1.50 for their room at 21 Mann Street. "Goldstein wanted me to brown him first," the immodest operator reported, "but when he saw my meat he said he did not want to get it dirty. Goldstein put my penis in his mouth," continued Zipf, "and held it there until I had an erection. Goldstein then sucked it off." Their conversation also produced admission that Goldstein used cocaine obtained from Richard.[39]

V

Rumors about Arnold's investigation accelerated following the April 4 arrest of Fred Hoage. He had been a stage and film actor before joining the navy, where he became close friends with the gang frequenting the Y.M.C.A., among whom he was generally known as "Theda Bara." Hoage's name had come up repeatedly, but no operator had sex with him. Preston Paul once reported an incident at the hospital, however, in which Hoage walked up to him while dressing, "rubbed his hands up and down on my trousers, on my penis looking skyward, and observed, 'isn't he a grand man?'"[40] McCormick later learned that Hoage lavished money and gifts on his friends, especially marines. He had bought a pair of expensive gloves for a man named Archer, whom he entertained during a lavish weekend in Boston. Hoage was also suspected of using his position in the hospital to acquire drugs. Late in March, for example, he offered to get cocaine for Clyde Rudy.[41] Exactly what precipitated Hoage's arrest is unclear, but on the 4th he was summoned to the master-at-arm's office for what he presumed to be a special assignment. Instead he found Pharmacist's Mate Third Class John Phillips with a revolver on his hip. "He told me to follow him," Hoage later recalled. "I did and was confined in the Training Station prison." The next day ointment, pills, powders, and other drugs were found among his personal effects; the pocket of his pea jacket contained a bottle of codeine and "some brown tablets."[42]

News of Hoage's arrest quickly produced rumors of an anti-gay investigation. George Richard, who raised the subject with Zipf, had heard through orderlies in Captain Campbell's office that the chief master-at-arms had been told to "hang around the Y.M.C.A. and catch the boys who were teaching immoral practices." Richard claimed that friendship with a chief paymaster who "had an awful [lot of] pull" would "save him if anything happened." Nevertheless, he intended to destroy "incriminating" letters as soon as possible.[43]

This report, together with the apparent willingness of Hoage to testify against his friends, persuaded Arnold, Hudson, and Drury to begin proceedings against other sailors about whom evidence had been collected. Promptly at 9:30 a.m. on April 8, 1919, the Court of Inquiry presided over by Murphy J. Foster resumed its hearings.

Lobby, Newport Y.M.C.A. during World War I. Here sailors gathered every evening for conversation, letter writing, church services, and other recreational activities. Some suggested sexual activities to one another; and often they ended up together in bed.

Credit: Rhode Island Historical Society.

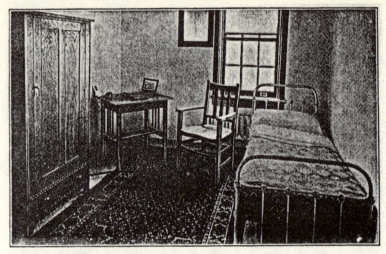

Upstairs sleeping rooms at the "Y" provided a convenient meeting place for sailors seeking a night's companionship.
Credit: Photo from the U.S. Naval Historical Center.

CHAPTER 3

Navy Justice

These hearings in some ways merely continued the work begun by Foster, Hibbs and Hudson two and a half weeks earlier. However, the evidence which Ervin Arnold and his operators had collected would now be used against individual sailors summoned before the court, charged, confined, and arrested. The same testimony ultimately convicted many of crimes sufficiently serious to earn them long prison terms. And the apparent success of this initial prosecution justified the extension of anti-gay sleuthing to civilians and earned it the endorsement of the Navy Department in Washington.

I

Proceedings began with yet another recitation of Arnold's hearsay evidence of homosexuality and drug use among patients and staff at the Newport hospital. He provided no new substantiating evidence and failed to mention the existence of his squad or its activities during the preceding weeks. As usual, the names of more than a dozen civilians, sailors, and marines were included, along with tantalizing details about their sexual proclivities.[1]

After lunch, however, the nature of the proceedings changed dramatically with the presence in court of suspect Frank Dye. Why he came first (or indeed the underlying strategy of the hearings) cannot be easily deciphered. The evidence against Dye was no stronger than that against most suspects. Perhaps he was expected to break under pressure and testify against other suspects. No sooner had he entered the courtroom than Dye discovered he was an "interested party" who had the right under the military justice system to attend the session, secure representation by counsel, offer evidence of his own, and cross-examine witnesses. In what became standard practice, he failed to object to the composition of the court and indicated that he did "not wish counsel."

Arnold continued his testimony by excerpting from his reports information pertaining to Dye. For the most part, the evidence was gossip. Only once had Dye allegedly touched Arnold's penis, told him "what a nice one" he had, and invited him out. The accused's single query concentrated on this event. "Where was I," he asked, "when I put my hand on your penis?" What seemed like a simple statement fell apart as Arnold explained that there really had been two incidents, one near the soda counter at the Y and a second in the basement of the Naval Hospital. "You were on duty with a mail bag on your back," added Arnold.

Arnold was followed by operator Charles Zipf. "I have met Dye on several occasions," he began, "and [in] nearly all of such occasions the conversations drifted to immoral subjects." While walking toward the Presto Lunch, Dye once threw his arms around him and asked him to dance. At the conclusion of a date on April 1, Dye had taken his penis "in his mouth and held it there until there was an emission." Having heard this testimony, the court changed Dye's status from an interested party to a defendant. Apparently shaken by the testimony of someone he had never suspected of being a detective, Dye failed to rebut evidence of having had sex with Zipf. The only other testimony came from Millard Haynes, who described Dye fellating him against a fence. The defendant departed for the brig without having made a serious effort at a defense.

Witness Floyd Brittain focused on Maurice Kreisberg. "I know that Kreisberg is guilty of immoral practice, such as sucking pricks," he began. "My only experience with him is that he sucked me off." When Kreisberg entered the room, he was notified of his status as a defendant and told his rights. Brittain used notes to describe the evening he and Kreisberg had sex along Cliff Walk. Unlike Dye, the accused sailor took no part in the proceedings and failed to cross-examine his accuser.

Operators Clyde Rudy and John McCormick later described how Rudy had sex with Kreisberg while McCormick watched from behind a curtain. "What do you mean by blown?" a court member asked. "Well," replied Rudy, "I presume he meant he did the same thing to them that he was attempting to do to me." To another question about the exact address where an episode occurred, McCormick responded that he could not remember the number, but it was the second or third house on the left side. At this point Kreisberg left for prison, and court adjourned for the day.[2]

II

The resumption of hearings did not immediately result in the suspension of operators' work. The very night the court reconvened, for example, Harrison Rideout and Zipf locked themselves in a dark basement room at the hospital. Rideout tried unsuccessfully for twenty minutes to arouse Zipf's passion before despairing that it was "no use at all." Embarrassment resulted when Zipf's key failed to open the lock, and he had to call the Steward on Watch (operator Haynes) to release them.[3]

During a dinner date with his steady, Duke Hawkins, at the Rhode Island Sea Grill, Dostalik feasted on steak, french fries, tomatoes, and apple pie. The subject of fidelity came up as Duke complained of rumors that Dostalik had been seeing another man. "When one loves another," the waiter went on, "it's hard to see him go out with anyone else." As they left, Hawkins paid the $1.50 bill, gave the waiter a twenty cent tip, and passed the change from $2.00 to Dostalik. They parted with a promise to meet the following Friday, but not before Duke revealed his knowledge that Dye had been arrested for "fooling with someone's mail."[4]

When court reopened the following morning, the focus turned to Harold Trubshaw. Operator John Feiselman took the stand. "I know that there is a lot of immoral practices," he opened, "but I have not studied the situation." In fact, Trubshaw was the only man he had "evidence on." He read from a report describing their night together at the Y. As the implications of the testimony became clear, Trubshaw was called in, informed of his status — first as an interested party, soon after as a defendant — and read his rights. Like the others, he declined legal assistance and failed to participate in proceedings. Next Zipf and McCoy described activities with Trubshaw the night of March 29. No one mentioned that Zipf had gone out with Reverend Kent the same evening, although the court seemed especially interested in knowing more about the elevator operator at the Y and, especially, about the Mr. Green who worked there.[5]

The second afternoon's proceedings concentrated on ship's cook David "Beckie" Goldstein. Operator William Crawford described a night with Goldstein on Golden Hill Street, during which the defendant was brought in and, as usual, declined counsel or to challenge the court's membership. Zipf told how he had gone with Goldstein to a room on Mann Avenue, following which Arnold presented further incriminating evidence. The only challenge to a witness came when Arnold was asked how he knew people in the Y were "soliciting and not merely asking them to go out with him." "That is the way they solicit," he replied, "as I have had dealing with this class before, and more experienced ones."

Throughout the afternoon, witnesses endeavored to teach the court the meaning of sexual terms used in testimony. "What do you mean," one officer asked Crawford, "that Goldstein wanted to get some?" "He wanted to get some from me," came the response. "He wanted to fuck me." Later Zipf explained that by "brown" he meant "pushing my prick in his ass." "What do you mean 'he went down on you?'" another officer asked. "I mean he sucked my cock," replied Zipf, who quickly corrected his language: "put my penis in his mouth and held it there until there was an emission." Not everyone apparently understood, for a few minutes later Arnold had to explain again that "getting down on someone" meant "he gets down on him and sucks another man's cock."

The remainder of the testimony dealt with Goldstein's public behavior. John Feiselman, for example, accused him of frequently "calling for trade" in the Y.M.C.A. lobby. "What do you mean," asked a court member. "He just said 'trade,'" responded the operator, who described an occasion during which the cook kept "tapping his fingers against the arms of our seats" and calling, "trade, trade." "What did he mean?" the officer again asked. "I suppose he meant immoral practices from what I have heard others say," replied Feiselman. Gregory Cunningham focused on a conversation about a "big drag" where Goldstein said liquor and "snow" would be served. Fred Hoage had also shown him pictures of sailors "embracing each other and in compromising postures." McCormick added that Rogers had told him that Goldstein used cocaine.[6]

In a rare instance of defiance, Goldstein proclaimed his innocence. "I, David Goldstein," he opened,

> ship's cook fourth class, U.S. Navy, stationed in the East Wing of Barracks "C," Commissary Department, U.S. Naval Training Station, Newport, Rhode Island, hereby state that I have never met the following named men who have testified against me

and he listed all who had appeared. "I did not," he concluded, "do the things these men said I did." With that, he, like the others, left for the brig.[7]

By the evening of April 9, the confinement of Hoage, Dye, Kreisberg, Goldstein, and Trubshaw precipitated panic among the gay sailors of Newport. Zipf discovered, however, that no one yet knew of Arnold's investigation or the identity of the operators. Arriving at Whitfield Court rooms shared by John Gianelloni and William Hughes, Zipf found a "great change" since his last visit. ". . . the room," he continued, "presented every aspect of a man's bed room rather than a ladies' dressing room." Gianelloni was deeply depressed as a result of the arrests and asked Zipf what he thought of them. ". . . heaven only knows" lamented the sailor, "what tomorrow will bring." Gianelloni was sure he could not sleep, so Zipf offered to get him morphine. Later he withdrew the offer allegedly because Gianelloni had failed to deliver cocaine as promised. Gianelloni was contemplating suicide and had obtained tablets from Hoage to take "should anything happen . . . [to] avert the trouble." "As the talk went on," Zipf reported, "Gianelloni got very much worked up over the subject." In contrast, Hughes was "in a state of profound gayety." He felt safe because the only ones who had "anything on him" were to be released from the service the next day. Thank goodness, he added, that the U.S.S. *Baltimore* was no longer in port, for its crew could "convict almost anybody." The best approach, Hughes had advised, was to say as little as possible.[8]

When court reconvened, Arnold testified against Samuel Rogers, with whom he had conversed in the hospital. After reading his notes, none of which reported new evidence or were based on more than hearsay, he added that during interrogation that morning Rogers said he had been initiated into gay life by a commissary steward named Johnson at the Melville Coaling Station. "He forced Rogers to the woods," according to Arnold, "taking his pants down, and forcing him by scaring him and main[ly by] strength to insert his penis in Rogers' rectum."[9]

For the first time since the sessions resumed, Rogers launched a long personal presentation. Trouble started, he admitted, the preceding July at Melville when he met George Richard whom he learned was a "cocaine fiend and a cocksucker." Richard persuaded him to take cocaine, and he (not the Johnson named by Arnold) introduced him to gay sex. One day they were picking vegetables when Richard asked if he could "brown" his friend. "I told him 'No,'" reported Rogers, "but finally he teased and begged me and finally forced me to do it." "That," he added, "is the first time in my life I ever did anything wrong." During a visit to Fall River, he learned that Richard had been a homosexual and female impersonator all his life. What was a female impersonator? asked someone on the court. "One that dresses up in girl's clothes," the witness replied, "and acts on stage, sings, and dances."

Through Richard, Rogers had met many other "fairies." "I got in their company," he explained, "I don't know why, but I used to go out with them. . . . I never met one until I came in the Navy." He was especially friendly with the group at the Y. Once, while attending a party on Golden Hill Street at which nearly everyone was drinking, Chief Brugs had proposed sex before becoming too drunk even to undress. He had a special affection for Harrison Rideout and William Hughes. "They have always treated me as a friend," he said, "and I had to look up to them and treat them the same." His closing words appealed for leniency: "I am sorry that I ever met George Richard because he spoiled me," he began,

I would like to add that I would not care for my folks to know anything about this; for that I would suffer everything, because I want them to know me as they think I am. This is something that I never did until I came in the Navy. I want it understood

he continued, "that I only took cocaine once and that liquor has never touched my lips." At 4:30 p.m. the court adjourned until 9:00 the next morning.

Rogers continued on the stand Friday morning and again Saturday. Apparently hoping that cooperation might win leniency, he provided numerous details about the activities of Newport gays. Goldstein and Richard came to a party in full-length ball gowns, women's lingerie, and wigs. When they danced, he remembered, they "kicked up high enough to show their bloomers." Every few minutes Goldstein would go outside with someone. "Some would come back buttoning up their pants," so he concluded that "he took them out in the entry-way and I think he sucked them off." Later he heard that Goldstein had eight men that night.

On and on he went, implicating one after another of his friends and adding Green, Kent, the elevator operator at the Y, and the "sporty" "nigger fellow" [presumably Duke Hawkins] behind the counter at the Y.M.C.A. restaurant. At one party, Goldstein had sucked off a man named Bowers while Dye ministered to Brunelle; then they went "fifty-fifty with the contents" of their mouths. "They swapped it just like swapping spit." He also knew that Fred Hoage had been going out with a "tall, skinny fellow" from the hospital. Once Rogers had delivered a note to the man from Hoage. How did he know that immoral purposes were intended? asked the court. "He winked his eyes, rolled them, and moved his body in different positions," replied Rogers, "So I thought by that it was what he wanted him for." Were there any homosexual officers? someone asked at the end of the sessions. Rideout had said that one physician was "queer," concluded Rogers, and "two or three that chums with him."[10]

The morning of April 14 Harrison Rideout confessed everything he knew about gay life in Newport, apparently hopeful—like Rogers—of winning favorable consideration. His record had been "perfectly clear" before joining the navy, and he had been "going with a woman making connections with her once or twice a week on the average." Nevertheless, he admitted having always "acted effeminate." Trouble began when he accepted dinner and later liquor from an enlisted man nicknamed Mary Tusche. "He gave me a drink," Rideout reported, "and started to embrace me and while I was under the influence of liquor I suppose he took advantage of me." Another time, Chief Brugs plied him with whiskey before he "inserted his penis into my rectum." His next sex partner had been operator Dostalik. "Dostalik was the last one I was with," he pleaded. "That is the absolute truth."

Rideout also introduced the court to gay life among civilians in Newport. The Art Association "reeks with it." "The women and these perverts," he continued, "get together and they talk." "You could find out a lot," he recommended, by watching the place. Especially prominent was a man who talked "just like a woman" and wore red ties. Another "little Portuguese fellow" was always after him, "said how good he was," and claimed he was "good for five times in two hours." Another "great big tall fellow" from a shop named The House that Jack Built dated sailors.

Rideout's testimony added still more tidbits to the court's knowledge of homosexual activities. Once Rideout had been out with a friend when Chief Brugs came along. The two entered the base barber shop where the friend "got down and sucked Mr. Brugs off." How did he know what happened? inquired the court. "I could hear the fellow sort of choking,'' he replied; "I could hear that oozing sound." He, too, suspected that one of the doctors was "queer." "He acted sort of peculiar," he explained, "walking around with his hands on his hips. His walk, his manner, was not masculine." Rideout concluded in language remarkably like Arnold's. "If a man was walking around and did not act real masculine, I would think he was a cocksucker." Another physician reportedly kept a "little short" orderly as his "chicken," and even Newport Chief of Police was suspect.

Rideout was the first defendant to counter operators' testimony. He had talked at length with Arnold, but much of what he had said was untrue. He had labeled himself a "frisker" who followed the fleet, he contended, only "to make myself seagoing." Descriptions of a trip to New York had incorrectly inferred sexual conquests. "The worse I could talk about myself," he admitted, "the more brilliant I thought myself."

The sailor's version of what happened with Zipf in the hospital basement differed considerably from the operator's. Rideout had requested an X-ray for tuberculosis, and Zipf had invited him down to have a beer and examine the plates. "Zipf took out his penis and tried to have an erection," continued Rideout, "and couldn't have it and I told him that I did not want anything that night. . . . There was no connection at all." Besides, he was not a "two-way artist" as reported. "I have never taken a penis in my mouth," only in the rectum. "I would not do that if I could help it."[11]

III

By the time court adjourned on the 14th, plans were under way to arrest the remaining suspects before they became too suspicious and escaped. Each evening after court adjourned, Ensign Drury stopped near Hudson's house on his way from quarters aboard the U.S.S. *Constellation* toward town. Arnold, summoned by phone, was already at Hudson's when Drury arrived. The brig would be emptied of other prisoners so each suspect could have a solitary cell there or aboard the U.S.S. *Boxer*, an old, leaky ship tied up at Newport. How long would it take his operators to begin locating suspects? they asked Arnold. Five minutes, he replied, then called the office to have everyone stand by while Hudson arranged for a hospital ambulance to transport prisoners.[12]

The massive round-up produced nine additional arrests at the

Y.M.C.A. and elsewhere. Included were Thomas Brunelle, Jeremiah Fowler, Elmo "Ruth" Gianelloni, William Gorham, Wade Hervey, William Hughes, Albert Kirk, George Richard, and Whitney Rosenzweig. The arrest the next day of Albert Viehl raised the total number of accused gay sailors confined since April 4 to eighteen.[13] New suspects were confined after being identified in court.

The arrests precipitated the first dispute over the legitimacy of Arnold's operation. The next morning Provost Marshall Brown protested to Lt. Commander Foster that the brig was overcrowded. "Where are all these fellows coming from," Foster asked Dr. Hudson. "They are the cases Arnold has been taking up around Newport," replied the physician. "Is Arnold still operating?" "Yes," replied Hudson, "Arnold is still working under Drury as far as I know." "What in the hell is the matter with Drury now!" exclaimed Foster, who apparently had no idea that that investigation had continued or that the witnesses heard the previous week were operators. "If they don't stop Arnold right away," continued Foster, "he will hang the whole state of Rhode Island."

Foster had assumed, it seemed to Hudson, that after his court recommended the use of more experienced, professional detectives, Captain Campbell had issued orders for Arnold and his volunteers to "knock off." "I remember he [Foster] got up and went outside the court and had a conversation with Drury," recalled Hudson. "What that conversation was I don't know."[14] Foster apparently carried his concerns to senior naval officials in Boston, but several days passed before orders reached Newport.

IV

When court sessions resumed, several important differences became apparent. As the focus moved away from those sailors with whom operators had allegedly had sex, the role of Arnold and his men diminished. Later defendants were also less passive than their predecessors. Instead of remaining silent or declining to participate, they exercised their rights to cross-examine accusers, and one even employed an attorney. Perhaps in part because of a dressing down from Foster, Drury pursued evidence less aggressively, as a result of which momentum slowed.

The approach of Stephen Brugs typified the new aggressiveness of accused sailors. While Brugs did not object to the court or utilize a lawyer, he called as witnesses everyone who accused him. "What proof have you got that I 'browned' you?'' he demanded of Samuel Rogers, who confessed he had only his own word. "During any of the times that you have stated that I have 'browned' you, has there been a witness to the act?'' No. Harrison Rideout received the same treatment. "Are you positive Hotchkiss sucked my prick?'' he asked, producing answers that he could "hear the noise and . . . see the shapes.'' Who was standing and who crawling? he inquired. "I could not tell,'' replied Rideout. Even Ervin Arnold was a subject of Brugs' interrogation: he reaffirmed his certainty that the man speeding off on a motorcycle was Brugs. Chief Boatswains Mate James Chase, who had allegedly been implicated with Brugs, denied knowing most suspects other than Rogers and Rideout, both of whom he characterized as "no more than good friends.''[15]

Several witnesses had referred to a marine frequenting the Y.M.C.A. who allegedly had a long-standing relationship with Mr. Green. Two different men who met the general description appeared in court. Both denied any personal knowledge of immorality in Newport, although one confirmed that marines often talked about homosexuality at the Art Association and the Y. Neither he nor the other suspect had visited the Y except to use the bathroom, and when the pair confronted Rideout, Rogers, and Richard, each was cleared of any suspicion and released.[16]

The longest, most elaborate defense was presented in the case of Neils Johnson, who ran the mess at the Torpedo Station. Johnson had never been mentioned by an operator, so the prosecution depended entirely on testimony from defendants Rogers and Richard. The counsel whom Johnson employed to represent him, Frank Nolan, thoroughly grilled each accuser. Rogers, for example, claimed that Johnson had once grabbed him from behind with both arms, unbuttoned his pants, and 'browned' him. "Who unbuttoned your pants?'' probed the lawyer. "He did,'' came the answer, referring to Johnson. "How could he have both arms around you and unbutton your pants?'' demanded Nolan. "Well, he did,'' was the best the sailor could muster. Moreover, George Richard claimed to have observed Johnson "browning'' Rogers near the station but admitted under close questioning that all he really saw were two figures moving under a blanket.[17]

Nolan hailed his client before the court for a carefully orchestrated defense. Johnson explained that he was married with children aged thirteen and seven. Both Rogers and Richard could be very effeminate, for which they were often chided by colleagues. Johnson denied both allegations against him: he had gone to the garden with Rogers one day, but they had returned with no untoward behavior having occurred. "Did you on that day grab him around the waist and unbutton his pants and commit sodomy?" asked the attorney. "No, sir." The blanket incident was merely playful "skylarking." Rogers had been picking up bedding being aired when Johnson came up and knocked him into the blankets. "And were you lying under the same blanket with Rogers that day at any time . . . ?" "No, sir."

The evidence against Albert Viehl was so sparse that he could never have been convicted had he not incriminated himself. As Viehl explained, he, too, had been initiated into gay life by the man nicknamed Mary Tusche, through whom he met Fred Hoage, William Hughes, Harrison Rideout, Chief Brugs, and other "fairies." He had been with Hoage two or three times, he recalled, before "he went down on me. They call it cocksucking." "I never had an experience before and I didn't know what he was after." Sometime later William Hughes asked him to put his "penis in his rectum." "Did you do it?" asked the court. "I did," he replied, adding that this was the "first time in my life I ever did anything like this."[18]

A much stronger case existed against Thomas R. Brunelle, whose hearing began Thursday afternoon April 17. Arnold presented opening testimony alleging both unnatural activities and cocaine use. No investigator testified, a change from earlier practice suggesting either that Foster refused to allow their further participation or that Drury chose not to depend on them. Brunelle admitted his sexual orientation and activities while steadfastly denying use of drugs. His meandering, almost incoherent testimony characterized numerous friends as pogues, cocksuckers, or "sixty nine" fellows. Hoage was "a very brilliant woman," a "good French artist." He "sucks a man all around the body." One man stripped naked and dressed in a curtain, while another dragged men one after the other to a hallway outside a party. "Gee, that was a big one!" he had once remarked. At one party, he admitted, "there was a little cocksucking done there and some cake passed around." "'Speedy' [Dye] has sucked me," he confessed, "and so has Goldstein." He denied having sex with Hughes. "We were known as man and wife," as he explained it, "but nothing was pulled off between us."[19]

V

Fred Hoage began his defense by questioning Brunelle. Just what evidence of drug use could he produce? Brunelle was no drug expert but argued that every time he had seen Hoage at the Y, he had appeared to "be under some influence." Evidence of his being a "French artist" was equally thin: "The way you jumped around the Y.M.C.A. and acted around the crowd" had convinced him. Hoage later cross-examined Rideout, Viehl, and Rogers. "On what grounds have you a right to surmise that I was doing anything immoral?" he demanded of Viehl, who had accused him of going into a room with men. "You wouldn't go and use anybody else's room if you were just going there to sleep," came the reply. "how did you know I was a cocksucker?" he asked Rogers, who responded that Rideout and Hughes had told him. "have you ever seen an immoral practice personally done by myself?" he queried further. "No."[20]

The most incriminating evidence against Hoage came the morning of Tuesday April 22. Pharmacist's Mate John Phillips listed the drugs and hospital equipment discovered among the sailor's effects the day after his arrest. A bottle of codeine and mysterious brown tablets had been found in his pea coat. Phillips had given the medicines to operator McCormick, who passed them to Arnold for transfer to Chief Pharmacist's Mate John Collins. The latter swore the pills found in the pea coat could "be nothing else" but codeine. Another bottle contained Dover's powder. Under cross-examination, however, Collins admitted he had never seen Hoage around places where drugs were stored.

Of all those accused by Arnold and his operators and hailed before the Foster Court, Fred Hoage presented the longest, most revealing, and ultimately the most incriminating defense. As the first man arrested, he faced unusual difficulties. Because neither Arnold nor any other operator appeared against him, he never knew what charges had been or were about to be made against him. In defending himself against any conceivable accusation, he brought up subjects and presented evidence of which the court had been previously unaware. When the inquiry reconvened the afternoon of April 22, Hoage launched into a monologue which consumed all that afternoon and continued the next morning. Cross examination the afternoon of the 23rd and all day the 25th filled more than seventy-five pages of transcript.

Hoage's troubles began, he opened, in June 1918 when he was assigned for duty at the Training Station Hospital. He worked with several other hospital corpsmen from Providence dubbed "the Yacht Club," each of whom went by the name of a popular female film star. He became Theda Bara. "The name has not been tasteful to myself," he contended; "in fact I did everything to discourage it." Inevitably, everyone hearing him referred to by this name assumed his sexual orientation and subjected him to "all the indecencies of one so named." No patient, nurse, or doctor with whom he worked had ever put him on report or reprimanded him for either poor work or immorality. "All nurses whom I have worked for," he testified, "will say that I have conducted myself in a perfectly gentlemanly manner among the nursing corps as among the patients."

Nevertheless, the defendant admitted having become friends with men "of a questionable nature." Most he first encountered at the hospital; later he accompanied them to the Y.M.C.A. and visited their rooms. He met John "Ella" Temple during a party at the Tokio Restaurant, after which a group visited the Jewish Y for singing and dancing. The two became close friends. "I . . . have [n]ever," continued Hoage, "seen him personally have any immoral action while I knew him although he is reputed to be such a character." He had also met Arthur Green at the Y.M.C.A. and had occasionally helped him sell stamps or give out mail. He had gone to Green's rooms but never for "immoral purposes."

Hoage had never become close with the group at the Y. During weekend liberty he usually left town. In fact, he kept to himself so much that he was called a "person heavily veiled" without real friends. He feared for his safety, because "rough necks" around the Y.M.C.A. cornered boys, "got them to mention certain things to them, invited them out, "and then on actual procedure of their immoral practice beat them up." One man called "Madam Choo Chin Chow" had been attacked, and he thought Goldstein had too. Never, he contended, had he told Brunelle that he was a "French artist" or desired a "sixty nine" party with him.

Hoage was equally adamant in denying drug use. He had been approached about getting cocaine from the hospital but declined on grounds that obtaining any was "utterly impossible." Richard had tried to buy drugs from him, but he had refused. "Of all parties that have taken place among the inverted gang," he concluded, ". . . I have never been at any of them or have ever supplied . . . intoxicating liquor or drugs."

Hoage explained that every relationship characterized as sexual was merely friendly. He had once sent a note through Rogers asking a marine to dinner, and they attended the Opera House together. 'I never had any immoral connection" with him "in any shape or manner," insisted the sailor, "nor to my knowledge did I even express such a desire." He had also taken others to dinner or the show, and sometimes he gave them "little tokens," loaned them money, or paid for the room in which they stayed. This was only because "I had a bit of money and was free with it. . . ."

He described one occasion in detail. Soon after his discharge, John Temple had rented a room at the Y.M.C.A. to which Britz and Hoage were invited. They played the piano for a time and talked about activities of such socialites as a Mrs. Robinson in Hartford and Mrs. Hamilton Fish Webster of Newport. Soon Temple left for tea at the Webster's, leaving Britz and Hoage alone in the room. Britz suffered from an "eruption" on his back, so Hoage agreed to massage it with zinc oxide and helped him remove blackheads from his face. Both were fully clothed, the door remained unlocked, and nothing sexual had occurred. Later that day, he, Hughes, Temple, Britz, Brunelle and another man pooled their money and sent Britz to Providence to buy liquor. Just as he returned, Hoage left to nurse a patient suffering from spinal meningitis; he took a half pint of whiskey with him. Unfortunately, the bottle fell through a hole in his pocket at the hospital entrance. He also became ill, "vomited all over," and developed a serious nosebleed, not from drinking but from smoking a cigar.

Another occasion he had been invited to a celebration involving men from the U.S.S. *Baltimore* but had not attended "because I realized what it would turn into." He had heard that those who attended "were all coked up and liquored up; in fact they were rolling them out of the door onto the lawn." The drugs, he thought, had come from a hospital corpsman at the Training Station. He accused Charles Zipf (whom he obviously did not know was an operator) of using drugs although he had no evidence to prove it. He also suspected a man who had recently shipped to France because he was "always ghostly pale and extremely nervous."

Hoage denied having ever had anything immoral to do with civilians at the Y.M.C.A. Neither Green nor Kent ever "mentioned anything pertaining to immorality" except to criticize some men who hung out there as "disgraceful." Green had taken " a great fancy" to one marine, but nothing "out of the way" occurred between them. He might have used the terms "Auntie Green" or "Auntie Kent," admitted Hoage, but "I have never accused them of being inverts." He had spoken to the negro elevator operator but knew nothing of immorality on his part. He admitted, however, that the elevator man first warned him that an investigation was underway.

Finally, Hoage turned to accusations that he was gay. "During my time in the dormitories at the Naval hospital," he commenced, "I have never had any immoral connections." "It is true," he added, "that I have been seen at the Y.M.C.A. often times with boys of ill-reputed fame, talking to them, laughing and joking with them." "I have even fooled as much as they," he explained, "what they call screaming and doing foolish things such as dancing, and having a general good time in a playful way." His only sexual impropriety occurred with the Greek known as Mary Tusche. The two met on the street and went to Mary's room where Hoage had rebuffed an attempt to "brown" him. "'What about putting it between your legs?'" the Greek had asked. "I had on my underwear," continued Hoage, "and I knew of no harm for him to put it there between my legs to satisfy him and so I said 'all right.'" Viehl stayed with Mary Tusche and might have had sex with him, but Hoage had never attempted "sucking him off" because of his "disagreeable odor and arrogant air." He also knew "Ruth" Gianelloni and "Salome" Hughes, but he had never seen or participated in immoral activities with them. "I want to say too" he concluded, "that I have heard a great deal about immorality among the boys that I have known, but personally I have never seen any of it take place. All that I know is hearsay."

Accounting for the presence of drugs and medical supplies among his clothing required more detailed explanation. Some items were harmless — zinc oxide for use after shaving, aspirin for minor pains, sulphur ointment for scabies, and a hot water bottle for an earache. A nurse, Miss Smith, had given Hoage the Dover's powder to return to the dispensary, but he put it in his pocket and dropped it into a drawer. The codeine had gotten into his pocket during the "hustle bustle" of an admiral's inspection. He had found the bottle with some rags while cleaning a drawer and counted six tablets inside. "Shortly after I had got the rags into the drawer," he explained, "they called "attention," and I ran to my pea coat [and] threw into the pocket of my pea coat this bottle." In his hurry to leave for Providence, he forgot to return the drugs to Nurse Smith. "I also want to say," he insisted, "that I have never used drugs in any form shape nor manner in my life in civilian life or in Naval life."[21]

During cross-examination Hoage admitted knowing more about gay life than his earlier testimony suggested. He had attended a party where "indiscreet things" took place; "it was," he explained "what they might call a faggot party, . . . a general congregation of inverts." Just how had he learned so much about "inverts"? probed a questioner. Had he read books? No, he replied, but "off and on in the stage work I have seen and heard of such things being mentioned as inverts." Then came the ultimate question: "Are you the only straight one in this crowd?" "I am not," replied the sailor, "saying that I am straight." What he meant became clearer when he denied having participated in a sixty-nine party. "A straight person," he went on, "must be straight and not reciprocate in any way." Just what was he then? "As they say in sets I have known," he confessed, "it is a dash of lavender." Then you have reciprocated in these sexual acts?" queried the court. "Depending on what they were," he answered, "I might have what they call, yanked someone off. . ."[22]

VI

The evidence of drug use by George Richard seemed substantial. Operator Clyde Rudy, whose testimony opened proceedings April 25, swore that Richard had given him envelopes containing white powder on March 26 and 28. The contents passed through Arnold and Dostalik to Dr. Hudson, who had pharmacist John Collins complete the required analysis. One contained only boric acid, Collins testified, while the other held cocaine hydrochloride. John E. McCormick described a Whitfield Court party he attended with Hughes, Brunelle, and Richard. Elaborating on his original report, the operator described how he and Richard watched Hughes and Brunelle fondle each other for some minutes before moving to the bathroom where McCormick's inability to achieve an erection limited their sex.

Richard's defense proved short, shallow, and unconvincing. He denied having "passed around" cocaine although making no attempt to deny having given drugs to Rudy. Rogers and Rideout, not he, had suggested that Green and Kent were queer; Goldstein had not worn women's clothes in his room; and he had not bought drugs from Eddie at the Tokio Restaurant. While technicalities might be raised, Richard could not counter the accusations either of his homosexuality or of his having distributed drugs. Perhaps he recognized his helplessness and chose, in effect, to plead guilty.[23]

William "Salome" Hughes, who played the female lead in a station play only months before, began to defend himself on Saturday the 29th. "Did I ever tell you I had been a pogue all my life?" he asked Samuel Rogers. "No," came the response. "I meant to say that you were a female impersonator." Later Hughes interrogated William Gorham. "Have you ever had intercourse with me at all?" he asked. A long discussion of what constituted "intercourse" followed, at the conclusion of which Gorham denied having sex with Hughes. Under cross-examination, Hughes further argued that he knew nothing of most suspected gays and had immoral relations with none of them.

Hughes took the stand in his own behalf. He chose to "deny the testimony" of Arnold and Brunelle without presenting detailed evidence to support his claim. In rebutting Viehl, he admitted having been invited to Mary Tusche's room with Viehl and another man. Viehl "lit the light and started to embrace me." Hughes, however, had "refused to have anything further to do with him." At this point his testimony became confused. He suggested having left immediately but added that he was afraid because Viehl became drunk and angry. He also worried that "he might try to extort money from me." Even more peculiar if the two men's relationship was innocent, Hughes complained that Viehl told him he was unmarried "which afterwards I found out was a lie."[24]

The afternoon session dwelt on evidence against Wade Stewart Hervey, who was accused of having participated in gay sex and giving cocaine to Richard who passed it to Rudy. Dr. Hudson moved from membership on the court to the witness stand to describe his training in fingerprint identification and to swear that the prints on an envelope were Hervey's. The sailor then presented his defense. About three months after having arrived at the Melville Coal Depot, Hervey explained, he had met Richard and Rogers, both of whom were "the topic of conversation because of their effeminate habits." Richard tried to present himself as a "cocaine fiend"; once Hervey had seen him try to persuade Rogers that licorice, wintergreen, or peppermint lifesavers were cocaine. Hervey admitted having had charge of small quantities of drugs and that a missing tube of cocaine had been found in Roger's locker. To prevent such incidents from recurring, the station custodian authorized him to keep the drugs in his personal locker. When cocaine disappeared again, Hervey accused Rogers who "insinuated" Richard's guilt. The culprit had never been identified nor the drugs recovered.

Turning to suggestions that he had participated in sex parties where drugs and alcohol were used, Hervey freely admitted to drinking but denied everything else. Once in mid-March, for example, "while in an intoxicated condition," he accompanied Richard to Golden Hill Street where he laid on a bed. Hervey's later recollections were "hazy," although he recalled singing, piano music, and someone playing a boatswain's pipe. By the time he awoke at 2:10 a.m., nearly everyone had left. There was talk of cocaine and alcohol, but Hervey knew neither who supplied nor who took them. If sex had occurred, he had been too drunk or sleepy to notice. He had also spent a night with Chaplain Kent and ridden in his car, but nothing untoward ever occurred between them.

The closest Hervey came to admitting drug use came as he described a request from Richard, whose chief promised to get him a good job in exchange for "snow." Would it not be possible, he asked Hervey, to put boric acid in a bottle and label it cocaine? Hervey agreed that the chief could never detect the difference, obtained boric acid, placed it in an envelope, wrote "cocaine hydrochloride" on the outside, and gave it to Richard. This envelope had gone to Rudy.[25]

Next morning the hearing focused on William N. Gorham, against whom Arnold had collected trivial hearsay evidence. For example, Gorham challenged the operators' report that during a boat trip he had boasted of having "had intercourse" with Rogers and Hughes. Had he actually used the word "intercourse"? Gorham demanded of Arnold. Yes, came the reply. "I made note of his words in the toilet of the boat after the conversation," Arnold reported. Just how accurate was the report from Brunelle that Gorham went "out with the gang," several of whom he "sucked off or had screwed?" It happened several times, Arnold recalled, "sometimes in the hospital, sometimes in the Army and Navy Y.M.C.A." And had he recorded each conversation? He had, Arnold reiterated, "just as soon as I could get away from the man and get to a place where I could do it." "Had anyone ever claimed that he had a tight rectum?" inquired Gorham. "No," answered Arnold, it was Gorham himself who had said that another sailor was "pretty tight but was good fucking."

The only witness Gorham summoned before the court was Thomas Brunelle, whose own defense included references to Gorham among others. Did Brunelle still claim, demanded Gorham, that he had claimed to have "broken in" Fowler? Yes, said Brunelle. Just what word had been used? Had he said he "had intercourse" with him or had "broken him in" or had "fucked him"? "You just said 'broken in' meaning that you fucked him," closed Brunelle, who admitted he had no personal evidence against Gorham. What about Arnold's reported conversation? "Did you tell Arnold that I had sucked off and screwed any member of the gang?" he asked. "No." ". . . had intercourse with Rogers at Whitfield court?" "I never heard you speak Roger's name." "Did I ever tell you I had intercourse with anyone else there or at any other place?" "No." In fact, Brunelle added angrily, "Arnold has been using my name quite often in this investigation, and it seems as if I were held up as a king of the gang." "I don't recollect to this day," he concluded, "that I said anything to him about Gorham that was true." "Were you in the habit of telling Arnold things about me that wasn't true?" demanded Gorham. "No."[26]

Men like Gorham and Hervey were minor victims of Arnold's sex sleuths compared to Elmo "Ruth" Gianelloni. In his first appearance in more than a week, operator Charles Zipf described the "feminine" attire found in Gianelloni's room, reported his descriptions of other "queens," and passed on "Salome's" admission of having had sex with men from the U.S.S. *Baltimore*. What was a "queen"? interrupted a court member. "Inserting the penis into the rectum," explained Zipf, adding more crudely: "fucking the ass hole." He seemed unable, however, to describe in detail the women's clothing or to explain who owned it.

Brunelle returned to the stand for cross-examination by Gianelloni. "How could you tell Arnold that I held a party in my room on Golden Hill Street when I never lived on Golden Hill Street?" he asked. "I never made that statement," came the reply. "Did I ever tell you that I had a 'sixty-nine' party with Grenelle?" Gianelloni continued. "You didn't say anything about a 'sixty-nine' party with Grenelle," Brunelle admitted, "but you said that he had sucked you and fucked you. That's your statement to me."

Gianelloni closed his defense with an impassioned statement of innocence. "The statements that were made against me are untrue," he opened. ". . . I never told anyone that I was a queen or a cocksucker or a pogue, because I am not." He had admittedly done "female stuff quite a bit" and was "effeminate in actions;" the name "Ruth" came from dancing in a production of *Intolerance* directed by Ruth St. Denis. Gianelloni denied every accusation against him. He had never used drugs, seldom drank, and had never became drunk. Yes, he and Hughes were roommates, but they split the rent, slept in separate beds, and seldom associated with gays. Occasional visits with men like Grenelle, Kirk, or Brunelle had been entirely innocent. In fact, Zipf had "teased" him at the hospital and "tried to get me to do things that I have never done with anyone." Later Zipf took him to the Parisian Restaurant, treated him to "several things," and once in the room "tried several ways to get close to me." "I did not attempt to do anything," Gianelloni concluded, "and gave him distinctly to understand that I was not that kind of person."[27]

Of all the cases heard by Foster's court, the evidence against Logan Palmatier was the weakest. Harrison Rideout claimed that Palmatier had once admitted fellating Viehl. Rideout repeated the charge in court; when Viehl was summoned, however, he denied having ever met Palmatier, much less had sex with him. "To my knowledge," Palmatier testified, "nothing in my actions would lead anyone to say anything like that of me because I have always behaved myself while in the navy, and in fact all my life." Before enlisting he had helped his widowed mother and sister run a pharmacy. "I am willing that any investigation should be made regarding my past life," he volunteered, emphasizing that the charges made in court were "absolutely false."[28]

Nearly as insubstantial was the evidence against Albert Kirk. Brunelle claimed Gianelloni told him he had been "blown" by Kirk, but he denied that Kirk used drugs, powdered his face, or did anything else to suggest he was a "fairy or pogue." Rogers claimed Kirk penciled his eyebrows but had no evidence that he "was a fairy." "Have you ever been out with me in your life? Kirk asked Gianelloni. "No, sir." Kirk admitted attending a party on Golden Hill Street for "about one minute." "I just merely opened the door, looked in and walked away." In his own defense, Kirk admitted having talcumed his face after shaving, but he never used eye shadow. "In regards to being a cocksucker myself," he continued, "it is not so and never will be." He had never seen cocaine and "would not know how to use it if I did have it."[29]

The same kind of case existed against Whitney Rosenszweig, about whom operator Preston Paul testified. "It was reported," he told the court, that Rosenszweig "was one of the crowd and they had been pulling funny stuff in Ward 'D.'" One night after lights out, a patient had come by Rosenszweig's bed. "He had the same line of talk as the rest of the crowd," continued the operator, "saying 'take it easy,' 'now it has slipped out,' and 'I had better use more vaseline.'" The visitor soon left, and "that was the end of that." Was he suggesting the two had sexual contact in the midst of a crowded ward? "No," replied Paul, "I don't think a thing happened except talk. The other party wasn't there long enough." The only added evidence of wrongdoing came from Rideout, who contended Hoage had "browned" Rosenszweig. When Hoage appeared in court, however, he denied having made such a statement. In his own defense, Rosenszweig claimed total innocence. He had never associated with Kent or had sex with Hoage or Rideout. The hospital incident amounted to no more than a man's "fooling" with him and punching him in the ribs. "That was all, and then he passed on."[30]

Next appeared Gunner's Mate Everett Lowe, who had allegedly dated Hoage. Lowe admitted receiving a letter through Rogers. "Here's a letter from 'Theda Bara,'" Rogers said one day. "I didn't know who 'Theda Bara' was," explained Lowe, "and asked who it was from, and he says 'Fred Hoage.' Then I knew who it was." The note was an innocent invitation to dinner; afterward they went to the show and the Y.M.C.A. "The man did not approach me in any way at all." Unlike Palmatier, however, Lowe worried because his record was imperfect. During his first cruise he had overstayed leave by nine days for which he had been court-martialed. "I seen my mistake," he explained, "and tried to make good." He was also embarrassed by cards advertising his availability as a lover; they had been printed in San Francisco at a time when he was going with two women and handing them out to dance hall girls. Imprudent and wild though he might have been, Lowe argued that he was innocent of the charges now brought against him.[31]

Finally, the court considered the case against Jeremiah Fowler. Once more, nothing but hearsay evidence incriminated him. Brunelle testified Gorham claimed to have "broken in" Fowler, suggesting this meant having "fucked him." Gorham admitted having made the statement but interpreted the words differently. "I simply meant going out with you and having a good time," replied Gorham. "Did you mean anything immoral by it?" "No." "Do you say to the court that you never had any immoral relations with me?" "I do." "We went to the theatre and home again," added Fowler, "and nothing immoral has happened at any time. . . ." Nor had he ever attended wild parties, drunk alcohol, or used drugs.[32]

VII

After more than three weeks of hearings, the Foster Court of Inquiry announced its findings at a final session the afternoon of May 1, 1919. The day opened as Judge Advocate Drury informed the court that many of those testifying had been "detailed through the Senior Officer Present under authority of the Commander" to collect evidence. Cunningham, Rudy, Brittain, Haynes, Paul, Zipf, Feiselman, McCormick, McCoy, Crawford and Dostalik were identified as investigators. This was the first time their duties had been publicly acknowledged and must certainly have astonished many who had been hailed before the court. The report was divided into "facts," "opinions," and "recommendations."

Despite all the testimony presented them, the officers were still not certain how prevalent either drug use or homosexuality was in Newport. There was, they concluded, "limited" cocaine traffic among naval personnel, but they had been unable to determine the extent of drug sale and use in Newport generally. "Certain immoral practices" existed among navy men "and others," but mainly these activities occurred in boarding houses and at the Y.M.C.A. although present "to some extent" at the Naval Hospital, Naval Training Station, and Melville Coaling Depot.

The court's opinions dealt primarily with drug use and civilian immorality. Narcotics kept at Melville were improperly supervised; "adequate measures" should be adopted for their care. A "more thorough investigation" by "proper authorities" was also required to ascertain the extent of drug traffic and identify ways to minimize it. The officers also believed that a more thorough investigation concerning the "alleged immoral practices" of Chaplain Kent, Arthur Leslie Green, and other civilians mentioned in testimony should be instituted.

The court brought forth a series of recommendations aimed at resolving such problems. Unmarried enlisted men should be prohibited from renting rooms in Newport, with enforcement responsibility assigned to the Training Station morale officer. Waiters and porters at the Y.M.C.A. should be replaced by "competent married women waitresses and chamber maids." No one except Y.M.C.A. officials should be allowed to stay at the Y more than two nights in a row or once a week. A "more thorough investigation" should be instituted "under broader authority than pertains to the Commander" to "minimize" the use of drugs and immorality "among Naval personnel and civilians and others in the First Naval District."

The court then turned to the men whose cases it had considered. Seventeen sailors were recommended to stand courts-martial charged with sodomy and scandalous conduct. Included were such highly dubious cases as those against Viehl, Gorham, Johnson, and Fowler. George Richard and Fred Hoage were also charged with unlawful possession of drugs, while Wade Hervey was accused of "unlawfully supplying narcotic drugs to persons in the Navy." Albert Kirk and Whitney Rosenszweig were recommended for dishonorable discharges. Only Logan Palmatier and Ray Lowe were found innocent and ordered released "with no further action."

Last, the court recommended that "a notation be entered in the service records" of each operator "in recognition of their interest and zeal" in conducting the investigation. Named were clerks Ray Gardiner and Preston Barker, who had done no detective work, in addition to Cunningham, Arnold, Rudy, Brittain, Haynes, Paul, Zipf, Feiselman, McCormick, McCoy, Crawford, and Dostalik. Its work finished, the court adjourned at 4:30 p.m., never to reconvene.[33]

VIII

Justice moves slowly in the navy, or so those men hailed before the Foster Court of Inquiry soon learned. Even though the panel of officers rendered its decisions the first day of May, months passed without formal charges having been made against the men. Meanwhile, everyone—even those against whom no charges had been recommended—remained imprisoned in the post brig or aboard the prison ship *Boxer*. When no action had been taken by mid-June, Newport commander Captain E. H. Campbell reminded his superiors of the need for prompt action. He complained on the 10th of

July, and on the 21st listed each man and noted how many days he had been confined. Rear Admiral Herbert O. Dunn, who commanded the First Naval District, passed on Campbell's concerns to Washington: "The Commandant cannot urge too strongly upon the Department," he wrote, "the necessity for some action in this case."[34] Again on the first of August, Campbell urged that the men either be charged and brought to trial or released. Dunn agreed.[35]

Not until August 21, 1919, did Navy Secretary Daniels approve the recommendations of the Bureau of Navigation and endorse the findings of the Foster Court of Inquiry. Courts-martial were ordered for fifteen of the men: Stephen Brugs, Thomas Brunelle, Frank Dye, Jeremiah Fowler, David Goldstein, William Gorham, Frederick Hoage, William Hughes, Neils Johnson, Maurice Kreisberg, George Richard, Harrison Rideout, Samuel Rogers, Harold Trubshaw, and Albert Viehl. Kirk and Rosenszweig were ordered discharged.

In the cases of two men, Elmo "John" Gianelloni and Wade Hervey, the reviewing authority found that the evidence failed to "produce definite dates and places necessary to properly charge" them. More information was needed, therefore, before they could be brought to trial.[36] Months more passed while Foster and Hibbs tried to collect sufficient information. Meanwhile, Captain Campbell became more and more concerned about the delays. The confinement of Harvey and Gianelloni for so long without charges having been levelled against them, he argued in early October, was "a hardship to the men concerned." More serious, it was "exciting considerable adverse comments" and was about to be raised publicly in newspapers, "bringing undesirable reflections upon the administration of the Navy Department."[37] The Harvey case became further complicated when Senator David I. Walsh (himself the subject of a homosexual scandal twenty years later) inquired as to when he would be tried. The sister of another sailor, Maurice Kreisberg, complained to Senator William Calder about the unseemly delays.[38]

The Harvey and Gianelloni cases demonstrated the quandary in which the Navy found itself. On the one hand, both had been accused of "extremely serious" crimes, and navy officials hoped to see them convicted. On the other hand, the original testimony in the Foster court had been so vague that detailed, specific charges were impossible, and the operators who had testified against them had subsequently been released from the service. For a time, navy officers in Washington hoped that civilian police agencies might help them locate witnesses and compel their presence for a court-martial. Ultimately, however, this proved impossible, and the Judge Advocate General concluded that it was "futile and inadvisable" to proceed with the cases. Both Gianelloni and Harvey were released from the brig and, restored to duty prior to discharge without charges having ever been formally instituted against them.[39]

Such was not the case for others, however. Between September 6 and December 8, twelve of the men stood trial. No operators appeared against them, however, and the only opportunities for cross-examination occurred when the testimony came from other defendants. Generally testimony delivered before the Foster court of inquiry was read into the record, and verdicts were handed down.

The disposition of charges against Stephen Brugs, William Gorham, William Hughes, and Maurice Kreisberg cannot be determined. They were probably found innocent or convicted of such minor charges that the time already served in prison completed their sentence.

Frank Dye was found guilty of three counts of "oral coition" constituting "scandalous conduct tending to the destruction of good morals." He was sentenced to 20 years imprisonment followed by a dishonorable discharge. Officials in Washington reduced the sentence to 7 years, and he received a Presidential Christmas clemency lowering the penalty to five years, three months.

David Goldstein, convicted of the same charge, was initially sentenced to 30 years confinement, but had his sentence reduced to seven years by the Navy Department. Christmas clemency further lowered it to five years, three months.

Fred Hoage's conviction for scandalous conduct was overturned because a witness against him, defendant Albert Viehl, changed his story between the time of the Foster court and the court-martial. He was found guilty of possessing drugs in violation of navy regulations and sentenced to 10 years in prison. Washington officials reduced the penalty to two years, and he was released and dishonorably discharged on October 15, 1920, on the recommendation of the Navy Clemency Board.

George Richard was convicted of one charge of "lewd acts," and ordered confined for five years. His sentence was lowered to four years by a Christmas clemency.

Samuel Rogers was found innocent of sodomy charges but convicted of being "under [the] influence of cocaine," for which the court sentenced him to 15 years imprisonment. The Navy Department reduced the term to 7 years, and a Christmas clemency further lowered it to five years, three months.

Harold Trubshaw was found guilty of three counts of "oral coition" and one count of sodomy, earning him a 20 year sentence. The Navy Department reduced the penalty to 10 years, and a Christmas clemency lowered it further to seven years, six months.

Albert Viehl was found guilty of three counts of sodomy and one of oral coition. Two of the sodomy convictions were overturned on review because of "defective findings," and his sentence of 20 years was reduced to seven. A Christmas clemency lowered his sentence to five years, three months.[40]

Thomas R. Brunelle and Jeremiah Fowler deserted from the navy and were never brought to trial.

No charges were ever filed against Harrison Rideout.[41]

Drag Queen in Newport. Sailors often dressed as women for training station plays, and some attended "drag" parties in full-length
gowns.
    Credit: *Newport Recruit*, U.S. Naval Historical Center.

Captain Edward H. Campbell, Commanding Officer at Newport.
At first he authorized the anti-gay campaign, but later he insisted he
had told its organizers to "knock off."
    Credit: *Newport Recruit*, U.S. Naval Historical Center.

William Hughes, drag queen and accused homosexual. "Billy" Hughes had played the female lead in a Naval Station musical only months before facing court martial for sexual misconduct.
Credit: *Newport Recruit*, U.S. Naval Historical Center.

CHAPTER 4

Section A., O.A.S.N.

Well before the Foster Court of Inquiry completed deliberations, steps had been taken to expand the pursuit of homosexuals within the navy. Instead of focusing primarily on sailors, Hudson, Arnold, and the "operators" now turned their attention to civilians. What eventually brought the Newport sex scandal into the nation's headlines, however, was its formal authorization by the Navy Department, including approval from both the Secretary and the Assistant Secretary of the Navy. What had once been a limited investigation at a single post now expanded throughout the northeast as Section A within the Assistant Secretary of the Navy's office. Because that official was Franklin Delano Roosevelt, the historical significance of the scandal increased materially.

I

Primary responsibility for expanding anti-gay activities seems to have rested with Charles P. Hall, the Red Cross field director who had provided Hudson a room for his headquarters and advanced expense money to the operators. What motivated Hall is difficult to discern. Perhaps continued dislike of staff members at the rival Y.M.C.A., whom he suspected of being gay, or more generally a Puritanical obsession with eliminating homosexuality encouraged his action. He could simply have recognized that money loaned the operators would never be repaid unless Hudson obtained appropriations from Washington. Or Dr. Hudson might have encouraged Hall's activities as a vehicle for continuing his crusade.

During April of 1919—while the Foster Court was underway—Hall contacted Rhode Island Governor R. Livingston Beeckman to condemn the deplorable moral situation in Newport. Was there nothing that could be done, he asked, to apprehend civilians, just as the navy had already arrested many enlisted men? For reasons which are not entirely clear, the governor chose not to contact local police officials; perhaps he shared convictions that the police were inept, corrupt, or inadequately zealous in pursuing sin. Instead, he felt certain that his longtime friend, Assistant Secretary of the Navy Franklin D. Roosevelt, would help. The 23rd or 24th of April, Beeckman called Roosevelt to ask if he would meet Hall. "Certainly," the Assistant Secretary replied. "This is a matter related to Newport," the governor told him, "and I think you should know about it, and I believe that an investigation should be made."[1]

Hall arrived at FDR's Washington office the next day. He described the efforts underway through the Foster Court of Inquiry and the Department of Justice but argued that conditions were worse than ever. "What do you mean?" Roosevelt asked. "Everything, drugs, prostitution, and perversion." Hall added that because of the "failure up to this time, I recommend that you should start a new investigation." Current efforts could not continue, he explained because by now the operators were "thoroughly well known" in Newport. Why couldn't civilian detectives be employed? asked Roosevelt. "Because a civilian stranger coming to a little bit of a place like Newport is spotted before he leaves the station platform," responded Hall. What should be done? Hall suggested nothing specific, but he recommended that Roosevelt talk with Dr. Hudson, whom he characterized as a "thoroughly trustworthy man with an excellent record," the right person to expand the investigation.[2]

In compliance with Hall's recommendation, Roosevelt ordered Hudson to Washington, and arranged to meet personally with him and Arnold. Travel orders arrived while the Foster Court was still deliberating the fate of accused gay sailors. Hudson explained the situation to Commander Foster, however, and was excused in time to take the five o'clock train to the capital on April 30. Next day he and Arnold met Captain Richard H. Leigh, Acting Chief of the Bureau of Navigation. They described "appalling" conditions in Newport and presented Leigh with a "mass" of "very confidential papers." "I looked through those papers," the officer recalled, "and I saw what I took to be abstracts of evidence which had been taken before the court of inquiry."[3]

The next morning, Leigh joined Arnold and Hudson in Roosevelt's office. Later Commander C. B. Mayo, head of the recently created Morale Division, came in as well. Roosevelt opened, as Hudson recalled, by reporting that he had heard many rumors about Newport; "where there was so much smoke, there must be some fire." Hudson presented the Assistant Secretary (also Acting Secretary because of Daniels' absence) with papers listing the names of suspected gays and the offenses with which they were charged. Like Hall, he argued that continuing the investigation along past lines would be counterproductive; civilians could not be effective in such a small town. It was best, Hudson suggested, for navy investigators to continue under new sponsorship.[4]

While everyone concurred that an investigation was necessary and proper, no senior officer was willing to take responsibility. Captain Leigh argued that investigating civilians was outside the scope of the Bureau of Navigation. Besides, Navigation "leaked like a sieve," so that everyone in the navy would soon know about any project housed there. The Morale Division had been organized in part to undertake just such activities, but Mayo protested that his office was still being organized and was inadequately manned. Undertaking major activities at this time, he insisted, would "seriously hamper the work of organization." The only reasonable alternative seemed to be the Office of Naval Intelligence. Its primary charge was collecting information from abroad, although expanded wartime activities included domestic surveillance. When Captain Leigh proposed to the Acting Director of Naval Intelligence, George W. Williams, that his office manage the project, Williams protested that he had no available funds. Roosevelt promised the needed money and proceeded under the assumption that Naval Intelligence would provide support and supervision. Captain Edward H. Campbell, commanding the Newport Training Station, also visited Washington where he learned of plans for the new "very confidential and secret" anti-gay campaign.[5]

The following Monday, May 5, Roosevelt signed orders for transmission to the Chief of Naval Intelligence. "The conditions in and around one of our Naval Training Stations," the letter began, apparently declining to name the site for fear of a leak, "is very serious indeed, in so far as moral perversion and drugs is concerned." As a result, he had assigned Hudson and Arnold to the Naval Intelligence office "in connection with suppressing these practices." An officer should be appointed with whom they could confer, but because of the pair's "special qualifications," FDR urged "every assistance be given them in their work, and that their knowledge of the situation, based on previous experience, be given every consideration." The bureaus of Navigation and Medicine and Surgery would issue needed reassignment orders. Matters related to subsisting and detailing sailors should be taken up with appropriate offices. "You will consult with me," he added, "as to the necessary funds for this investigation." To insure secrecy, he ordered that "this be the only written communication in regard to this affair." As if to further obscure the matter of reporting responsibility, he suggested that an old friend, Lieutenant Stewart B. Davis, be contacted and asked if he would return to active duty to assist in the investigation.[6]

Upon receiving Roosevelt's letter on the 7th, the new Director of Naval Intelligence, Admiral Albert P. Niblack, expressed serious reservations about the plan. As early as March, Secretary of the Navy Daniels had ordered that with the war ending, Naval Intelligence should limit surveillance activities to foreign countries. Such domestic activities as these contradicted standing policy. Second, he questioned the advisability of employing amateur detectives for work that required the "best professional experience, because they were going up against expert criminals." It would be highly preferable, Niblack and Williams agreed, to employ a "regular detective agency."[7] Niblack made no attempt to hide his objections, and even Hudson recognized Williams' lack of enthusiasm. "I got the impression," he recalled, "that he did not much approve of the whole proceeding. . . . [he] had not made up his mind what to do, to go ahead or try to stop the whole thing."[8] Naval Intelligence chose to employ a detective agency while moving as slowly as possible to activate Hudson's plan. Not even Roosevelt, however, learned of this seeming refusal to comply with instructions.

Four days later Williams appointed private detective George E. Rowe to look into the situation at Newport and recommend appropriate action. He reviewed previous work by the Justice Department's J. J. Daly who concluded that Arnold's evidence was "largely hearsay" and "very much exaggerated." In Newport he interviewed Dr. Hudson at his home. "Lt. Hudson was very much surprised to learn that I had been directed to make this investigation," Rowe reported to Naval Intelligence, since he understood that Roosevelt would arrange to have him "assigned to the Secretary of the Navy's office to conduct this investigation." Hudson reviewed the history of the anti-gay activities, however, and presented a set of recommendations, later committed to writing, as to how he, Arnold, Rudy, and the other operators should be secretly reassigned to New York to continue their sleuthing.

Rowe's report, like Daly's, raised numerous questions about Hudson's ability to direct a campaign against Newport gays. "Lt. Hudson is not an experienced investigator but is interested in work of this character," Rowe concluded. "My impression is that he is sincere, but inclined to have rather exaggerated and imaginative ideas concerning the manner and form of conducting investigations." Hudson's plan was so impractical as to justify no further comment. Rowe proposed having two experienced, uniformed naval detectives sent to Newport so they could mingle with military personnel. They would "keep in each other's company constantly in order that one may corroborate the other." A second pair should be assigned parallel duties, but neither set should know of the other's existence. All should work under a Naval Intelligence officer headquartered at Providence or Fall River. No identification cards should be issued to any operator. Even if this approach was adopted, Rowe was pessimistic about the chances for success. "It should be borne in mind," he reported, "that it is extremely difficult to prosecute an undercover inquiry after an open inquiry and arrests have been made, . . . for the reason that such open action invariably tends to make suspected persons more careful and discreet and prospective witnesses more careful." Rowe had originally planned to conduct an independent investigation himself, but given Dr. Hudson's attitude, he concluded that such an attempt would produce "duplication, friction, and embarrassment to the case, to say nothing of needless expenditure of money. . . ." Instead, he returned to Washington, reported verbally to Williams, and went back to Pittsburgh to prepare the report he submitted May 19.[9]

Meanwhile, Hudson grew increasingly frustrated at the slowness with which the scenario was unfolding. In mid-May, after finishing work with the Foster Court, he received orders transferring him to the Naval Hospital in Brooklyn, New York. From there, he telegraphed Williams, whom he thought would see that further orders assigning him to head an investigation were issued. Hudson's superiors at the hospital had no idea of what was to transpire, however, and put him in charge of a ward. The doctor dared not reveal his plans, although he tried to convince the hospital commander that a permanent assignment was impractical since he would only remain a few days. He looked at me, the physician later admitted, "as if I were out of my head." Every day that passed without new orders became more embarrassing.[10]

Hudson's endeavors to speed up his transfer met with increasing frustration. He tried contacting Roosevelt's friend Stewart Davis at a New York telephone number. Davis was never home, however, and all he could learn was that his return was expected in a day or two. When Davis finally returned from his Long Island summer home, Hudson asked him to call Roosevelt. He also instructed Arnold, who along with other operators had been granted thirty-day leaves of absence, to Washington to find out why the plan had stalled.[11] Davis finally telephoned Roosevelt the last week in May to report that there "seemed to be a hitch' in getting Hudson's orders and urged his help in "hurrying . . . up . . . [a matter] of great importance."[12]

These efforts gradually produced results. May 30 Hudson received a telegram asking him to meet Captain Williams at the Hotel Astor the next day. The doctor had difficulty convincing his commander to allow him off duty to attend the meeting, since he could provide no details. The officer finally relented, though, and the pair met as planned. Hudson voiced frustration that "nothing had been done," and Williams apparently agreed to look into the matter. He also expressed misgivings about Davis' role in the operation, suggesting that because of his close friendship with a controversial admiral he "did not have a very good standing in Naval Intelligence." As soon as Hudson returned to the hospital, Arnold called with news that Roosevelt wanted both of them in his office the next morning. Hudson's request for travel leave precipitated a "hard argument" with his commander. Was there any written evidence to support the request? he demanded. The only proof Hudson could produce was Williams' letter introducing detective Rowe, but it was adequate.[13]

II

Meetings June 5 and 6 led to major changes in the administration of the investigation. Everyone admitted that either because of the reluctance of Naval Intelligence to follow orders or, more charitably, "a general crossing of wires," the expanded operation had "not gotten off its feet." A "full discussion" among Hudson, Mayo, Williams, Leigh, Campbell, and Roosevelt focused on how the work should be administered. Someone even suggested Hudson might be officially stationed in Hawaii, but the ultimate decision was that rather than assign the anti-gay squad to any bureau or division within the navy, it should report directly to Assistant Secretary Roosevelt's office. Despite continuing objection, Roosevelt ordered Naval Intelligence to provide identification cards; Arnold and Hudson took Naval Intelligence oaths.[14] The letter that served as Hudson's credential was post-dated from early June to May 15 to prove to his commander "that he was not a liar" and "substantiate the fact he was acting officially in making these trips."[15] By June 12, 1919, Section A of the Office of the Assistant Secretary of the Navy—shortened in Navy parlance to "Section A, O.A.S.N."— had been established.

Organizational details fell quickly into place. Roosevelt authorized discretionary funds from his accounts to pay expenses and offered to issue Hudson a general warrant. The doctor deferred on grounds that he knew "nothing about keeping accounts" and requested the help of a paymaster. He hoped to have the services of James M. Baker, with whom he had served aboard the U.S.S. *Leviathan*. Orders transferring Baker generated "quite a disturbance," however, because his commander at the Washington Naval Yard valued the sailor's expertise as a steel estimator and objected to losing him. As a result, Lester Hill was assigned to keep the financial records.[16]

Steps also proceeded to have detectives assigned to Hudson. June 6 Roosevelt signed orders transferring men to Hudson "for special duty until such time as he may request their detachment." All records were given directly to Arnold, so no one at Newport would know where the men were going or for what purpose. Included were many who had served earlier, including Rudy, Paul, Crawford, McKinney, Phillips, Dostalik, and Haynes. Zipf withdrew to resume medical studies; W. I. Crawford requested release as well, but Hudson refused because he was needed to testify against Kent when he was arrested. Nurse Elizabeth Baxter served only until general orders discharged all females. New men appointed to Section A included Thomas Conlon, H. K. Brown, Dudley J. Marriott, James Scanland, Joe Minnick, James Goggins, Chesleigh (Gilbert) Healy, August Bena, Claude McQuillan, Urban Young, Thomas Chaney, and George Steck.[17]

The new numbering system Hudson utilized reflected the more complex organization of the enlarged staff. Arnold became number

1000, and each of six supervisors under him (Rudy, Scanland, Marriott, Brown, Steck, Cheney, and Bena) was numbered serially from 1001 to 1007. Men working under them used the same last numeral, with the third digits arranged serially. Thus Paul as number 1011 was operator number one in the squad of Rudy, who was 1001. As the fourth man in Scanland's (1002) squad, Phillips became 1042. Only M. C. Crawford retained his original number of 3-5.[18]

A new office outside Newport was needed from which to administer the investigation. Hudson persuaded Roosevelt to authorize a location midway between Washington and Newport in New York. The real motive was that Hudson's wife required medical treatment there. At first, headquarters consisted of a single rented room in the Hotel Gerard. Hudson preferred a basement or first floor room from which operators could come and go without arousing suspicion.[19] Federal regulations required use of government facilities wherever possible, so on June 14 the secretary's office requested quarters in the New York Custom House. During a visit to these offices, Hudson confirmed that while the Shipping Board might soon vacate part of the building, no space was yet available.[20] As a result, he received authorization to rent several rooms at the Hotel LeMarquis, where he already lived. Desks, chairs, typewriters, and an adding machine came from the naval supply center. Some men remained in New York, but most worked in the Newport area under Rudy and Arnold, who set up a base at Fall River, Massachusetts. Everyone maintained regular communication by phone or through a post office box in New York.[21]

III

Despite these organizational changes and more formal authorization from Washington, Section A's activities so closely resembled what they had done the preceding several months that distinguishing between them becomes difficult. As in the past, operators frequented places where gays were known to congregate, struck up conversations with suspects, and whenever possible accepted invitations to attend a movie, eat at a restaurant, walk along the beach, or visit rooms. Not infrequently operator and suspect ended up enjoying sex together. Reports detailing what occurred were routinely mailed to New York, where they were typed and filed for future use. The only substantial difference was that sleuthing focused almost entirely on civilians.

While Section A was being organized, operators continued collecting evidence against Reverend Samuel Neal Kent at the Army and Navy Y.M.C.A. May 10, for example, Malcolm Crawford spent half an hour talking with Kent, during which he accepted an invitation to go for a car ride the following week. As they departed, Kent offered to help the sailor with his coat. Even such an innocent act was ascribed sinister implications. "He held his hand against my back a few seconds," reported the detective, "as though he was caressing a girl." Several days later Crawford agreed to join Kent for a play at the Community Theatre and to stay overnight with him. "He said he was sure I would enjoy the evening and that he would call it a date," Crawford told his superiors, once more inferring a great deal more than the invitation necessarily implied.[22]

Much more substantial and potentially damaging reports about Kent soon accumulated. The afternoon of May 15, Charles A. McKinney joined the chaplain for a drive along the coast toward Fort Adams. As the operator described it, almost immediately Kent indicated what "a great pleasure" it was to meet "a young man like me who had been brought up with the better class; that he liked my companionship and thought we would understand each other very well after getting acquainted." Soon Kent's hand slipped over McKinney's, "squeezing very tight all the time." Next it moved to his leg, "inching up and feeling up higher all the time, until he finally reached my penis." "He laughed," remembered Crawford, "and said I was some boy. I squeezed his hand between my legs a little," he added, "and it pleased him immensely." Kent wanted assurance that McKinney "was a boy he could trust," to which the operator cynically replied that he kept his mouth shut. They parted with a handshake and an agreement to spend a night together the following week.[23]

The next night Crawford kept his previously arranged date with Kent. Following dinner and a play, the pair went to the Parish House. Preston Paul kept watch outside until after midnight, noting what lights switched on or off and observing Kent remove night clothes from a dresser. Crawford had already retired when Kent asked if he would join him. A positive answer prompted the cleric to "jump into bed" beside the sailor. As they talked, physical contact gradually increased. "He was rubbing one of his legs against mine," Crawford recalled. "Had one of his arms around my neck and would squeeze me as if he couldn't control himself. He could hardly talk." Kent admitted that he "liked it 'backwards'" and complained that some sailors he had in bed had been dirty. "While talking," the report continued, "he was pulling me closer and began playing with my penis. He tried to jerk me off but I wouldn't let him." After fifteen minutes, Kent protested that everyone else "gave in to him" and returned to his own room. Next morning after breakfast, they parted with promises to meet again.[24]

McKinney's opportunity with Kent came May 20, when he accepted an evening invitation to the chaplain's apartment. No sooner had the sailor removed his coat that Kent "became very affectionate, putting his arms around me and trying to kiss me." The two moved to a couch where "loving up" began. "Pretty soon he laid his hand over and began rubbing my penis and wanting to know how big it was and all the particulars," reported the operator. McKinney declined to unbutton his own trousers, so Kent helped. "He had great sport for quite a while rubbing it and playing with it," according to the report, until eventually "nature took a hand in the case and the discharge went all over his hand." Kent continued "playing with the peter" until McKinney left. He promised to stay all night the next time. "Will notify headquarters in advance if possible," he promised in closing, "when I am to meet him again."[25]

From the 22nd of May (immediately after Hudson left for New York) until Section A was organized formally in June, no operator collected evidence in Newport. Thereafter, activity quickly accelerated. By June 13, Charles McKinney was back in Rhode Island. He ran into Kent, who had just returned from a ten-day trip to New York, Bethlehem, and Boston, almost immediately. "Said he had a wonderful time,' reported the sailor, "and stayed all night with a woman a week ago Thursday." The pair drove out of town to inspect the site of that night's circus performance before heading for Kent's apartment. Soon the sailor seated himself on the lap of the chaplain, who "commenced trying to love me up." "Then," continued his report,

> he unbuttoned my pants and commenced playing with my cock. While he was playing with it, he asked me if I had ever had it sucked and I told him no but I'd like to and asked him if he wanted to. He laughed and said he didn't do it. He said he's had his sucked lots of times but he wouldn't tell who did it. I

asked him if it was good, and he said it all depended on who was doing the sucking, that some knew how and some didn't.

A call from the church rector forced the pair to suspend their sex to go downstairs. Soon they returned to town.[25]

Four days later McKinney met Kent again. Before long, the two were in bed hugging, kissing, and playing with each other. "When it raised," reported the operator, "he tried to pull me over on top of him and put it between his legs." McKinney objected and, while the fondling continued, asked the chaplain "what his game was, did he want to suck it or what did he want to do?" Kent declined oral sex unless his partner reciprocated. "if he wanted to suck," retorted the sailor, "he'd have to suck by himself." Did he get "any pleasure playing with another man's cock?" the operator asked. "He did get some," came the answer. "It made him feel good to know he was doing something for another man." Shortly after, McKinney grew "tired of letting him play with it" and moved to his own bed. Next morning Kent proposed further sex, but McKinney declined because he did not have "much pep." The pair talked about a possible trip to New York and separated with promises to meet again.[26]

Operator Henry Dostalik visited New York with Kent. In the course of a conversation July 8, he told the chaplain that he planned a trip there soon to await discharge. Kent said he needed to go, too, so they agreed the sailor would leave a note at the Y.M.C.A. if they could travel together. Dostalik obtained approval from his superiors and notified Kent, and the pair met the evening of July 10 at 9:35 on the Fall River boat. Small talk on the deck and a shared bottle of ginger ale preceded their going to bed together. Dostalik reported that Kent "started to kiss me, pull me close to him," and say what a "nice buddy" I was. The operator continued his abbreviated report:

> Started to pull my penis and play with it and mentioned as he would want to jerk me off, but would only a little while and then he would stop and say, ["]Oh, let's don't get through as you won't like me after that.["]

Kent wanted to "suck tongues," but the sailor pleaded that he was "getting tired" and tried to move to the upper berth. "Just a little while longer," urged the chaplain, as he fondled the man, inserted his erection between his legs, and commenced "to work it up and down. . . ." Dostalik protested that he disliked sex that way, claiming that he enjoyed "the back way" but "not as good as the french way." The sailor eventually moved to his own bed. "Grunting" suggested Kent had "jerked himself off."

Next morning the chaplain tried repeatedly to awaken his guest and get him into his bed. Protests of sleepiness proved unconvincing, and after being kicked from below, Dostalik complied. Once more the chaplain played with him till he stiffened, slid his penis between his legs, and began moving up and down. The sailor's complaints resulted in an attempt to turn him over and "do it the back way." That, too, proved unsuccessful because the chaplain found Dostalik "too big" to allow painless entry. Finally, amid protests that he wanted to go out on the deck, Kent masturbated the sailor and wiped the discharge up with a towel. Efforts to "start the sailor again" continued until the boat berthed in New York. The pair spent the day sightseeing, after which Dostalik saw Kent off to Newport before calling the New York office to report his success.[27]

Efforts to collect evidence against Arthur L. Green, Kent's associate at the Y.M.C.A., proved less fruitful. Operators watched him nearly every night and occasionally trailed him through the city. They overheard him make what seemed to be incriminating statements. Once, for example, he referred to himself and Kent as "a couple of middle aged ladies" and urged a sailor not "to throw us down for some good looking women." He was seen in the company of marines whom he bought dinner and took upstairs to rooms in the Y.[28] One operator reported that Green kept company with an actor from the company that performed "Jack and the Beanstalk." "Green and Gidrey are pulling off 69 parties together at different times," reported another detective. When Green quit the Y.M.C.A. in mid-May, a detective lamented: "It will be practically impossible for me to make any headway on the case of Green, that is getting in with him. . . ."[30] Another man who saw Green near the U.S.S. *Boxer* described him as "very suspicious" and inferred that he was attempting to get gay sailors off the prison ship. Never, however, was any substantial evidence of homosexuality ever collected.[31]

IV

While operators devoted more effort to entrapping Kent and Green than anyone else, many other suspected gays became their prey during late June and early July. In all, Paul, McKinney, Crawford, Scanland, and Goggins filed reports on a navy librarian who frequented the Newport Art Association. The only evidence against him, however, was an allegedly "feminine" demeanor and repeated expressions of concern about the imprisoned sailors aboard the *Boxer*. Once he described the jailed men as "fine fellows" and volunteered that he had "such good times with them." Nevertheless, he declined every operator's suggestions to have sex.[32]

After his transfer to Section A, Preston Paul became one of the more sexually active operators. His exploits included an unusual heterosexual encounter. June 19 he dated a yeowoman from the supply office. The pair went to her apartment where she played the piano before falling into Paul's arms and beginning "some heavy loving.' The operator was soon on his back in a couch with the yeowoman pushing "as close as possible" to him. "We loved around," he reported, "and every time I would push up to her, she would push back." When Paul "tightened up on her," she asked what was the matter. If the squirming did not stop, he protested, "an accident" would be unavoidable. "After that she was worse than ever," he continued, "so I let her go and about that time I ruined a pair of drawers." She laughed. The pair remained together till midnight, during most of which time she was undressed. "I'm not sure," the sailor added, "but think that she also had a discharge with me as just after that she went upstairs between 5 and 10 minutes." They parted like the gay couples, with promises to meet again."

Paul did not limit himself to women. The night of July 8 found him at a popular rendezvous called Forty Steps along Cliff Walk. A man named Anderson, a servant in the Whitney house, offered him a cigarette. Hand squeezing began as they walked together, and when they stopped at a watch tower, the man's hands slipped across the sailor's pants. "He asked me how was my lily," Paul reported. Anderson hugged him, bit him on the neck, and remarked that he had "an awful big cock." Further sex was delayed until they reached a dark tunnel further along the walk. "He then started hugging me," Paul recalled, "and opened my pants and played with my penis. He kept remarking what a nice big one I had so I asked him if he didn't like big ones and he said he did." The sailor protested being jerked off, so the servant continued hugging, kissing, and biting. "He then got down on his knees," the report continued matter-of-factly, "and started to suck me off. After I had a discharge, I pulled away from him, and he spit the load out. . . ."

Anderson wanted to continue, but because Paul thought someone was coming, they smoked and talked instead. Anderson admitted having had sex with a sailor who called himself Boyd (actually operator McKinney) but Paul was "the nicest fellow he had been out with for a long time." Before they separated, the operator took all the man's cigarettes and matches, agreeing to meet him again the next night. "He promised me that he wouldn't go out with anyone but me in the future," continued the report, "if I would let him be with me two nights every week."[34]

Three nights later Paul returned to Forty Steps by 9 o'clock. Anderson had apparently forgotten his promise of fidelity, for he invited Paul to join him and friends for whiskey. They headed for the Bath Road apartment where Nelson, a butler for a wealthy Newport family, lived. Drinking continued until 11:30; Paul claimed he only consumed enough to confirm the liquid was alcoholic. All three competed for the right to bed the visiting sailor; Nelson won out for having provided the room. When the others left, he began fondling, with the usual affect, and then pulled the sailor between his legs. "He had a hard on also," reported the operator, "and tried to put it between my legs but I would roll off him." Suggestions of a "69 party" having been spurned, the butler washed his new friend's penis, applied salve, and began sucking. Paul did not report whether he ejaculated, although he claimed that he got up and left after Nelson tried once more to insert himself between his legs.[35]

Two days later Paul was waiting for Swanson at Forty Steps when he met Jack Kelly, a New Yorker visiting his chauffeur brother. Kelly initiated the conversation; Paul "bummed" a cigarette from him; and the sailor soon felt a hand moving "very lightly up and down my pants over my cock. I was sitting on the rail," he continued, "so I stood up and he started to run his ass around me." Nothing was said, but soon the New Yorker reached down and grasped the sailor through his pants. "He was very much excited by this time," Paul recalled, "and tried very hard to coax me to go for a walk." The sailor protested that he was too tired and needed to get back to his ship, although he agreed to return the next night.[36]

The date went exactly as planned. He and Kelly talked briefly, then walked along the south side of Forty Steps and over the edge of the cliffs to sit on a rock. Fondling began almost immediately. "He became very passionate, and said I made him very hot," reported the operator. "He kept saying what an awful big tool I had and then unbuttoned my pants and pulled my cock out. He played with it a while and then all of a sudden hugged me and said I'm 'going off.'" His own passion satisfied, Kelly dropped to his knees to fellate Paul, then spit the proceeds onto the ground before wiping him with a handkerchief. Paul—who was never modest—quoted Kelly as saying he wished he could have him in bed "as I would be wonderful stripped." The pair arranged another date the following week, but it never materialized.

Charles McKinney reported four sexual encounters in just over two weeks. He had apparently tried to meet a man named Sherman for some time before finding him at home on June 27. He knocked at the door on the pretext of seeking a room to rent but soon directed the conversation to sex. Sherman said he did not care if boarders brought girls home, but he himself would rather "be out with the right kind of boys." McKinney responded that he, too, "liked the men if they were the right sort." "This seemed to make a hit," observed the operator. As a result, Sherman showed him through the house and offered him a loft for $4.00 a week. The conversation then turned to different ways men enjoyed sex. Sherman listed the French way, the Turkish way, and "some other" way McKinney could not remember. The Turkish way, he explained to the operator, was "going in behind." Sherman indicated an interest in having the sailor "stick it between his legs or under his arm sometime," but at first explained that he had no time today. He became nauseous from oral sex, although he had a friend who was "very fond of doing it the French way." All this talk having stimulated erections on both men, McKinney allowed Sherman to unbutton his pants, pull out his penis, and play with it "a while." It was so big, the immodest operator boasted, that Sherman said he "never could get it in him the Turkish way."[38]

The night of July first found McKinney loitering around the public toilet in Washington Park. He waited till a "young fellow" came out of the facility, sat near him on a bench, then sauntered slowly toward Touro Street. The man said "hello," and asked if McKinney was lonely. He identified himself as a servant in town for the summer with a wealthy Ruggles Avenue family. The pair walked till they found an isolated street called Sunnyside Place. "When we got to where it as real dark he said we should stop there," reported McKinney, "and he unbuttoned my pants, played with it until it got hard, then got down on his knees and sucked it." They separated by 12:30 with promises to meet again.[39]

The next week the same Anderson with whom Paul had sex

"picked up" McKinney at Forty Steps. They found what was thought to be a secluded spot near a beach house and had begun fondling when someone came along. The search for a darker place led them to a side street where a noise again interrupted them. At yet a third location, McKinney reported, "We didn't see anyone so he unbuttoned my pants, played with it a while, and wanted to know if I could stand it every night." "I told him," the sailor responded, "maybe I could." Anderson promised to buy whiskey if McKinney would return the following Wednesday, but the operator refused to commit himself.[40]

Paul introduced McKinney to another of his conquests, the butler named Nelson. The two spent the night of July 13 talking and playing with each other along Cliff Walk. Nelson described a recent party where participants "did it every way known," talked of picking up sailors in New York's Central Park, and told of having taught "all the different tricks" to a country boy from Vermont. They later adjourned to Nelson's house where all efforts to get McKinney aroused failed. "He wanted to pull off a sixty-nine party, and said that if we did that it would get hard," reported the operator, "but I told him I didn't have any pep and would meet him some other time." McKinney left before midnight and prepared his report in time to turn it in at 1:30 a.m.[41]

John Phillips had much less success tracking down gays. Like Paul, some of his encounters were with women. Ladies in taxicabs frequently "motioned" for him "to go out with them." One afternoon two women who had been sitting in Washington Park suggested he follow as they got up to leave. He sat next to them in the Colonial Theatre. One girl whom he had seen before pushing a baby carriage admitted her child was illegitimate and claimed she used to "keep sailors" in her house. He also witnessed women picking up sailors near the Naval Hospital and at the beach. Eddie Harrington, the waiter in the Tokio Restaurant, had talked of some "very fast" women. A man named Simmons also gave out the phone number of a local woman who charged $3.00 for visits to her room.[42]

Phillips also observed the availability of whiskey in Newport. The night prohibition went into effect, he spotted several bottles of liquor near the Y.M.C.A. and followed two men who had carried a sack of bottles to a house on Farwell Street. On the way back, he met a couple of sailors who bought liquor from them. Once a "very drunk" man asked Phillips if he would like a drink. A negative response brought a threat: "If you don't, I will knock your flat hat off." Phillips took the bottle, but, as he explained, kept from consuming any. "I placed my thumb over the mouth of the bottle as though I were drinking," he recalled, "and I didn't drink a drop and I passed the bottle back to him." The two talked for several hours, during which time the bottle passed to half a dozen passers-by.[43]

In addition to prostitution and liquor, Phillips discovered homosexuals. The evening of July 5 he was sitting along the beach with another sailor when he spotted a "well-dressed" man who was "very nervous and . . . continually spitting." When the operator started toward town, the civilian followed, and after a brief conversation began fondling the sailor. "At his suggestion we moved several times," according to Phillips. "Finally he unbuttoned my trousers, pulled out my penis, and sucked same." Later the man identified himself as George S. Collins who lived in Providence but frequently visited Newport during the summer. He invited the sailor to visit his home, promising that if he brought a friend, "another fellow" could be invited. "He knew plenty of them."[44]

Little did Collins suspect that throughout the evening operator Joe Minnick had tracked him and Phillips. "I followed them for perhaps 3/4 of a mile where they went out on a small point and laid down on the grass." When they moved again, Minnick followed closely, once passing within six feet. "They were talking," he recalled, "and having a hell of a time." Back in town, Phillips introduced Collins to Minnick. Since the Y.M.C.A. was full, Collins accepted Minnick's invitation to spend the night together. "When we arrived at [my] room," he later told superiors, "I told him to make himself at home which he did by proceeding to strip off." The pair sat on the bed in their underwear reading the papers and talking. Finally Collins proposed they complete undressing. "I made the excuse that I had a beastly headache," reported Minnick, a freshman operator whose first encounter this may have been. "You better lay still and cool off and you will feel better," responded the civilian. "We lay that way for a few minutes," he continued, "when he reached over and began playing with my privates. He then slid down and took it in his mouth and began sucking." In an unusual refusal to allow completion, Minnick shoved his partner away and "gave him a punch in the ribs." Collins dressed and left to find a room elsewhere.[45]

Another man against whom both Minnick and Phillips sought evidence was a black named Chauncey Miller. Minnick first met him the night of July 6 in City Park on Thames Street. "He appeared to be very intelligent," observed the operator, "as he brought up history, mentioning Greek, Itallion [*sic*] and all the foreign composers and opera singers.'' Miller invited Minnick to his "club," which turned out to be a series of dark, empty rooms. The place had been busy before the war, Miller explained, but was "very quiet now." They drank ginger ale and smoked cigars until Miller "slid over," began "laying" with Minnick, and attempted to unbutton his trousers. "I pushed him away," said the operator, "and told him it was too damned late."[46]

Several nights later, Phillips spotted Miller standing in the doorway of the club and accepted an invitation inside. After touring the rooms, they settled near the pool table to drink ginger ale. Miller smoked cigars as they chatted about "music, actors, actresses, plays, etc." Later, as other patrons departed, they moved to a couch in the reading room where the conversation turned to "diseases of men and women, etc." Soon Miller's hand moved across the sailor's pants, unbuttoned the fly, extracted his organ, and began massaging. How far they went or what Phillips did in response was not mentioned, but the evening must have been enjoyable, for the operator left with an invitation to return when a bedroom could be reserved.[47]

Phillips also worked closely with another new operator, James F. Scanland. He first met suspect Dan O'Connor the night of July 9 at Forty Steps. They began talking about what a "fine evening it was" and walked together. Before long they found a secluded place where O'Connor began fondling Scanland. Their love-making stopped, however, when Phillips passed with a civilian and, as the report put it, "caught us in the act." They arranged a date for the following Friday, with Phillips promising to bring a shipmate and O'Connor agreeing to come with a friend named Eckman.[48]

Scanland met O'Connor at 7:30 p.m. in front of the Post Office. They talked, enjoyed supper together, and bought postcards. At 9:30 they met Eckman and Phillips [number 1042]. "We went down Catherine St. straight to the beach and laid down on the beach," recalled Scanland, "me with O'Connor and #1042 with Eckman." "They were laying about 12 feet from me," he continued,

and I stood up once and saw #1042 getting his cock sucked by Eckman. All this time O'Connor was playing with my penis and saying he wished we were in bed with no clothes, and then his passion would rise so that he could take it in his mouth. He caressed and played with my penis for at least 15 min[utes].

Once he was alone with Scanland, Eckman proposed that they "drop over the wall here and gave a good time." "We did," recalled the operator, "and right away he started to unbutton my pants and says, 'I know you are all right as you are a friend of Dan's' . . . so he went ahead and started sucking me off." Meanwhile, Phillips and Eckman walked to Bath Road, where they "stopped for a few minutes." Soon after the two couples reunited, the civilians ducked out through heavy shrubbery and the operators headed back to prepare accounts.[49]

The next night Phillips returned to Cliff Walk to meet O'Connor. They walked along the beach, purchased cigarettes, met several women acquaintances of O'Connor's, and rode on the "rolly-coaster." Nothing significant happened until they were inside the Old Mill, where O'Connor put one arm around the sailor's waist while the other fondled his groin. They walked past Atlantic Beach to a pasture where they stopped under a tree. "He requested that I sit down and be comfortable," according to Phillips,

> I had no sooner than sat down when he started feeling of my penis and trying to love me. In a very short time he unbuttoned my trousers and took out my penis and played with same.
>
> He made the remark that the only way he liked it was for someone to put their penis between his lips, at the same time requesting me to do it. This I refused to do.

They returned to the beach and parted with an agreement to meet again the 14th with Eckman and Scanland. Phillips' report was unusual in describing O'Connor, thus providing a unique description of dress among Newport gays:

> Hat: straw with dark band of two stripes.
> Suit: Dark, looked to be blue serge.
> Cravat: Blue with white dots.
> Collar: Long pointed turned over.
> Age: About 27. Weight: about 175. Height: about 5' 8 1/2".
> Hair: Black, combed down tight. Two gold teeth in the upper side of mouth. Looked to have same in lower. Had watch in front pocket of coat fastened by chain to lapel of coat.[50]

Another of the new operators assigned to Newport was Dudley J. Marriott, whose only encounter came with a suspect named Baxter. July 15 he had been sitting on a bench in Touro Park, then walked over to the nearby Channing Memorial church. Baxter "came along

and just passed the time of day." He appeared to be a gentleman,"
according to the operator, "and I felt I gained a valuable acquaintance, that is, a man I would like to speak to. He was a well-cultured
man in every respect." Baxter invited Marriott to his "studio,"
which turned out to be a shack "out on the rocks" in back of the
Clive residence. Exactly what transpired was never reported. Baxter at least fingered the operator, and they may have gone considerably further.[51]

Of all the new men participating in Section A, James L. Goggins
was the most active. Nearly every night he hung around Forty Steps
on Cliff Walk, and most times he ended up meeting someone. Relations were frequently so casual that he could not even identify contacts by name. "I was lying on the grass just north of the Forty
Steps," a typical report opened. About 11:00 a civilian laid down
near him, moved close, began to rub his leg against the sailor, and
suggested moving to a secluded clump of trees. "He unbuttoned my
trousers," reported Goggins, "and took my penis in his mouth."
The man, who came from Boston, worked in the commander's office at the Torpedo Station, and lived at 37 Everett Street, never
revealed his name. Goggins labeled the report simply "Cocksucker." When the pair met again several days later, they found a
secluded grassy spot inside a high board fence. Attempts to have
sex proved futile. "He unbuttoned my trousers and played with my
penis," according to the detective. "He excited no sexual passion
in me," so they quickly parted, with the civilian showing no interest in future meetings. Still Goggins failed to get a name.[52]

July 5 Goggins returned to Forty Steps. A man called Frank sat
down near him and asked for a cigarette. "We talked for a few
minutes," the operator reported, "when he began feeling around
and offered to such me off." When the sailor asked how much it
was worth to him, the man produced a dollar bill which was all he
had. "Then he sucked me off," continued the report. Meanwhile, a
friend named Jack took up with operator Thomas Conlon nearby.
The four returned to town where the civilians gave them a pint of
whiskey kept in their Salvation Army hotel room, and all agreed to
meet again the following Sunday.[53]

Several of Goggins' later encounters were with Frank's friend
Jack. He and Conlon, for example, met Jack and a man named
Gibson the evening of July 14 in front of the Community House on
Hill Street. During their conversation, Jack began rubbing the sailor
through his pants. He "asked he how much I weighed," the opera-
tor reported. "I told him. He said that was just the size he liked."

Nothing more occurred that night or when they ate together at the Boston Lunch the next evening. The 18th, however, Jack invited Goggins to his room in the Salvation Army Hotel. "Jack took off his coat and vest and came over and began hugging me and biting my neck," wrote the operator. "He began feeling my penis, then he unbuttoned my trousers and took it out. He played with it for about 15 minutes." The subject soon turned to anal sex, as Jack asked Goggins to sleep with him. Jack said "he would like to put his penis in my rectum. I laughed and asked him if he wanted to cripple me. He said he had done it to others and they never said it hurt. He said he would like to get me drunk, when he could slip it to me." Such talk and the accompanying caresses apparently had no affect on Goggins. "My penis did not get hard," he reported, "so he said to save it till tomorrow when he would meet me at the beach."[54]

If the pair met, no report of what happened exists. They went to the show the afternoon of July 19, however, and later met friends of Jack named Gibson and Pond. As they rode from Washington Square in a 1919 Chevrolet, Pond began feeling through Goggins pants. After dropping the others at Forty Steps, the pair drove on to an isolated location. "He stopped the car," reported the operator, "and unbuttoned my pants and took out my penis and began playing with it." Pond took his own organ out and suggested he would like to "stick it" in the sailor's rectum. Goggins declined, so he "got out of the car and jerked it off." They returned to the beach and picked up Jack and Gibson, who joined them for ice cream at the Convention Hall.[55]

V

As evidence accumulated against suspected civilians, Arnold began to formulate plans for a mass arrest. As early as July 6, supervising operator Clyde Rudy visited Arnold at Fall River to develop a strategy. They apparently feared that some suspects would flee or that locating them once warrants had been issued might be difficult. Since Section A lacked personnel to keep everyone under surveillance, they requested the Provost Marshall's office to assign them ten additional men. Two groups of five were ordered to meet at the Y.M.C.A. where Rudy "lined [them] up in a room" and, as he recalled, "gave them a little talk." The men were assigned specific suspects to "shadow' and warned not to get too close or arouse anyone's suspicion. "These men are bad man, but they are men that you want to stay shy of," Rudy said. "I told them they could be of service for the good of humanity and the Navy in getting rid of them." After a detective pointed out suspects, the "shadowers" kept suspects under surveillance on two-hour shifts from 9:00 a.m. until late at night. The men stayed at the Y, which issued them special tickets to receive meals.

Meanwhile, Arnold endeavored to obtain arrest warrants. He consulted Joseph C. Cawley, a Providence attorney assigned by the Justice Department to assist with the case. From reviewing operator's reports sent to New York, Cawley concluded that sufficient evidence now existed to make arrests. On his advice, Arnold made an appointment with Newport City Solicitor Jeremiah Sullivan. The case was discussed at a meeting attended by Sullivan, Arnold, operators Millard Haynes and Thomas Chaney, Newport Mayor Mahoney, and Chief of Police Tobin. Cawley was expected as well, but he never arrived. "They went over the reports," recalled Arnold, "generally looking over each report, to pick out what charges they could prove against the men." Finally the mayor spoke up. "Mr. Sullivan, you are the City Solicitor," Arnold remembered his saying. "I will leave this matter up to you; what ever you do I will sanction it. . . ." The mayor left, whereupon Chief Tobin said he had read the reports but would have to have the allegations proven to him. Arnold considered the chief's language "very insulting." He apparently said so, for Tobin became angry and left, telling the solicitor that "if he wanted him he could find him."

By 6:00 p.m. Sullivan, Chaney, and Arnold had drawn up a list of men they wanted arrested. The three ate together, then went to Tobin's office where Sullivan presented the list and asked the chief to swear out a total of sixteen warrants. A man whom Arnold recalled as Kelliher having prepared the documents, arrests began immediately. Tobin proved fully cooperative, even driving through town with Arnold to identify and apprehend suspects. Not everyone could be found that night, however. When Arnold left for New York the next morning to report to Hudson, he ordered operator Phillips to Providence to arrest one suspect. He went to Narraganset Pier after another.[56]

More serious, Reverend Kent had disappeared. Beginning July 21, operators fanned throughout Newport in search of him. Minnick spent a day around Washington Square trying "to find Kent or get information as to his whereabouts." Next day at the parish house, the sexton informed Urban Young that the chaplain was "out of town for a few days." He was still "on the street looking for Kent" the 26th and spent the 28th doing the same. Goggins and Conlon watched boats arriving at the Fall River pier, while McKinney met every train coming into Newport. Marriott thought he spotted him in a car headed down Spring Street, but he proved mistaken as no lights appeared in the Parish House. Finally, at 3:30 p.m. on July 31, 1919, Samuel Neal Kent was arrested on Thames Street.[57] With his apprehension, the major work of Section A, O.A.S.N. came to an end.

Rhode Island Governor R. Livingston Beekman urged Franklin
Roosevelt to clean-up Newport.
   Credit: Rhode Island Historical Society.

The Navy "War Council" in 1918. Josephus Daniels (seated), Franklin Roosevelt (third from the left) and many other senior Navy officials helped plan and authorize the Newport anti-gay campaign. Credit: *Newport Recruit*, U.S. Naval Historical Center.

Cliff Walk borders the coast between Newport's most fashionable homes and the sea.
Credit: Photo by the author.

Cliff Walk was best known as a romantic area for straight couples, but gay Newporters also found it a convenient place for making contacts — and more.

Credit: *God Packed My Picnic Basket*.

CHAPTER 5

On Trial in Newport and Washington

The arrests of the Rev. Samuel Neal Kent and other civilians inaugurated a second phase in the navy's systematic persecution of gays. Military investigators collecting evidence for Erastus Hudson and Ervin Arnold now faded into the background as virtually all sleuthing ceased. "This old investigation petered out"; operator Clyde Rudy recalled; "no work was actually done."[1] The focus of events turned instead to those government agencies that would determine whether the evidence was sufficient for conviction. Moreover, as the general public became aware for the first time of what had transpired over the previous months, defenders of the accused organized to demand justice, initiating the process by which the Newport scandal achieved national prominence.

I

Of those against whom evidence had been collected, none was more important than Rev. Kent. Born in 1873 and reared in Lynn, Massachusetts, he attended local grammar schools before matriculating at the famed Boston Latin School. The Kents were poor, so higher education seemed impossible. Instead, young Sam found work at the shoe making firm of William Porter and Son. Herbert F. Walker, who superintended the business, recalled that Kent "came as an office assistant," the lowest rung on the business ladder, and progressed through "purchasing, shipping, and charge of the packing room." By the time Walker retired in 1904, Kent directed all these activities for the company. Sometimes he went "on the road" selling. His reputation was excellent, beyond reproach, and his employer considered him unusually trustworthy. One summer he led a dozen boys on an extended camping trip to Sebego Lake; for two years neighbors chose him to represent them in the Lynn Common Council.

A lifetime in the shoe business promised limited fulfillment for Kent, so he began seeking a new career. For a time, in partnership with Pitt Parker, he ran a Lyceum Bureau to arrange plays, speakers, and musical performances. A theatrical career was soon abandoned, however, in favor of a stronger call to the ministry. In the fall of 1908, at age 35, Kent enrolled in the Episcopal Theological School adjacent to Harvard University in Cambridge, Massachusetts. There he came to the attention of Professor Phillip L. Rhinelander. "I was trying to establish connections with Harvard men," he recalled more than a decade later, "get them over to my house, talk to me, especially on Sunday evenings." Kent's age proved an asset, as did his temperament, experience, and "general knowledge of how to approach young men and influence them for good." His success was remarkable, and soon the flourishing St. Paul's Society attracted many Harvard students to the professor's study for sabbath evening discussions. Respect for Kent grew. His reputation, recalled a schoolmate, was "a thoroughly good one"; "excellent in every particular," noted a professor.[2]

Kent's experience and reputation won him rapid advancement following his 1911 graduation and ordination as an Episcopal priest. For two years he had charge of a small church in Arlington, Massachusetts, after which he directed young people's programs as assistant rector of New York's Church of the Holy Communion. His superior, Rector Henry Mottett, explained that he planned social activities for boys and young men "to secure the strongest possible hold religiously upon them." "Now," he added, "that was very largely what Mr. Kent did to interest himself in the social side of their life . . ." What was Kent's reputation? Excellent, Rev. Mottett concluded: "Everyone who got to know Mr. Kent and who remembers him today, remembers him with the profoundest respect and gratitude because he is a perfectly splendid manly man among boys and men."[3]

By early 1913 Kent had been named housemaster at Leonard Hall, a Bethlehem, Pennsylvania, residence for boys planning to enter church work. There he served as counselor and spiritual advisor to more than a score of teenagers. The school was adjacent to Lehigh University, whose president, Henry D. Drinker, met Kent, was impressed with his abilities, and in September 1916 persuaded him to become university chaplain. "I considered Kent to be a good man, a gentleman, and a man whose word you could rely on," Drinker recalled. "I believe him to be a thoroughly good, honest, man. That was his reputation in our community." A Lehigh professor recalled that Kent had been "extremely industrious and diligent," not only fulfilling his pastoral duties but undertaking such added tasks as managing a local Shakespeare production. A university graduate whom Kent steered toward a ministerial career and helped enroll at his alma mater remarked that "words could not portray . . . the high esteem in which Mr. Kent was held at Lehigh University."[4]

The outbreak of World War I created an insatiable demand for men of Kent's experience and ability. Never one to hold back when he could serve, he spent the summer and fall of 1917 as chaplain at Fort Niagara. As soon as Lehigh ended the next school year, he accepted appointment from the Episcopal War Commission as civilian chaplain at Plattsburg, where he was frequently the only protestant minister. "Very often," recalled a colleague, "he came over to Company N, and he would sit on the bed there and discuss questions with the boys; occasionally he would take them out for an automobile ride." Young soldiers appreciated his valuable services and his friendship. "I have often heard boys mention what a good friend he was," an observer noted, "how he helped them out of difficulties." He was in every way "a very valuable man in the community," winning special praise from his post commander for "the excellent influence . . . [his] presence had on the work and progress of the camp."[5]

Kent's success at Niagara prompted further advancement, this time to Fort Adams and four other small coastal facilities run by the army near Newport. He reached his new station in September 1918, reported to the commanding officer, and began establishing himself at each post. A visit to Chaplain W. G. Cassard soon changed the focus of his work. The influenza epidemic that engulfed America during 1918 had hit the huge Naval Training Station where Cassard served especially hard. Two hundred men an hour were arriving at the hospital, many near death; with several regular and volunteer chaplains, sick, too few clergy were available to counsel the sick, comfort the dying, or console the bereaved. "Is there not any possible way," Cassard asked Kent, "that you could change you work to come over to the naval hospital?"

Kent's requested reassignment having been approved by the Church War Commission, he began work at the hospital as Cassard's official representative. The first few weeks were especially traumatic as he comforted as many of the sick as possible, talking gently, writing letters, or providing spiritual assurances to the dying. He endeavored to see every patient daily and spent more time with the critically ill. Exposure to influenza was constant. The situation was almost too terrible to describe. "I hope never to see anything like it again," Kent lamented. By early October, the crisis having begun to pass, Cassard expressed his personal gratitude to Kent. "When you came to us, we were facing an emergency of a very serious nature," he wrote. Hundreds were ill, many were dying, and few could render chaplain's services. "You came to us at this critical juncture, and the service you have rendered has been of . . . the most helpful character," earning the thanks not only of the chaplains but of surgeons and nurses and the men themselves.

No sooner had the epidemic among naval personnel subsided than conditions worsened at the army posts to which Kent had first been assigned. Visits to the army hospital as well as other buildings used as emergency medical barracks kept him continually busy, and when the regular chaplain fell ill, the commander assigned him additional duties as acting chaplain. New responsibilities included holding regular services in the auditorium of the base Y.M.C.A., calling on soldiers in their barracks, visiting prisoners in the stockade and, as Kent recalled later, "doing anything that I could do to assist the men in any way."[6]

Demobilization following German surrender reduced the pressures and workload. Rather than restrict his activities to either army or navy personnel, Kent was asked by the War Commission to do whatever he could among all the thousands of service men in the Newport area. Hospital visits continued. He also spent several hours each day at the Army and Navy Y.M.C.A. Exactly what did he do? someone asked. "Serving the boys, listening to what they had to say, any complaints they might make, trying to be friends with them," was his response. Perhaps the term "Big Brotherhood" expressed it best. Kent's role, explained another Y.M.C.A. employee, was "to do a good turn wherever he could and for whomever he could." "Pop Kent is a good soldier," the boys often remarked; "there is a fine man; there is a good fellow."[7]

II

Such a successful career did not, however, blot out the nightmare that began with Kent's arrest the last day of July 1919. Almost from the day Arnold began loitering around the Y.M.C.A. he concluded that the chaplain was homosexual and set about trying to demonstrate his guilt. Nearly every operator tried to make friends with him, and wherever possible they accepted invitations to dinner, the theatre, car rides, or overnight stays in his apartment. In all, the Bill of Particular prepared against Kent listed eleven occasions between May 15 and July 10, 1919, when sailors had witnessed his "lewd and scandalous" behavior.[8]

Not surprisingly, the first court proceeding were inaugurated against Kent. He was sufficiently prominent by comparison with others that his conviction would virtually assure the successful prosecution of others. If it could be proven that a minister of the gospel had participated in homosexual activities, it should be simple to convict servants, librarians, restaurant workers, and other alleged gays. In addition to Kent, charges were also brought against Ernest Vernon, alias Brown. For reasons not readily explained, his name appears in none of those operators' reports included in the record, so nothing about his background or alleged crimes is known. Possibly Vernon was one of the anonymous civilians with whom operators had contact or he had given out a different name.

The trials that occurred August 22 and 23 raise as many questions as they answered. According to Rhode Island law, district trials were not held in a "court of record," so no official transcript of the proceedings exists. Kent's attorneys from the firm of Sheffield and Hervey employed stenographer Charles L. Wood. He later described himself as new at the profession and admitted that because of difficulty in keeping accurate records, mistakes might well have crept into his work. Dr. Hudson asked Arnold to find a stenographer from the Naval Training Station, but the man taking notes for the government left the service before transcribing them. No one completed the task.[9]

Another issue clouding the trial was the impartiality of Judge Hugh B. Baker, who heard both cases. As an appointed official, some claimed he was "a political judge." Others labeled him "corrupt" or "incompetent." Assistant Secretary of the Navy Franklin Roosevelt characterized him as "a political appointee who knows very little about law, and before whom it is difficult to obtain the proper kind of justice, especially from the point of view of the government or the state." Hudson objected that the trial had been held in open court where witnesses had to describe their intimate sexual relations for everyone to hear. "In most courts," he argued, "a case of that nature is in a closed court, because of its effect on the morale of the community, and I certainly believe this should have been a closed court. . . ." The judge disagreed, however, and denied admission only to women, whom even he apparently believed deserved protection.[10]

The prosecution's strategy seemed simple and reasonable. Operators Charles Zipf, Charles McKinney, Malcolm Crawford, Urban Young, and James Conlon apparently testified in one or both trials. Each described how they had met the accused and detailed the sexual activities they claimed to have occurred between them. Some witnesses proved especially effective. Conlon, Hudson recalled, "practically took the court off its feet" when he testified.[11]

The approach taken by the defense seriously undermined the navy's case. Attorneys employed by Kent and Vernon presented character witnesses who declared their clients' moral purity. Vernon's friends provided alibis for the times when crimes allegedly occurred. Explained Arnold: "two or three women" testified on his behalf. One said she had seen him "in the house sometime before the alleged act and sometime after the alleged act." Clergymen who had known Kent since his youth confirmed his good reputation and denied that he was capable of gross immorality.[12]

Cross-examination of operators aimed to show that the accused had been entrapped. A critical issue arose when the defense probed the existence and activities of the undercover detective squad. The first operator refused to answer on grounds that his Naval Intelligence oath prevented revealing such information. The judge, however, ordered the man to testify. Furthermore, the defense attorney's hard-hitting questions intimidated several prosecution witnesses. "I also heard in that court," recalled Arnold, "what I considered a threat to one of the witnesses which scared the man so he left the stand, and I had to go out in the hall and talk to him before he would go back on the stand."[13]

As details of the operators' activities emerged, the issue of entrapment became central to the defense. Under close, probing, unrelenting pressure from Vernon and Kent's attorneys, naval witnesses admitted that they had been ordered to allow themselves to become sexually involved "to the limit" if necessary to collect evidence. Later they tried to explain that the word "order" had not been used in its military sense. "I was talking to a group of laymen . . . and civilians that used the words 'ordered' and 'advised' indiscriminantly," complained Zipf. "In fact as to an actual military order, there was none."[14] Charles McKinney admitted that he had said, "My instructions were to be with Mr. Kent as much as possible, and to let him play with my penis and to allow it until . . . [I]had an emission." Later, he denied the truth of this statement, explaining that "in the Newport trial of Mr. Kent it was my first appearance in any kind of court." He continued:

> I testified for several hours . . . standing on my feet the whole time, and was forced to break my secret oath in the court, and under the stress of severe cross-examination by Mr. Hervey. . . . I permitted him to lead me in that case and answer practically the way he wanted me to answer, simply because I was excited and didn't know what I was doing.[15]

The revelations in the Newport trial excited strong emotional outcries from both sides. "I wasn't disappointed at the prosecution," insisted Hudson, "but I was disappointed with the tactics used by the defense attorneys. . . ." After McKinney testified, one observer commented that he "should be tarred and feathered and run out of Newport."[16]

The vigor of the defense together with revelations about the work of the anti-gay squad proved fatal to the prosecution. At the conclusion of Vernon's trial, his attorney evidently moved for acquittal based on insufficient evidence. Judge Baker agreed. Within days, after having heard testimony similar to that against Kent, Baker ruled him innocent.[17]

III

Only days after Kent's acquittal, Hudson visited Washington to inform Roosevelt of what had happened. "He was very much disappointed," Roosevelt recalled, "because he and his investigators had been unable to convict Rev. Kent and another civilian in the two trials held in Newport." The Assistant Secretary later confessed that as an Episcopalian, he had been "rather glad, personally" to hear the news. Why, he probed, was Hudson so sorry? "Because I still believe," he replied, "that Dr. Kent is guilty and more than that, I believe that the trial was a miscarriage of justice and was badly conducted." He went on that this had not been a court of record and that the judge was a political appointee and probably "incompetent." No doubt the government should find some new way to bring Kent to a second trial.[18]

Hudson was not, however, the only visitor to Washington. Early in September two prominent Rhode Island citizens arrived at the Navy Department to see Roosevelt. Rev. Stanley C. Hughes was a prominent Episcopal clergyman assigned to Trinity Parish, Newport while Hamilton Fish Webster was a wealthy townsman in whose home sailors had frequently been entertained. Once inside FDR's office, the pair bitterly attacked the navy for having persecuted Kent. Roosevelt responded politely that he was "much disturbed by what they reported." When shown what purported to be a record of the Kent trial, he was surprised, since he had been told by Hudson that no transcript existed. "I said nothing about it," he later admitted, "because I had too much official business to attend to that day to read the testimony." Nevertheless, before ushering the visitors to Captain Richard Leigh, he told them: "If anybody has been guilty of ordering things like that done," "he ought to swing for it." This did not fully satisfy the Newport representatives, however. "Of course, the Navy Department must make amends to Mr. Kent," they added, asking Roosevelt directly: "What are you going to do about it?" "If offenses of this kind have been going on," he responded, "they will be immediately stopped." In all, FDR later recalled, the men could not have been in his office more than six or seven minutes.[19]

Many more details poured out during the lengthy meeting Hughes and Webster enjoyed with Captain Leigh. Kent had been arrested, they complained, "handcuffed on the streets of Newport, and tried in court and found not guilty. . . . and [t]he[y] wanted an apology from the Navy Department." Their evidence consisted of what purported to be testimony from the trial and letters attesting to the chaplain's good character. The men departed briefly, during which Leigh perused these materials. On one hand, he became convinced that the accused were guilty of committing "acts of that kind" with sailors. Just as serious, however, he recognized that operators had "gone further than was right and proper." When the Newport men returned, Leigh promised to recommend the appointment of a high-ranking officer to investigate the case.

A conference between Leigh and Roosevelt produced agreement

on a two-fold plan. First, they summoned Hudson to the Navy Department and ordered that "if this was going on, that it was to stop immediately." The doctor, of course, denied ever having utilized improper methods and pledged that they "would not occur in the future." Second, they appointed Captain John D. Wainwright from the Philadelphia Navy Yard to investigate the Newport situation.[20]

Captain Wainwright began to prepare his report almost immediately. Collecting evidence proved difficult because operators refused to tell him anything about their work. In frustration, he telephoned Hudson to complain. The physician explained as commanding officer of the section that the men were "under orders to maintain secrecy and not divulge information." He suggested that Wainwright talk to hospital commander Captain Gates, Newport City Solicitor Jeremiah Sullivan, Attorney Joseph Cawley, Lt. Commander Murphy J. Foster, and Red Cross field director Charles Hall. He also agreed to let him interview as many operators as were available in Newport; the remainder met him in New York. "I had quite a talk with Captain Wainwright," explained Hudson, "and went over the whole situation." The investigation had been made especially difficult, he continued, because of the operator's "lack of authority"; arrest powers would have made a clean up possible "in a much more ideal way." Moreover, he continued, "the perverts are very careful to do things in secret where they are not observed."

The report completed September 17 and submitted to Captain Leigh the next day emphasized the positive aspects of the anti-gay investigation. The investigating group had been headquartered in New York, according to Wainwright, but had carried out operations in New London, Connecticut, Providence and Pawtucket, Rhode Island, and Fall River and Boston, Massachusetts. He made no mention of Newport, and no reports describe activities in any other city. In each location, investigators working under chief operators received written and oral instructions, those related to "the detection of moral perverts being given orally." Orders prohibited soliciting persons "to commit an immoral act," he noted, adding the unbelievable statement that no operator "had asked or solicited any immoral act from any person." Detectives sometimes wore uniforms and other times civilian clothes; all worked "voluntarily and of the[ir] own free will," and no one ever complained about the work.

Wainwright also discussed the sexual activities operators had undertaken. "When an attempt was made upon an operator by a moral pervert," he told the Navy Department, their instructions were "not to permit to go the limit, although some operators have stated that they were not to go the extreme unless necessary to get evidence." A list included the names of men who "had immoral acts attempted to be performed upon them by moral perverts." Each, he continued, had "perfect marks in their records of sobriety and obedience" except Conlon, who had once overstayed a leave. They performed the work willingly, although paid nothing more than their regular rate plus three dollars a day for subsistence and reimbursement for incidental expenses. "The files and records of the headquarters," the report concluded, had been "kept in an approved manner" and someone was "on watch at all times to receive messages and to guard the premises" in New York.

In discussions with Captain Leigh, Wainwright expressed full confidence in Arnold and Hudson. He was "thoroughly convinced of [their] honesty and sincerity," reported Leigh, and "felt that they had the good of the service at heart and . . . were using their best efforts to stop these very bad conditions." Was he absolutely certain investigations had ceased? asked Leigh. No, responded Wainwright; he was not "positive about that." As soon as Wainwright left his office, Leigh drafted a telegram to Hudson that he carried to Roosevelt for approval: "Discontinue present work," it directed, and "report to Bureau of Navigation with Arnold Monday morning September twenty-second."[21]

IV

Neither Leigh nor anyone else recognized that while these events transpired in Washington, Hudson and Arnold had been preparing for further prosecution of Kent. Soon after visiting FDR, Hudson returned to Providence to meet with attorney Joseph Cawley. "I went over the whole situation with him from all angles," recalled the doctor, "that is the political situation, the church situation, the Newport situation, and a great many different situations which had arisen at this time." Later he called on Charles P. Hall, the former Red Cross official, now retired to Pawtucket, Rhode Island, whose intervention had helped precipitate the creation of Section A. "He wanted to know how things were going," according to Hudson, "and I told him about the trial in Newport." Hall was "quite disgusted" by what he heard and suggested a meeting with Episcopal

Bishop James DeWolf Perry, one of the most respected clergymen in New England. He had known Kent for many years and headed the Church War Commission that employed him at the Army and Navy Y.M.C.A.[22]

Hudson accepted the idea and returned to Cawley's office to telephone the diocese for an appointment. When he and Arnold arrived at the bishop's office, they identified themselves as attached to the Assistant Secretary of the Navy's office and indicated their interest in "moral conditions in and around Newport." As soon as Kent's name was mentioned, Perry became "very, very angry" that the pair still thought him guilty. Hudson argued that he was convinced of the chaplain's guilt because of evidence including testimony from Dostalik and a man named Britz had not been presented in court plus other "character testimony" heard by the Foster Court of Inquiry. "I told him that it was common knowledge that he was a man of that type," explained Hudson, noting that he himself had observed Kent "feel up certain boys" at the hospital.

After all, continued the doctor, detecting perverts was simple. "If a man was walking along the street in an effeminate manner," he explained, "with his lips rouged, his face powdered, and his eye brows pencilled, . . . in the majority of cases you could form a pretty good opinion of what kind of man he was, and that in the majority of cases you would be right in forming the opinion that man was a 'fairy.'" "Didn't you tell the Bishop," an inquirer later asked, "that you could detect a degenerate at sight, at a glance, and that if you saw a man walking along and observed the actions, not hastily, that you could tell pretty well that man was a 'fairy.'" "That," responded the doctor, "is common knowledge." Arnold confirmed the doctor's arguments, leaving the impression that he claimed "the power of detecting sexual degeneracy at sight."

As the discussion continued, Perry mellowed. He confirmed his own desire to see Newport cleaned up, although refusing even to look at materials on Kent that Hudson had brought with him. At first, the bishop ordered the two men out of his office, but they talked further while walking toward the exit. Hudson argued that the twenty witnesses against Kent could not all have lied. Ultimately, Perry "apologized for his hasty action," asked that his "rudeness be excused," and shook hands. The navy would provide Perry with as much information as he wanted, promised Arnold, including the transcript from the Foster Court of Inquiry, access to files of Section A, and the opportunity to question operators in person. Perhaps a committee of two or three officers and an equal number of clergymen could be formed to review the case. Perry seemed "so pleased with that arrangement" that Hudson reported afterward to Hall: "I think we have made a hit with the Bishop."[23]

The last had not been heard from Bishop Perry, for the same month he appeared in Washington. Unlike Hughes and Webster, he was not content to see the Assistant Secretary. So as soon as Secretary of the Navy Josephus Daniels returned from Hawaii, on September 21, he found Perry outside his office. Daniels claimed the first time he learned that the Newport investigation had extended beyond naval personnel came as the bishop described efforts to prosecute civilians, including Kent. The evidence collected, however, had been "characterized as improper," as a result of which Kent had been acquitted. The navy, Perry continued, should "write a letter or make a public apology." Something should also be done about enlisted men who in the process of gathering evidence had been immoral. "I was shocked," admitted the Puritanical Daniels, "to be informed that any enlisted personnel in the Navy had practiced what Bishop Perry said these men had practiced in obtaining evidence."

Daniels summoned Admiral Richard Niblack, Chief of Naval Intelligence, who knew more about the case. "Of course, I can make no apology, and I can make no statement until I have all the facts in the matter," Daniels told Perry. "We must have all the information," he went on, explaining that he had never heard of Kent but would "look into it." Niblack was less cautious. "Mr. Secretary, he told Daniels, apparently while Bishop Perry was still present, "I would advise you not to make an apology as the evidence in this case is very strong."[24]

The government's intentions became clearer during a visit to Newport by Niblack. After a lecture at the Naval War College, he telephoned his "great personal friend," Rev. Stanley C. Hughes. He would only be in town a few hours, Niblack said, but "he wanted to know why he [Hughes] was so much interested in the Reverend Samuel Neal Kent. . . ." Niblack warned the rector that he "was putting himself in a very bad position by mixing himself with the case." Hughes' request for an explanation was met by the suggestion of a meeting.

In their time together Niblack admitted that the navy should apologize if Kent were innocent. That could only be true, however, if witnesses perjured themselves, which seemed unlikely. "It was up to the church, he went on, "to not put itself in the position of allowing a minister of the gospel to rest under any suspicion. . . . The only way" to settle the question finally "was to try the case again and then if the case was not successfully prosecuted, there must be something criminally wrong with the evidence."

Hughes' reply demonstrated the Newport clergy's strong support for Kent. He described the chaplain's work "in the highest praise" and argued that from close association with Kent he was sure "these stories could not be true." Evidence presented at Newport was ridiculous, he continued, as he "charged the witnesses with perjury, and in fact, ridiculed the whole proceedings and character of the evidence as being irresponsible." The two men agreed on nothing, of course, and Niblack left convinced that Hughes "sincerely and honestly believed that the Reverend Mr. Kent was absolutely innocent of the slightest suspicion of the charges. . . ."[25]

By the time Hudson and Arnold returned to Washington the third week in September, nearly every naval official associated with the Newport case had become convinced of Kent's guilt. Discussions regarding future action occurred during meetings among Hudson, Arnold, Leigh, Niblack, Roosevelt, Cawley, and Daniels. At a staff session September 25, the only one who demurred from further prosecution was Captain Leigh, who feared publicity generated by a new trial would adversely affect recruitment. "It would not look well," Hudson recalled his having said, "if people wanted to make an issue of it from a moral standpoint." "I did say," Leigh remembered, "that it would be bad for the Navy." Admiral Niblack argued that the "methods being used were the right methods." He later confessed embarrassment at his earlier "belittling" of Hudson and Arnold and felt compelled as an active Y.M.C.A. supporter to see that organization vindicated. "It seemed to me outrageous that the institution's usefulness could be jeopardized by any connection with immoral practices." When the meeting moved to the Secretary's office, Niblack argued that "it was imperative that the Department take up the further prosecution of Reverend Samuel Kent to demonstrate that he was guilty." Daniels was sufficiently "horrified" after hearing a review of the evidence to order Hudson and Leigh to raise that possibility with the Justice Department.[26]

That same day Arnold, Hudson, and perhaps Leigh met with Assistant Attorney General Robert P. Stewart. Stewart knew nothing of the case, so they explained it to him, noting that Cawley had been appointed a special assistant and informing him that Newport ministers had demanded an apology. Stewart was angry because his overcoat had recently been stolen by a minister. "Tell the Navy Department that if any more preachers come down there looking for apologies," Hudson recalled him saying, "to send them to him and that he would take care of them. . . ."[27]

Stewart prepared a letter ordering Cawley to expedite the case. Noting that Hudson and Arnold had come to his office inquiring about prosecution, he informed the Providence lawyer that "this serious matter demands attention from yourself and whoever is in charge of these prosecutions." If evidence was ample, he should "proceed promptly and vigorously to prosecute. . . ." Shortcomings should be detailed so the navy could determine "whether or not the deficiency can be supplied." "You will keep in mind," continued the letter "in the institution of these actions if any local situation might affect the judgment or decision of the United States Commissioner" from whom an arrest warrant would be requested. The obvious implication was that the case could be transferred to a more compliant commissioner or taken before a special grand jury to insure indictment.[28]

Cawley proposed prosecuting Kent (and perhaps other civilians) under a wartime statute extending federal jurisdiction to immoral behavior near federal installations. "During the present emergency," read the law,

> it shall be unlawful within such reasonable distance of any military camp, station, fort, port, canton, training or mobilization place to engage in prostitution or to aid or abet prostitution or to within such solicit for the purpose of prostitution or to keep or set up a house of ill fame, brothel or boarding house.

The specific clause under which Kent could be prosecuted made it illegal "to receive any person for the purpose of lewdness, assignation, or prostitution into any vehicle, conveyance, place, structure, or building."[29]

As suggested by Stewart, Cawley visited Washington to propose his plan to navy officials; Captain Leigh suggested the matter be discussed personally with Secretary Daniels. He was unavailable the morning Cawley arrived, but by afternoon everyone associated with the case congregated in the secretary's office. Cawley explained his strategy, summarizing the federal statute to be used and evaluating the strength of the evidence. As the meeting ended,

Leigh recalled, "instructions were given to proceed with the cases."[30]

V

By the time necessary preparations were completed, however, Kent had left Newport. A newspaper reported that he had been temporarily reassigned to an Episcopal parish at Warwick, Pennsylvania, so Arnold hurried to Philadelphia to obtain an arrest warrant. U.S. Commissioner Henry Maltzberger having issued the warrant October 13, 1919, Arnold and U.S. Marshall Matthew Kelley began searching for the chaplain. They met at Reading, took a train to Elverson, and hired a taxi to the tiny village of Warwick. "I stayed in the automobile," recalled Arnold, "and he went to the parish house." No one answered raps at the front or side doors. Inquiries about Kent's whereabouts at the post office and general store nearby produced suggestions that a "lady down the street" might know Kent's whereabouts. She could report no more, according to Arnold, than that he "had gone home and that his sister was sick, or something to that effect."[31]

Arnold organized a massive search utilizing nearly all his operators. After studying railroad schedules, W. I. Crawford concluded that anyone travelling from Philadelphia to Elverson had to change at Coatesville, so he staked out the station there. "Met all the trains," he reported on the 15th, "and hung around the hotel the rest of the time." Charles McKinney took up duties at Reading. Clyde Rudy watched the home of Kent's mother in Lynn, Massachusetts. A post office employee there revealed that Kent had neither received nor inquired for any mail. "Faked a telephone call to the Rev. W. A. Lawrence," he continued, and learned that the Episcopal rector had not heard Kent was in town. Most of his time was spent around the Breed Street residence of Mrs. Kent, "a very old woman." Rumors that Samuel had gone to Detroit sent H. K. Cheney scurrying there. The register at the Hotel Statler listed him as a guest October 10, but an acquaintance confirmed his departure the 13th.[32]

The most successful detective was Preston Paul, who was assigned to the Elverson railroad station. The morning of October 17 he learned from the ticket agent that Kent had "gone west" the previous week and "should be back most any time." When the 10:55 train arrived, Kent disembarked. "He was at one end and I at the other," reported the detective. "He recognized me. Came toward me with a faint smile, shook hands, asked when I got out of the service and what I was doing." Paul fabricated a story that he had been discharged the month before, worked for a Philadelphia producer of exzema lotion, and was trying to make sales to dry stores, Kent explained he was preaching "in that part of the country" and regretted that he could not talk further because his sister was with him. Daring not reveal his intentions or attempt an arrest, Paul parted with a friendly handshake and instantly phoned Arnold who ordered him to Warwick. He found Kent with his sister at the local undertaker's. "I then drove back to Elverson," he went on, "and watched all trains, coming and going."[33]

Arnold's team closed in on their target. McKinney sped with a U.S. Marshall from Reading to Elverson, where they joined Paul for the taxi ride to Warwick. Inquiring for Kent at the undertaker's, however, they learned he had left. If he were not at the parish house, the lady at the general store might direct them. The house was empty, and the storekeeper sent them on to a Mrs. Fillman's, where Kent took meals. She confirmed that he had arrived that morning, "ordered his dinner in a hurry," and left in the church's 1916 Ford touring car saying that his mother was ill and he would have to send a telegram about future plans. The three waited in Warwick till 6:15 hoping Kent would return before notifying Arnold that they prey had vanished. "Send two men," Arnold telephoned Hudson at 7:00, "as Samuel got away in fast automobile. . . . keep watch everywhere. . . ."[34]

Next day, Arnold's Reading headquarters intensified the search. Phillips combed hotels in Allentown, Bethlehem, South Bethlehem, and Kutztown to no avail. In Reading, they learned Kent had stayed in Room 333 the previous Thursday with a "Dr. M. Kent, Battle Creek, Mich." Paul learned from the Warwick telephone operator that Kent had called Mrs. Fillman from Pottstown at 8:30 the previous night to say he would be gone "for a day or two." "We are endeavoring to get hold of the telephone operator at Pottstown," Arnold added, "to determine for certain whether he did phone to Warwick at 8:30 last evening." When Arnold wired Harrisburg to get the license number of the missing car, he found none registered in Kent's name. He also requested that the U.S. District Attorney in Philadelphia send a marshall to Reading but received no reply. "I studied road maps last evening," Arnold told Hudson, "and today sifted out every possible escape he can make."[35]

Naval operators also solicited the help of local law enforcement officials. Arnold distributed a "general alarm" to the chiefs of police in Reading, Harristown, Bethlehem, and Chester, Pennsylvania, as well as Battle Creek, Michigan. It described Kent as 5 feet 11 inches tall, weighing 170 pounds; "wears Episcopal uniform," he went on, "nose glasses, top of head extremely bald, wears ring third finger of left hand, sometimes third finger of right hand, sallow complexion, round face rather full. Hair grayish tint. Walks with a quick step, very erect." The notice added that Kent had "escaped" from Warwick October 17 in a 1916 Ford. Travelling with him was a "middle aged woman," Dr. M. Kent. "Do not want woman." All police communications, according to Arnold, included instructions that "this matter was strictly confidential."[36] Arnold constantly reiterated his conviction that Kent would soon be apprehended. "I cannot understand how he can remain loose very long," he reported. "As far as I can see, it is a matter of only a few hours before something will show up." Nevertheless, he had to admit that Kent was "a very slippery man."[37]

After Kent missed church the 19th, the villages of Elverson and Warwick swarmed with yet more sailor-detectives. Phillips and Arnold interrogated the Elverson ticket agent, who said he knew Kent but that he had never bought tickets from him. "Told him I was a Government Agent," Arnold revealed to Hudson, "and that matter was strictly confidential." The agent agreed that he "would be only too glad" to keep Arnold informed if Kent were spotted. The next day he had a "very confidential conversation" with the owner of the Elverson Hotel, who told him that Kent had frequently gone to Philadelphia with Mrs. Fillman "without the knowledge of the husband. He," continued the report, "told me this came from a number of intimate friends of his who knew this to be absolutely true." The hotelkeeper agreed to board three operators for $1.50 a day and rented Arnold a car for $3 daily.

Arnold and Phillips drove to Warwick to continue investigating. First they interviewed Mrs. Morger, wife of the undertaker. Arnold introduced himself as "representing the U.S. government" and secured her promise to keep their conversation "absolutely confidential." She could not provide the license number of Kent's car but revealed it had been left in Pottstown. "If anyone was trying to shelter or hide Mr. Kent," warned Arnold, "and that if later it was found out, they would be very apt to get into serious trouble." "For her own good and the betterment of the community in general," he urged Mrs. Morger to let him know if Kent was located.

Next stop was the home of Mrs. Fillman, whom sailors instantly characterized as a "cocaine fiend." After having introduced himself, Arnold secured a pledge of confidentiality and asked the woman what she knew of Kent's whereabouts. Kent and his sister had said they were going to Boston, she replied; before that, the chaplain had been in Lynn to see his mother. Mrs. Fillman did know the car's license number, however, and declined to board Arnold's men. When she was unable even to name the local Episcopal bishop, Arnold concluded that she knew where Kent was. "She seemed to be inclined to contradict statements at different times," he reported, noting that he had warned her not to reveal his and Phillips' identities but to tell inquirers that they were "friends of Kent's stopping at Elverson."

Not satisfied at trying to intimidate Kent's friends, Arnold sought to use other federal employees to collect information. He informed the Warwick postmaster that he was "a government agent on confidential business" carrying a warrant for Kent's arrest. "I told him that, being a government man himself, it was to his advantage to assist another government man." He had seen Kent only occasionally, the postmaster asserted, the last time being the previous Friday when he "left in a hurry." He also revealed that Kent's mail was being held and agreed that if he received any letters to or from Kent, he would notify the Elverson constable or the federal marshall in Philadelphia.

Then they snooped around the parish house. Someone entered Kent's room to steal a photograph of the chaplain which was mailed to the New York office. In the garage was Kent's Buick, still bearing its Rhode Island license but freshly painted.[38]

Telegraph and telephone operators at Elverson proved especially accommodating. Mr. Schofield at Western Union provided copies of telegrams to and from Kent or his sister. He also promised that if he sighted Kent, he would hold him until the marshall came. The telephone operator promised that if Kent called or anyone else asked about him, the call would be tapped into the Elverson Hotel so one of Arnold's men could eavesdrop. "I think," Arnold concluded at the end of the day, "this completed a very good trap in the search for Kent."[39]

Following Arnold's return to Reading, operators Crawford, Steck, and Minnick remained in Elverson and Warwick. The postmaster provided them with the return addresses on all of Kent's mail. "The postmaster . . . has agreed to let us see any mail that comes into Warwick, P.O. for Kent's most intimate friends," Steck reported. When Mr. Morger, the undertaker, returned, he proved "very disagreeable." As a result, his home along with the Fillman residence, the parish house, Kent's car, and the post office were put under twenty-four-hour surveillance. Steck became "very friendly" with Miss Marion Ames, the operator for the Conestoga Telephone Company in Morgan Town, three miles outside Elverson. "Through our short friendship," he reported, "she has agreed to listen in on all calls to Warwick and in case anything is said about Kent she will let me know." She was 23, frank, and according to Steck, liked him "very much."[40]

Nothing worthy of reporting occurred until the night of October 22, when Crawford observed a car stop in front of the Fillman house. "We could see the man and the Fillmans in the house," he reported, "and Steck went to one of the windows and I to another." None of the conversation could be understood, although Mrs. Fillman allegedly said "I expect a letter tomorrow." "I will hold this letter until I hear whether you've heard or not." There was no evidence that the meeting had anything to do with Kent, although suspicions that the visitor was "next to Mr. Kent as an official of the church" seemed adequate for Arnold to portray this part of some vast plot to protect the chaplain. Both Morger and Fillman, he concluded, seemed to be "working in conjunction with Kent."[41]

Meanwhile, similar snooping occurred elsewhere. In Lynn, for example, postal and telegraph officials intercepted messages to and from Kent or his mother. The telegraph office agreed to review past files and provide copies of anything relevant. D. J. Marriott in Providence unsuccessfully endeavored to persuade the office managers of the Postal Telegraph System and Western Union to allow him to search through their files.[42]

Each passing day further enlivened Arnold's fertile imagination. When a car was stolen at Pottstown, he immediately pinpointed Kent as the thief. Someone claimed to have spotted a man looking like him on a Pottstown Street at 9:30, and at 9:45 thieves stole the car. A military recruiting party whom the operators told about Kent recalled having seen a minister who resembled him eating at a Pottsown restaurant. A recruiter named Brown said that "as soon as Kent spotted him, he grew red in the face and nervous." The man and the woman with him left quickly, "jumped into a Ford, and drove away."[43]

News of the search also began to interest newspapers. The evening of October 23 a reporter from the *Philadelphia Press* called on Arnold and operator Bena. They provided a description of the fugitive and suggested that people in Warwick knew his location but would not reveal it. Three times Arnold claimed to have warned the reporter not to publish anything "as the government was not ready to allow the matter to be published." The man allegedly agreed, although he argued that publication would not interfere with an arrest.[44] The next day, however, stories were printed in both the *Philadelphia Press* and *Philadelphia Bulletin*. When he heard a story was about to appear in the *Pottstown Ledger*, operator Phillips contacted the paper. He learned that a local news item from Mr. Morger in Warwick merely noted that Kent had left town for a few days.[45]

In Lynn Clyde Rudy found no ploy unacceptable in collecting information. The morning of October 31 he presented himself at the home of Kent's mother. She was too sick to see him, but he was able to talk to her nurse. Introducing himself as "James Martin," he said he was a travelling salesman who had known Kent at Newport. "At first she was very careful what she said," he reported, "but . . . I did not ask where he was but only acted as sorry he was not there. . . ." The information he sought soon leaked out. Kent was stationed in Warwick, the nurse revealed, but because of "bad health" had gone to Grand Rapids, Michigan. It would be nice, she added, if he sent him a card there. In the meantime, Rudy left his pseudonym so Mrs. Kent could forward it to her son. "I believe this is worth investigating," he concluded, "as before I left she seemed very much pleased that I had called."[46]

Other evidence already hinted Kent might be in Michigan. Acting on a suggestion from Dr. Hudson, U.S. Attorney Francis Foster Kane in Philadelphia wrote Bishop Perry and Bishop Phillip Rhinelander of Pennsylvania that a federal warrant for Kent's arrest had been issued and solicited their assistance in apprehending him. On October 27 Kane met personally with Rhinelander, whom he had known since boyhood and whom he considered a "very conscientious man." The bishop argued that Kent had already been acquitted on the basis of evidence from "witnesses [who] had in each case been sent to him and had solicited him." "They regard the trial in Rhode Island as a vindication of Kent," he went on, "and the termination of what in their minds was unjust persecution." If the "facts had been fully presented to the Navy Department," according to Rhinelander, no warrant would have been issued. He added that following the trial, Kent's "nerves underwent frightful strain" as a result of which the Bishop had offered him the tiny parish at Warwick. He did not know where Kent currently was, although he might be at his mother's.[47]

The very next day, however, Kane received a telegram from Bishop Perry revealing the truth about Kent's supposed disappearance. "Person of whom you write," the bishop cabled, "left recently for Battle Creek Sanitorium not eluding arrest, but notifying all concerned especially in Philadelphia and Rhode Island of his moves. He inquired whether warrant issued. Left for Michigan on physician's advice, believing there was no warrant." A request for advice on how to proceed produced a response that Kane could "not advise defendant as he represented the government." Kane telegraphed this news to Hudson and prepared a long letter explaining his relations with Bishops Rhinelander and Perry. "Now, I suppose, the matter will be one for the United States attorney in Michigan to handle and not myself," he concluded. Two days later Kane learned that Kent could be reached in care of his sister, Dr. Maude Kent, at the Good Health Publishing Company in Battle Creek.[48]

Hudson and Arnold quickly sought to open their case in Michigan. In accordance with orders from Hudson, Arnold and operator Dudley J. Marriott hurried to Grand Rapids. Roadblocks quickly developed, however. The U.S. Attorney was not home, and the marshall told Arnold that Battle Creek was outside his district. By the time the navy men reached Detroit, it was too late in the day to accomplish any business, but the next morning Arnold tracked down U.S. Attorney John E. Kiname at the Post Office building. Then the U.S. Commissioner before whom Arnold took his case refused to swear out the warrant because no grand jury had indicted Kent, Arnold lacked the original Rhode Island warrant, and Kent's name had been improperly affixed to the Pennsylvania warrant. Anxious telephone calls and telegrams among Arnold, Hudson, Kane, and Michigan officials occurred the next day in time for a warrant to be issued.[49]

Accompanied by several operators, Arnold arrived in Battle Creek on November 3, burst into the famed Sanatorium, and arrested Chaplain Kent. By 1:25 the morning of November 4, 1919, he wired Hudson to report his success. Released from jail on a $5,000 bond, Kent apparently waived an extradition hearing and headed east toward Providence for yet another trial.[50]

Samuel Neal Kent, Chaplain at the Newport Y.M.C.A. and the
central figure in the Newport gay scandal.
Credit: Lehigh University Library.

The Newport County Courthouse in which Kent's trial on Rhode Island state charges occurred is on the right. Directly across the street (left) is the Y.M.C.A. Credit: Photo by the author.

CHAPTER 6

The United States versus
Samuel Neal Kent

The trial that began at Providence the fifth of January 1920 differed substantially from the one at Newport the previous August. These proceedings occurred in a federal court presided over by Judge Arthur L. Brown and heard by a jury of twelve men, so allegations of local bias or corrupt decisions would be more difficult to prove. An official transcript recorded proceedings. And whereas the earlier case had avoided public attention, beginning on January 6, 1920, the influential *Providence Journal* as well as several Newport papers reported on the trial, initiating an interest in the sex scandal which brought it to national attention.

I

The prosecution depended almost entirely on the testimony of Arnold's operators, the first of whom was Charles B. Zipf. Special Assistant U.S. Attorney Joseph C. Cawley led him carefully through a description of his relations with Chaplain Kent, focusing on the night of March 29th they spent together. Early that evening, the sailor told Kent that he was "lonely" because a close friend had recently left the navy. An invitation to spend the night followed.

"How close were you to him during the conversation?" asked Cawley.

"I was close, and he came ever closer," responded Zipf. ". . . I was standing and he edged over along the desk until his leg was right against mine, and he was pushing his knee up against me in the most suggestive manner."

The pair moved to Kent's room where "ordinary conversation"

preceded preparation for bed. "He threw back the covers, told me to get into bed," responded Zipf, quickly adding, "asked me."

"Did you?"

"I did." "Well the next was—took place was lewd in the extreme," he went on; "with his hands he found my privates, penis, and tried repeatedly to throw his arms around me. . . . He tried to kiss me." Their conversation, as Zipf recalled, was "suggestive along—suggestive to the effect—I don't exactly know what to say, how to express—that I do unnatural things to him. . . . I refused to do that." Nevertheless, Kent "continued his acts until there was a discharge." Zipf spent the night in another room. Next morning they parted following breakfast, with promises to keep their activities secret. "He said that when two fellows thought a great deal of themselves that they did these things. . . . he didn't frown on them at all. He seemed to think they were all right."

Zipf's admission that he had returned from the parish house to the Red Cross building enabled Kent's principal attorney, Rathbone Gardner, to broaden the discussion to include the navy's anti-gay investigation. "Were you, Mr. Zipf, under orders to investigate vice conditions?"

"Yes, sir."

"You were in the performance of your duty when you met Mr. Kent?"

"Yes, sir."

"Why did you single out Mr. Kent?"

"I had been ordered to do so."

As the prosecution resumed questions, Zipf described an April meeting during which the chaplain allegedly "attempted the same thing." The defense protested that no such incident had been included in the indictment, so it could not be brought up. Cawley replied that he was trying to show "the disposition on the part of this man." "I submit," he continued, "that it is a well known principle in a case of this nature where disposition, inclination, is an element that we are not confined to the specific conduct which we have complained of in the indictment." Others could be introduced "for their corroborative value as to intent, as to disposition, inclination." "This is not an indictment for being [a] lewd, wanton, or licivious person having a certain disposition," countered defense attorney Gardner. "It is an indictment for having on a definite day, committed a definite act on a definite man." Judge Brown, agreeing with Gardner, ruled that descriptions of other alleged acts were

"incompetent" unless "something was said concerning the previous matter which was in the nature of an admission."

Zipf also described a meeting after the arrest of the gay sailors.
"I don't want you to say anything about this, what happened,"
Kent had pleaded.

"No," replied Zipf.

"You promise?" reiterated the chaplain.

"Yes."

Gardner's cross-examination focused almost entirely on the
Newport investigation. According to Zipf, it had been organized by
the District Commander and directed by Arnold. "Did he have
charge of the boys who were also engaged in it?"

"Yes, sir."

"And you received your instructions from him?"

"Yes, sir."

"Did Arnold tell you that you were obliged to perform this duty,
or did he offer you an opportunity of performing it?"

"Orders were orders in the Navy."

"Then you understood that you were under compulsion to accept
this appointment to proceed under this investigation of vice conditions in Newport?"

"No, I imagine I could have got out of it if I had really tried."

"Then you didn't want to get out of it?"

"Not particularly so."

"You liked it, you liked the work?"

"No; I liked the principal of the thing."

"Were you told," persisted Gardner, "that it was your duty to
allow your penis to be held?"

"Not as a duty; no, sir. . . . We were to obtain evidence."

"And if it was necessary to obtain evidence you were to allow
your penis to be handled?"

"Yes, sir."

"And you were to allow that handling to continue until there was
an erection?"

"Yes, sir."

"And an emission?"

"Yes, sir."

"And that you were to suck parts or allow yourself to be
sucked?"

"No, sir, not to suck parts."

"Now that there may be no misunderstanding about your instructions," probed the lawyer. "Were you not told that you were to allow yourself, your instrument to be sucked if necessary?"

"If necessary, yes, sir."

"That was a duty which was imposed on you as a member of the navy?"

Zipf objected to the word "imposed" on grounds that he had "eventually" declined to continue as an operator. "How many victims had you had," asked Gardner, "and how many people had you reported before you declined?" Zipf's memory faded rapidly; the best he could estimate was "three or four."

"As many as six?"

"I don't know."

Gardner also asked why Kent had been singled out for special attention. "I was ordered to," replied Zipf.

"Who ordered you to do it?"

"Higher authority," he responded, denying knowledge of who issued the command, although it had been transmitted by Arnold. "He told me to get evidence on Kent."

"What were your instructions as to how far you were to encourage?"

"To encourage nothing by word of mouth or by action."

"You understood," the questioning continued, "from that that you were ordered to go further and act if you could, the purpose of which would be evidence against Kent?"

"If Kent would go through it; it would be evidence."

"You were to induce Kent to go through it?"

"Yes, sir."

Gardner's questions about what happened the night Zipf spent with Kent forced admission that more than a hundred people had been present in the lobby of the Y.M.C.A. during the chaplain's activities. Zipf also confessed he had voluntarily crawled into bed. "There was no force exercised to get you to do so?"

"No, sir," replied the ex-operator.

"There was no persuasion?"

"Yes, sir," maintained Zipf; there was "suggestive persuasion" that occurred "by words, by action."

"It was left to you to decide whether you would go or not?"

"No; it had been decided for me."

"Were you not compelled to accept that decision?"

"If I was to do my duty, it was."

"You did that as part of the duty assigned you by your superior officers in the Navy of the United States?"

"Yes."

Gardner demanded more details about Zipf's relations with gay sailors at the Y.M.C.A., asking in particular if he had been "buggered and permitted . . . [himself] to be buggered."

"No," replied the young man. "I testified that I had buggered, but I never permitted myself to be buggered."

Zipf insisted that only once had he buggered anyone, whereupon Gardner raised a final question. "Before you were called upon to go into this work," he inquired, ". . . did you have an opportunity to consult your parents?"

"No, sir," replied Zipf.

"Have you a mother living?"

"Yes, sir."

"You think she should have been pleased at this?"

Zipf never replied; for a prosecution objection having been sustained, the operator stepped down.[1]

II

Much the same scenario unfolded as Charles R. McKinney described his role in the investigation. "They were on moral perverts around Newport," he explained, "and we were investigating to find out who they were, and conditions of that sort."

Why had he joined?

"Well, I knew some fellows that had been doing that work before."

Was his participation voluntary?

"Yes, sir."

McKinney reported that during an automobile ride in mid-May, Kent had "acted all right" until they reached a remote area. First he had rubbed his hands, then dropped to his leg, and worked up toward his crotch. "How long did that last?" asked the prosecuting attorney.

"For several minutes," he replied, until traffic on the road increased. Later Kent complimented McKinney as "some boy" and suggested they become better acquainted.

A chance came five days later when they met at the Y.M.C.A. and went together to the parish house. McKinney was seated on a couch when Kent put his arms around him and tried to kiss him "to show me how glad he was that I came down to see him." Despite the operator's professed resistance, Kent's hands soon found his organ and began playing with it, as he recalled, for "quite a little while until I got tired."

"What did he say while indulging in this practice?" asked the lawyer.

"He remarked about the size of it and the different characteristics of it and wanted to know if it had ever been sucked, and one thing and the other like that and it was a dirty conversation all the way through." By ten o'clock, Kent escorted McKinney home.

In mid-June they met again. Kent drove to the circus grounds outside Newport, and later the pair spent half an hour in the chaplain's apartment, during which McKinney claimed the clergyman again tried hugging, kissing, and fondling him. A telephone call ended the encounter.

Several days later he accepted yet another invitation, agreeing this time to stay the night. Soon the men were in bed together. "As he got ready," recalled the witness, "he got a towel in the bed with him. I asked him what the idea was of the towel. He said we might need it. I laughed." Before long they were rolling together in tight embrace. McKinney found himself on top, with kent's penis inserted between his legs. The sailor objected to this as well as suggestions that they suck one another. Ultimately, Kent "kept on moving me up and playing with my penis until finally I discharged, and after that I went to my own room and went to bed." "What pleasure was there in playing with somebody else?" the operator asked. "It made him feel good to think that he was doing some other man some good," came the answer. The two parted the next morning, never to meet again outside a courtroom.

Following the noon recess, defense attorney Abbott Phillips opened the cross-examination by inquiring why McKinney had joined the squad. The only "friends" he named in the group were Haynes and Rudy; he also admitted knowing the nature of the work before agreeing to serve. "You knew it included sucking and that sort of thing, didn't you?"

"I knew that we had to deal with that, yes, sir."

"You knew it included sodomy and that sort of thing, didn't you?"

"Yes, sir."

"And you were quite willing to go into that sort of work?"

"I was willing to do it, yes, sir."

"And so willing that you volunteered for it, is that right?"

"Yes, sir. I volunteered for it, yes, sir."

Enough! interrupted Cawley. "That has been answered!"

"I asked him 'sodomy,'" explained Phillips.

"You knew it included buggering fellows, didn't you?" he repeated.

"Objected to," reiterated the prosecution lawyer.

Judge Brown interrupted: "I do not know as it is necessary to use quite so much voice in these matters. You can speak plainly." He allowed the defense to continue, however, and Phillips repeated his "buggering" question yet a third time.

"It didn't require me to do it, no, sir."

"You were not required to do that?"

"No," insisted McKinney. "No, sir."

"Your requirement—you were to suck the part?"

"No, sir."

"Being sucked?"

"Yes, sir."

"You were sucked weren't you? In doing this sort of work?"

"Not by Mr. Kent, no, sir."

"By others?"

"Yes, sir."

"Several?"

"No, sir."

"How many?"

"One, no there were two times. . . . Yes, sir."

Phillips redirected his cross-examination to discrepancies between what McKinney had said at Newport and what he now claimed to be the truth. "Didn't you testify down there at least four sucked you?" he opened.

"I don't remember."

"Will you deny it?" demanded the lawyer.

"No, sir, I might have testified, but I don't remember it."

"But if you did testify so, under oath, down there, it wasn't true. Is that it?"

"I don't remember whether I said it or not?"

"It is not true is it?"

"If I said it, it was a mistake."

Having stumbled onto what seemed like a productive line of questioning, Phillips persisted, quoting Newport testimony in which McKinney admitted having been ordered to do the work rather than volunteering. When the sailor pleaded forgetfulness, interrogation intensified. "Can't you remember what you testified to in the District Court at Newport?"

"No, sir."

"You can remember what the facts were, can't you?"

"I can't remember my answers to questions."

"In the district court [at] Newport," he continued, "didn't you testify that Arnold ordered you to work on Kent?"

"No, sir."

"Will you deny that?"

"I don't recall saying that."

"Can't you remember anything you testified to in the District Court at Newport?" the attorney demanded.

"That has been so long ago that I have forgotten," explained McKinney. "I don't remember it."

Phillips quoted McKinney's Newport testimony that he had been ordered by Arnold to "follow, and look out for Kent." "did you so testify?" he asked.

"I don't remember the exact words but Arnold instructed me to look out for anybody of that character. He didn't say Mr. Kent especially or mention any other names especially."

"If you testified," Phillips insisted, "as I have just read, that Arnold told you that you were to follow, look out for Kent, that wasn't true, was it?"

"I don't remember Arnold telling me that, no sir."

"I will ask you once more whether you deny this testimony that I have read as given by you in the district court last August at Newport?"

"I don't remember what I testified to there, sir. I can't remember the answers I gave."

Phillips probed whether McKinney volunteered for the work because "he liked it so well" or whether he had been ordered into it. The operator claimed he had asked Hudson several times to be released. "I wanted to get out of the Navy," he insisted. "I wanted to be discharged. . . ."

"This is not what I asked you," interrupted Phillips. "I asked you if you ever made any attempt to get out of this same work, this sucking business, this sodomy business."

"I do not," interrupted Judge Brown, "think it is necessary to use such terms."

"Of course," retorted Phillips, "you have to use these terms because we are in it. It is not very pleasant for any of us."

The defense attorney asked again and again whether McKinney had ever requested "to get out of this sort of work, without calling it what it is."

"No, sir," the operator finally confessed.

McKinney's denial that Arnold or Hudson had ordered him to allow himself to be played with and sucked proved no more convincing. No order had ever been issued; each man was to use his "own judgment, go as far as necessary to get convicting evidence." Yet at Newport McKinney had admitted that Dr. Hudson and Mr. Arnold told operators to let themselves be played with until emission. McKinney could only argue that he had forgotten.

More inconsistencies arose as Phillips probed McKinney's recollection of encounters with Kent. The descriptions of his first car ride changed regarding the length of the trip, the topics of conversation, and the way fondling began. If he knew Kent wanted sex, Phillips asked, why had he agreed to spend the night with him? Or if he had wanted good evidence, why had he not tried to have his activities corroborated by another operator? McKinney admitted he could not remember whether or not he had left a message for Kent. Phillips protested: "Can't you remember what happened except this little story you let in this evidence?" Was it not true, he insisted, that Cawley had coached him in what to say? No, insisted the witness, although he admitted reviewing material with Hudson and Arnold and re-reading his operator's reports. After one more instance when McKinney forgot whether or not Kent had a red light in his room, Phillips erupted: "Can't you remember anything that you testified to at Newport last August?"

"I didn't make any notes in that court down there to read over."

"What did you testify to? A lot of things down there that were not true?"

"I don't remember what I testified to down there," constituted the operator's best answer.

To show that sailors thoroughly enjoyed sex with their victims, Phillips endeavored to determine how many times McKinney had been fellated. At first he said four; later he admitted that without referring to reports, he could not be certain.

"You can't remember things like that?" queried the attorney.

"That actually did that; no, sir."

"It would not make any impression on you, would it?"

"There may have been two, three, or four. I don't recollect how many there were."

"A fellow doing that, that would not make any impression on you, would it?"

"Certainly it would make an impression at the time."

"So you don't remember whether four did it to you, or thirty-four, or two, or how many did it to you. I suppose so many did it to you you can't remember?"

"You have asked the number. I wouldn't say how many there were."

"You were so willing to have it that it didn't make any impression on you one way or the other. Is that it?"

Prosecutor Cawley rose to protest. "The question is improper," he insisted. "This witness is entitled to some protection."

"When a man comes here," replied Phillips, "and voluntarily says that he volunteered for this sort of work and allowed these things to be done to him, I think, your Honor, we are allowed to go into it."

The judge overruled the objection, allowing any question, "so far as there was a basis in what was presented before me." Complaints about operators being asked how well they liked their work were also rejected. Phillips returned to earlier questions about how many men had fellated McKinney, quoting Newport testimony that there had been four.

"I don't remember that."

"Do you remember a single thing that I have read to you from the district court?"

"I think I have, yes, sir."

"What do you remember that I have asked you about the district court, that you remember?"

"Well, I don't remember the questions now," he responded. "There were so many things you asked me."

As if to drive the final nail into McKinney's testimony, Phillips inquired whether he had ever told Kent he belonged to the special squad. "No, sir." How then did he explain that he hung around all day without working. McKinney confessed he had left the erroneous impression that he had been discharged from the service. "I will ask you whether or not it was a fact, whether it was necessary or not to practice certain deception to get evidence upon him?" continued Phillips.

"I thought it was necessary."

"As a result you did it?"

"Yes, sir."[2]

Before further testimony against Kent could be introduced, two defense witnesses certified Chaplain Kent's good character. Rev. Henry Mottett, rector of the Holy Communion Church in New York, had been Kent's superior there. "I should say he was held in absolute esteem and respect," he testified. "Not a breath" against him had ever been heard. Cawley tried to argue the abnormality either of the advanced age at which Kent entered the ministry or his interest in youth work but to no avail. The best he could argue was that Mottett had only defended Kent against negative charges. Defense Attorney Gardner objected, to which Mottett responded that "everyone who got to know Mr. Kent and who remembers him today remembers him with the profoundest respect and gratitude because he is a perfectly splendid man among men and boys."[3]

President Henry S. Drinker of Lehigh University, where Kent had charge of the preparatory dormitory and served as chaplain, testified next. "My wife and I knew him well," said Drinker, "and we knew his reputation in and about Bethlehem and among the young men at that locality. It was one of the very best," he continued; "I never had cause to think of Mr. Kent otherwise than as a Godly straight forward man in every way." When Cawley endeavored to demonstrate that Drinker saw Kent so rarely that his testimony was unreliable, the president responded that he knew him well.[4]

III

Operator Henry Dostalik had barely taken the stand before the first day concluded. When court resumed the sixth of January, the twenty-year-old sailor was the lead witness. Like others, he rehearsed his relations with Kent, in his case describing a boat trip to New York. Because the federal statute under which Kent was charged limited jurisdiction to ten miles from a military post, testimony centered on the exact location of the boat in relation to the Training Station. A critical question became whether Kent had lured Dostalik into his room for lewd purposes before or after the boat passed the limit. Dostalik reviewed arrangements for the trip, described how he and Kent had entered their room for a ginger ale, and told of their having crawled into bed. "He started feeling of my penis, and he continued for quite a while," testified the operator, "and he would pull me on top of him, and put my penis between his legs and wanted me to get there that way. I tried to push away. I told him. No, and in one instance I told him I didn't like it that way." Kent indicated a preference for "the back way," and when Dostalik declined, he proposed "the French way." Dostalik told how he had picked up fellows "just by talking to them" and had them do it to him that way. Kent tried initiating sex again the next morning, but the pair left the ship for a day in New York with nothing more having occurred. As they parted after sightseeing, Kent returned home with promises to write.

"You had been a decent clean boy up to the time you enlisted in the navy?" began Gardner's cross-examination. "And never indulged in any of these practices?" A negative reply stimulated a further query: then why had he become part of the investigation? Because he spoke four languages and was a "finger print expert," explained Dostalik. He denied having been "solicited" to enter Section A but admitted that Dr. Hudson "had asked me if I wanted to go into it."

How had operators been instructed? Dostalik reported that they had been told to use their own judgment in determining how far to go in obtaining evidence. "Were you not told either individually or with a group of others," demanded Gardner, "that if necessary you were to allow men who you were investigating to handle your penis?"

"I was not told that, but I was told to get evidence enough to be convicted, enough to convict or lead to conviction."

"Didn't they tell you that you should allow your penis to be handled, that you should allow it to be handled until there was an erection or emission, if necessary?"

"No, sir; they didn't tell me that" he said, adding that "if necessary . . . that was understood."

"And it was understood also that you were to suck, or permit yourself to be sucked, if necessary?"

"Yes, to permit it — they told me, prevent it as much as possible."

"To play with my penis and if that was enough, if I could get away from him without his knowing, to get away, and if I couldn't to stay until he got through, so he would not get suspicious."

"Told you 'to get through'; you mean, till you had an erection and an emission, or had an erection and emission and sucked?"

"Yes, sir."

"And up to the time of your instructions from Dr. Hudson you were a perfectly clean boy?"

"Yes, sir."

"You never had an experience of that kind?"

"No, sir."

Cross-examination concentrated on Dostalik's other activities in the anti-gay squad. He, too, had forgotten how many men he had "gone through the same sort of performance with" but thought three or four.

And how much time had he devoted to the work?

Fourteen hours a day for nine months.

"You mean to say you worked fourteen hours a day just talking to people to see what sort of people they were and whether they would be likely to indulge in vice of this character?"

"Yes, sir."

"How many people did you interview altogether of which you obtained four?"

"I don't think it was over six when I was taken off."

Dostalik added that he had spent six months on his fingerprint studies, leaving only three for tracking down gays.

"For three months you were working fourteen hours a day investigating the conduct and character of six people?"

"Yes, sir."

Gardner turned next to the time Kent and Dostalik had spent together. The operator admitted that he could find nothing wrong with Kent cashing a check for him and confessed that he had lied to the chaplain in order to get himself invited to New York. Permission to go had ultimately been granted so late that he had not even had time to collect clean underwear or a toothbrush. Dostalik stuck to his original story of what had happened on board the ship, and, since he apparently did not testify at Newport, the defense could not follow the line of questioning pursued with Zipf and McKinney.

Did the same kinds of sexual activities attempted by Kent occur with others? asked Gardner. A positive response led to more questions about these incidents.

"One with each, that was all," replied the operator.

"Did you commit buggery or sodomy with any of these men?"

Cawley's objection having been overruled, Gardner asked again.

"I don't know, sir."

"You don't know?"

"No, sir."

Had Arnold told him to "work on Mr. Kent?" Gardner probed following a brief recess.

"Yes, sir," he answered first, then corrected himself: "Well, I don't know. It was understood at the beginning of it that I was to work upon anybody."

"Mr. Arnold told you, as you testify, to work on Kent. When did he tell you that?"

"I don't remember when he told me that."

And why was it that he had volunteered for the work? Dostalik now denied ever having volunteered; he had merely told Arnold and Hudson that "he would work, help them out."

"And they didn't ask you do to it even?"

"No, sir. They asked me if I wanted to do it. I was willing to help them out. . . . For the good of the cause, I saw the good of the cause in it."

"For the cause you were willing to go the limit?"

IV

The final operator appearing in the Providence trial was 28-year-old Malcolm Crawford, a Mobile, Alabama, native who had joined the navy in January of 1918. Like the others, he described how in early May Kent invited him to ride in his automobile; they had not gone that day, but on the fourteenth the pair went to the theatre and afterward to Kent's apartment. The discussion having rapidly turned to sex, the chaplain tried to "love up" the sailor. "He tried to kiss me and played with my penis, and I would not let him," according to the sailor. "The operator moved to his own room for the night, and next morning they shared cereal and coffee before parting.

Perhaps confident at how effectively he had shaken previous witnesses, Phillips opened aggressively. "You seem to enjoy coming in and testifying to these things, don't you?"

Cawley objected, whereupon Judge Brown observed that he "saw nothing in the witness' demeanor" to justify such a question.

"That witness smiled all the way through his examination when he was telling about these dreadful things," he retorted. "I will leave it to the jury whether I am right or not about it."

When Crawford volunteered for this duty, Phillips continued, how much had he known about the work?

"I had an idea," he responded, "but I didn't know."

Had he ever tried to secure release?

"Yes, sir," but Arnold refused. The request had not been made until two months ago, however, and then not because he disliked Section A but because he had a job at home.

"Then why didn't you apply to get out of it sooner?"

"I don't know," replied Crawford. "I just wanted to stick it out, when I got into it. I wanted to see it through."

As Phillips launched questions about what the operator said during the Newport trial, assistant prosecutor Peter Cannon protested.

"There is no good my reading from the record to these fellows," complained Phillips, "and have them say they don't remember, the way Mr. McKinney did, one hundred times."

"I don't think," retorted Cannon, it is necessary "to make remarks like that."

Contradictions quickly heaped one on the other. Crawford said he joined the squad in April; now he said May. He claimed to have been "detailed" to the job; now he said he volunteered. He once denied having applied for the post; now he admitted he had.

"That was a lie, wasn't it?"

"It wasn't a lie."

"Haven't you just told me you volunteered and applied for this work? Applied for it. Didn't you tell me a moment ago you volunteered and applied for it, didn't you?"

"I volunteered."

"Answer my question!" demanded Phillips. "Didn't you tell me before this jury a moment ago when I asked you whether you volunteered and applied for it, didn't you say yes a moment ago?"

"I didn't apply for it."

"Didn't you tell me so a moment ago?"

"Well, I mean I was asked to go into this organization and agreed to."

"What is it now — that you did tell me so — that you didn't tell me the truth?"

"The truth is I was asked to go in and I agreed to it. I didn't go out working. They detailed me to put me on the job."

"When you volunteered, didn't you have to go to these men, tell them you would like to do this work?"

"I didn't volunteer then, no, sir; because I was asked to go into it. They picked out certain men in the station. I was one man who was picked out. To my knowledge, I didn't go to them, ask them to put me in the organization."

What instructions had been given operators? Crawford recalled Dr. Hudson having told him to "go out and look for a forger," but he recalled no orders regarding homosexuals. He remembered written instructions "to get evidence against these men, these immoral perverts."

"Were you told in these written instructions, over Lieutenant Hudson's signature, to subject your private parts to being played with until you had an emission, if necessary?"

Cawley objected that this was not cross-examination, but Judge Brown overruled him.

"Answer my question," demanded Phillips.

"Not that far, no sir," responded Crawford.

But in Newport, according to the transcript, Crawford admitted having been told by Hudson to "subject your penis or anything like that to another man."

"Did you so testify in district court—yes or no?" he demanded.

"Yes, I think I did."

"So that what you have been telling he here was not true?"

"You said about the limit till a discharge?"

"Is that what I said? Didn't I ask you a moment ago if Hudson gave you any orders to submit your private parts? Didn't you tell me no? . . . whatever you may have said before, are you going to leave it as the fact that this man Hudson gave you specific orders to submit your penis or anything like that to other men. Is that a fact?"

"Yes, sir, that is a fact."

While denying Arnold ever gave him more specific instructions on how to proceed, Crawford confessed that he had been told to "get evidence against Kent." "What I mean by 'get,'" he explained, "I wasn't supposed to go force him to do it. . . . I was supposed to go out and see Kent and let him do the lewd."

"Arnold told you to?"

"He told me to go out, yes."

"Get evidence against Kent?"

"Not to get him—what I mean that way."

"Will you stick to anything? Will you say that you did say is it a fact that Arnold told you to get evidence against Kent?"

"He meant to go out, try to get evidence."

"Try to get evidence against Kent?"

"Try to get evidence against Kent; that is like it."

Phillips demanded to know if the operator had led on Chaplain

Kent; the sailor denied any provocation. "Kent knew nothing about you at that time, as far as you know?"

"As far as I knew, he didn't."

"So there was no reason for Kent to believe, after it started, in playing with your privates as you claim he did at that time, that you would not haul off, give him a crack in the eye?"

Cawley objected but when overruled, Crawford replied: "Of course, I couldn't tell what he thought."

"So that your story is—I want to get this correctly—that you went up there to his room, talked about his church work, and then suddenly he began playing with your privates without your encouraging him or saying a word to him or without his having any knowledge, as far as you know, that you would stand for that kind of business. Is that correct?"

Crawford claimed not to understand the question even when repeated, and Cawley objected that it contained "too much" to allow a yes or a no answer. "I don't understand it' I don't understand," muttered the sailor. Phillips reread the question yet again. "That is fact." Crawford conceded.

The court recessed for lunch, and after only minor queries in redirect examination, the prosecution rested.[6]

V

Far less dramatic than the operators whom Cawley presented were the clergymen, business leaders, friends and colleagues—fourteen in all—who appeared as character witnesses for Kent. Bishop Phillip Rhinelander had known Kent since he was a student and certified his reputation as "of the highest description." The prosecution's only successful rebuttals came in securing admission that the bishop had not realized the transcript of the first trial he had seen was unofficial and that he had no way of ascertaining Kent's reputation in Newport during 1919.[7]

Raymond Walters had known Kent at Lehigh, where they worked together on a Shakespearean tragedy in 1916. He emphasized Kent's industry and energy and argued that no one had ever questioned his morality. The only cross-examination consisted of suggestions that actors were especially vulnerable to accusations of homosexuality.[8]

No more successful was the cross-examination of Henry Washburn, who attended theology school with Kent. Cawley alleged that he had known him insufficiently in recent years to testify as to his current character. Harold Fair, another Lehigh colleague, credited Kent with helping him become a minister, while Howard Rider reported what a valuable asset he had been to the college community. A boy often mentioned "what a good friend he was to him, how he had helped them out of difficulties." From a still earlier period of Kent's life, retired Lynn shoe manufacturer Herbert Walker, for whom Kent had worked, portrayed him as "clean morally and trustworthy." Never had his "personal purity" been questioned.[9]

Other witnesses worked with Kent in Newport. Charles Forster, rector of Emmanuel Church were Kent lived, had never heard his reputation questioned, although Cawley forced admission that his acquaintance was "casual" and that to some extent he had "a general interest" in the outcome of the case. Edwin Andrews, Frank Sharwell, and Thomas Harvey from the Y.M.C.A. verified Kent's effectiveness with servicemen and argued his reputation as excellent. Retired Judge Darius Baker, a member of the Episcopal Church War Commission, had heard "pleasant laudatory" comments about Kent, who was "looked upon as an earnest Christian man and was much interested in young men."[10]

The next two witnesses had already played significant roles in the case and would continue their interest long after the Providence trial ended. The Rev. James DeWolf Perry, Episcopal Bishop of Rhode Island, had known Kent for nine years, beginning while he was still a student. "He was, so far as I could tell," testified Perry, "universally esteemed and he had the confidence of all who liked good men." The only questions about him came from Arnold and Hudson.[11] A final character witness was Rev. Stanley C. Hughes from Trinity Episcopal Church in Newport. He had known Kent since his arrival in town and traced his valuable work at Fort Adams, among influenza victims in Newport, and at the Y.M.C.A. His reputation was "excellent."[12]

Before Hughes' testimony ended, a bitter controversy arose as prosecutor Cannon demanded a copy of the Newport transcript used by Gardner and Phillips to question operators. "Our own transcript, your Honor please," argued Gardner, "we think that we are under no obligation to furnish the other side. They had their own stenographer there and took their own notes as they saw fit." Judge Brown found the request reasonable. No copy was not at hand today, responded the defense attorney, adding that it was only "a long memorandum of parts" of the prosecution's evidence. Brown admitted he was not sure he could compel production of the document, although a summons could be issued. Besides, argued Gardner, no transcript related to Hughes' testimony had been made.

But did it exist? demanded Cannon.

"Are you afraid Mr. Hughes testified differently in the district court?"

"Not in the slightest degree."

"Then produce the transcript."

"If the other side wish the evidence of Mr. Hughes as far as we have got it," responded Phillips, "I will go over and get it for them"; Hughes had not testified to anything different here than in the district court, however. Phillips explained that the transcript did not "purport to be . . . complete or correct." Cannon withdrew his request while accusing the defense of "trifling with this Court and jury" by using such a document to make "these government witnesses appear to be telling untruths."

After a few more minor questions, Rev. Hughes stepped down so the defense could call its star witness the Rev. Samuel Neal Kent himself.[13]

VI

The forty-six-year-old clergyman's testimony began with a carefully prepared autobiography tracing his childhood, describing his employment in a Lynn shoe factory, and explaining his growing interest in religious work. Following seminary he had charge of a small church and worked in New York before going to Lehigh, then to Plattsburg, and finally in September of 1918 to Newport. Vivid descriptions portrayed work among influenza patients, interspersed with commendations from associates; he characterized his activities at the Y.M.C.A. as "big brotherhood." Kent frequently invited young men to his apartment; many stayed overnight. "When boys got a short leave of absence, when they didn't have to report for duty for a day or so," his attorney asked, "what was your custom with such boys if you happened to know them?"

"A boy I knew pretty well I told him he could stay up with me."

"Did a good many accept your invitation?"

"A great many, sir."

Phillips reviewed one after another the chaplain's relations with operators. Charles McKinney had accused him of "immoral conduct" in "broad daylight" driving along Ocean Drive.

"Is that true or false, Mr. Kent?"

"Absolutely false, sir."

"Did you do any such things that McKinney claimed you did when riding around Ocean Drive in your automobile with him?"

"Never."

The night McKinney said they were together, Kent escorted a lady to a Harvard Choir concert and returned home without ever seeing the sailor. Sometime later, McKinney called several times to see him, indicating a desire for "a good long talk . . . about his future." They met one evening after Kent conducted singing at Fort Adams and addressed a women's meeting at the parish house. After a discussion during which the chaplain encouraged the sailor to continue his education, McKinney accepted an invitation to stay the night.

"We prepared to go to bed," reported Kent, "and I saw that the cot was arranged for him. I got a pair of pajamas for him. I myself had got ready to go to bed, entered my bathroom which is between the bed room and the study, and went to bed." McKinney seemed to be undressing, and the two talked briefly while he was in the bath.

Then, without warning, the sailor entered Kent's room, crawled into his bed, and—as Kent testified—"asked me if we could not have a good time. He put his arms around me, rubbed his self up against me, his parts. I noticed that he had an erection . . . I repelled him with all the force I could. I asked him what he meant by doing such a thing, what he took me for, what he was there for." Eventually, Kent forced the sailor out of bed. "I couldn't give you the exact sequence in any way," he confessed to the jury, "because I was excited and do not remember just the way it developed, but I got him out of the room, told him to stay, and shut the door."

Kent was thoroughly shaken. "I didn't know what to do," he confessed. "I have never been in such circumstances before and never came across a man who had tried such a thing." He considered fleeing the house or reporting McKinney to someone or just trying to talk with him. He concluded, however, that he was in no "shape to do it."

After a sleepless night, he awoke early and immediately ordered to sailor to get his clothes and leave. They drove to the town center in silence. "I stopped and told him to get out and go on his way," testified Kent. "I didn't have anything more to do with him."

As for Zipf, Kent recalled his once having stayed overnight. "At that time did you have any improper relations with him of any kind, Mr. Kent?''

"No. Sir."

"Did anything unusual or out of the ordinary at all happen the night when he did stay over night with you?"

"Nothing, sir."

Much the same scenario applied to Crawford. Kent remembered taking him to dinner, after which they attended a performance at the community theatre before going to Kent's apartment. Crawford stayed all night, and the two ate breakfast together in the morning. Nothing unusual, improper, or immoral occurred.

Kent already knew Henry Dostalik well when they began talking about a trip to New York. "I had seen enough of Dostalik," the chaplain concluded in retrospect, "so that I feel now he knew perfectly well in the position that he put himself, that I would do the ordinary thing which I would do with any other man that I knew as well as he, and told him that if he was going down on that boat he could use the extra berth in my state room . . ." The two met on the boat, put their things in the cabin, and joined other sailors on deck before departure. Later they drank ginger ale and talked before undressing.

Then the sailor "began to get familiar." "He tried to be affectionate, put his arms around me, lay over against me. I noticed that he had an erection." Such actions surprised and disturbed the chaplain. "What are you doing, boy?" he exclaimed. "Don't you know such a thing is wrong for you? Get out; go into your upper berth—and that such a thing is not right for any body." The sailor compliantly moved to his bed for the night.

Next morning Kent lectured Dostalik when he again became affectionate. "Now, see here," he opened; "It is time that you understood what is good for you and what is good for a chap who has a tendency such as you seem to have. You want to cut all this out. You want to be a good clean chap." He suggested "fresh air" and sent him outside while he dressed. They planned to talk later, but a full day's sightseeing left few opportunities for the kind of "sexual hygiene" lecture Kent felt was needed. While atop a Fifth Avenue bus, the cleric indicated that he was "surprised and ashamed" of what had happened the night before. "Keep clean and live a good life," he urged the sailor, and "get married to a good girl." As they separated at the pier, Kent admonished: "Now I want you to be a good boy. Go home, and live to marry a good girl and be a good citizen. I hope to hear some time that you are just everything you ought to be."

Cawley's cross-examination aimed to demonstrate that Kent had lured youngsters into his quarters to engage in sex. The cards he distributed were introduced, and questions were raised about his relations with operators. How could he have berated Dostalik for his behavior and yet spent a day with him during which he introduced him to several "respectable" people? Could Kent have physically expelled McKinney if he wanted?

"I haven't been for some time very fit," replied the defendant. "I should not want to run up against any healthy young man in a physical test."

The critical question was whether Kent or the operators were telling the truth. "You heard the testimony that Mr. Crawford gave here?" asked Cawley.

"Yes, sir."

"And the occurrence that he has testified to didn't occur, did it?"

"It did not, sir." The same held true for events described by Zipf.

"It is an absolute falsehood," insisted Kent. "I say it is absolutely false."

"Whether the statement is made or not," demanded the prosecuting attorney, "you do not admit that you had any such improper relations with anybody down there, do you?"

"I do not."

"You deny you had any such improper relations not only with the men that have testified, but with other service men?"

"I do deny."

Cawley began to question Kent's relationships with other sailors. Hugh Francis Quinn was a seventeen-year-old who had been part of the Training Station cast of "Jack and the Beanstalk." Kent's attorney objected to raising his name because no charges related to Quinn. Judge Brown permitted the interrogation to continue until he became convinced that nothing "material to this issue" was being raised.

"At that time did you place your arm around Quinn and squeeze him?"

"I object to that," complained Gardner.

"I don't recall," interjected Kent.

"Wait a moment!" shouted Gardner.

The attorneys gathered around the bench. The discussion, which was not recorded, continued in the judge's chambers until the 4:20 recess.

When the trial resumed at 10:00 the morning of January 8, Kent was still on the stand, Cawley immediately raised questions about Quinn. No sooner had he uttered the first sentence than Gardner objected.

"I think that is not within my ruling," replied Brown, apparently referring to decisions the previous day.

Cawley, nevertheless persisted in asking Kent if he had put his "hand on Quinn's knee and squeezed it." Gardner's objection was sustained.

Interrogation shifted to yet another man, Joseph E. Tooze. "Didn't you try to feel his legs," Cawley asked Kent.

Gardner protested.

"This is not within my ruling," replied Brown. "Objection sustained."

"I think your honor, if your honor will pardon me," interrupted Cannon; "I think that shows the character of the acts that this man is charged with. . . ."

Gardner's objections were once more sustained.

Cawley proceeded along parallel lines about two other sailors. Kent admitted knowing one of them and having entertained him in his apartment. When Kent was asked if "the back . . . of [his] hand and fingers rested on his fingers?" Gardner protested. The objection was overruled, so the defendant had to answer:

"I have no recollection as to my conversation, . . . and it is absolutely untrue that I ever did anything improper." The judge interrupted to exclude references to sex between Kent and the sailors.

"Is it absolutely true," demanded Cawley, "that your hand rested in the position I have inquired about? It must be so."

"I never did a thing of that sort, sir."

Cawley also argued that mention of Kent's earlier acquittal was meaningless because Judge Hugh Baker might himself be a pervert and because his father, Judge Darius Baker, served on the board that oversaw the Y.M.C.A.

"He lives with his father, does he not, in the same home?" asked Cawley.

Yes, confirmed Kent.

"He is not married?"

Cannon objected. "What is the bearing of Judge Baker's residence and marriage?"

The judge disallowed the question as "objectionable" and "not in cross-examination."

"It appears," countered Cawley, "here it has been suggested by certain witnesses who have taken the opportunity to state several times that these proceedings in Newport led to an acquittal." No objection had been raised at the time, but now the prosecution claimed that Kent's relations with the Bakers furnished "a possible reason why those charges might have been looked upon a little . . ."

The court interrupted before the sentence was complete and ordered it excluded. "Is there any intent," demanded Gardner, "to suggest that Judge Hugh Baker is a dishonest judge or a dishonest man?"

"Gentlemen," protested the bench; "the ruling has been made."

Cawley now asked whether many of the sailors arrested for immorality "congregated from time to time at the 'Y' and other places that were notoriously immoral.

"Not to my knowledge," replied Kent.

Was he "on terms and friendship and intimacy" with the arrested men?

Objection.

Sustained.

"Is it not a fact, Mr. Kent," Cawley persisted, "that at the time, to your knowledge, your reputation suffered from the connection of your name with the names of these men who were apprehended in the Navy, these service men, and tried on these immoral charges?"

This time the defense's objection was denied, so Kent answered: "I never knew that my reputation was under suspicion." After the arrest of the sailors, he learned that his "name had been connected with the investigation." The only question that ever came up, he continued, was the appropriateness of civilian chaplains visiting those jailed aboard the *Boxer*. He raised the issue with Rev. Hughes, who disagreed with naval policy restricting jailed men's access to chaplains. "My words," he continued, "were that 'Our Lord did that and that was the least we could do.'"

"Did you not, Mr. Kent," continued Cawley, "say to Mr. Quinn that it was a shame to confine these boys, that this practice came to them naturally and they could not help it?"

Gardner objected but was not sustained.

Kent admitted having employed an attorney at the time of the *Boxer* cases but denied having ever made such a statement.

Kent admitted having employed an attorney at the time of the *Boxer* cases but denied having ever made such a statement.

Finally the court ruled that the interrogation had gone "too far afield altogether." "Let us," the judge urged, "get back to this case."

Cawley asked Kent about his "escape" from Warwick. Complaints that the subject was irrelevant stimulated the judge to comment: "So far it is a mystery what you are driving at. If you will indicate what you propose to put in, perhaps we could shorten this." Cawley defended his right to "conceal" his strategy, and approaches to the bench won him permission to continue. Lengthy questions rehearsing in detail Kent's activities after his acquittal at Newport tried unsuccessfully to secure admission that he knew he had been indicted and was avoiding apprehension. "Why can not you ask him directly whether or not he fled to evade justice?" the judge finally asked.

"At any time, Mr. Kent, did you flee to evade justice?" asked Phillips.

"Never," he replied just before stepping down.[14]

VII

Perhaps recognizing the degree to which the operator's testimony had been shaken, Cawley's prosecution team endeavored to buttress their stories and, perhaps more important, to demonstrate that Kent had immoral relations with men other than operators. Their first rebuttal witness was Dr. Erastus M. Hudson, who began to describe the work of his investigators. Defense counsel immediately objected. "The defendant's character witnesses were allowed to go into details as to their knowledge of this man, their opportunities for knowing," complained the prosecution, so Hudson should be able to detail "what work he did, how he came to know about this man's character." The judge proved unsympathetic: "It is mere repetition of proven things," he ruled, which are "already in proof by the government as to the positions of these young men." As a result, Hudson limited himself to rebutting Bishop Perry's description of their meeting. Even then Cannon protested that the evidence failed to refute anything Perry had said. Gardner then asked his witness to characterize Kent's general reputation, "whether it was good or bad as to personal cleanliness."

"Well," replied the doctor, "he is generally known by what they call 'queer.'"

"I think that answer should be stricken out, your Honor, please," demanded Gardner.

"You asked," responded the judge, "what the reputation was and he said—the question is what the speech of people is."

"I said," repeated Hudson, "he was generally known that he was queer."

"I move to strike out that answer," Gardner repeated.

"That is not responsive and may be stricken out," ruled the judge.

Unwilling to abandon what seemed to be effective testimony, Cawley tried again. "I will ask you, Doctor, whether or not his reputation for personal cleanliness was good or bad."

"Bad . . . in the moral sense," replied Hudson.

In his cross-examination, Gardner forced admission that his knowledge stemmed from little more than casual gossip among officers and enlisted men. Yet more damaging to the prosecution was Hudson's confession that a chief machinist's mate such as Arnold "usually had charge of the engine room of a destroyer" and had no special training related to detection.

The next witness was Hugh Quinn, whose name the prosecution had repeatedly raised. He had only met the chaplain four times and had portrayed himself to a member of the defense team as a "character witness." The only damaging information provided was that "the boys" did not rate Kent's character "very good."

Lambert Britz, another rebuttal witness, had been assigned to the Torpedo Station when he met Kent and accepted an invitation to his room. His recollection of dates was so imprecise, however, that he could not recall whether the encounter occurred in February or July.

"I ask you Mister Britz," Cawley opened, "on this occasion when you went to his room and while you were there with him, if he took hold of your penis, sucked it, remarked about the size?"

"I object," interrupted Gardner.

"You may answer," the judge replied.

"Yes, sir, he did."

"This is a matter that I have indicated that I will grant an exception on," continued Judge Brown.

"Exception!" exclaimed Gardner.

"I will ask you, Mr. Britz, whether or not this reputation that you have spoken of that Mr. Kent bore down there, was notorious or not."

"Objected to." "Objection sustained."

"I will ask you whether or not, Mr. Britz, any nickname was applied to Mr. Kent generally there in Newport?"

Counsel for Kent again objected, whereupon the judge ruled that enough had already been said about the chaplain's "general reputation." Neither question was ever answered.

Britz had never been an operator and had not testified at the Newport trial. Nor had he ever encouraged Kent's actions, claiming "it was a terrible surprise" when the chaplain initiated sex with him.

"What did you do?" asked attorney Phillips, "Knock him down?"

"No, I didn't knock him down."

"Were you accustomed to have fellows do those things on you?" he probed further.

"No."

"Never had anything like that happen to you before, had you?"

"Yes, I did."

"Oh! You had. Now is that a fact, Britz, that you had been one of those operators down there around out getting evidence?"

"Was I an operator getting evidence? No. . . . ."

"You say other fellows had tried the same thing on you down there?"

In an effort to preserve the credibility of his witness, Cawley objected. "This is immaterial." "I think," ruled Judge Brown, "that is objectionable."

"Was it a common thing down there to have men doing those things on you, you fellows in the service?" persisted Phillips.

"No."

"But it had happened to you before, had it?"

"Yes, it had."

"Now, did you give Mr. Kent the old Harry for trying anything like that on you?"

"No; I was too dumfounded. I got away as quick as I could, used an excuse. . . . I told him I had an engagement for the next dance."

Britz admitted having met Kent on three previous occasions, during which no sexual advances occurred. "But this time, without saying a word, he suddenly grabbed you?. . . . Is that the fact?"

"He made plenty of advances which I didn't want to believe."

"And grabbed hold of you as you said?"

"Yes," agreed Britz.[15]

Next Cawley called Lloyd Dean Lawrence, apparently the second corroborating witness whom the judge agreed to hear. A twenty-two-year-old Iowa native who served at Newport until September 1919, Lawrence characterized Kent's reputation as bad and began to describe a visit to the chaplain's rooms. Gardner protested but was overruled on grounds that the supporting testimony even though not directly associated with a charge against Kent could be allowed. As it turned out, however, the testimony was worthless; nothing occurred between the two except hand holding, during which Kent's fingers momentarily "rested on . . . [the sailor's] privates." Furthermore, Lawrence admitted that from earlier observations at the hospital he knew what to anticipate from the chaplain. Why, if he suspected him already, had he accepted the invitation? "I had never come in contact with such a man personally," replied Lawrence. "I wanted to see if such a thing was possible."

"You want the jury to understand," the defense counsel summarized,

> that you had no connection with Mr. Hudson or Mr. Arnold, or with the vice investigation that was being carried on, that you heard from people in the hospital that Mr. Kent was an immoral man, that you thought you would like to see how such a person behaved, and so you immediately accepted the invitation of this immoral man to ride with him and dine with him and go to his room, and when he got to his rooms that happened which you thought might be going to happen. Is that it?

"Yes, sir."

Cawley's redirect examination provided additional detail about the meeting to buttress his argument that Kent had been the aggressor. The pair had talked generally until the subject of girls came up. Lawrence thought a minister was the wrong person "to tell a girl's troubles to," whereupon Kent urged him to forget he was a minister and replaced his chaplain's uniform with a bathrobe.

"I will put my arm around you," Lawrence recalled his having said, "and while holding hands, you will tell me about this girl."

"When he was holding me," continued the sailor, "the way he held his hand, he tried to draw me over on him. I resisted, drew back, paid no attention to the drawing back of his hands, and his fingers rested over my penis, he rubbed my hand that way with his hands would be going over my penis."[16]

VIII

Final court proceedings followed the noon recess. Attorney Phillips attempted to limit the government to a single count instead of separate ones for each occasion on which Kent had allegedly committed immoral activities, conviction on any one of which could result in imprisonment. "The ground," he argued, "is that all are separate courses of action."

"We feel," responded Cawley, "we have sufficient evidence here to support a verdict of guilty on each count."

Judge Brown denied the motion.[17]

The attorneys then presented final arguments. Nothing of what the prosecution said was recorded, but a local newspaper quoted Phillips as claiming Kent was "not the man that ought to be here before you[.] He has not offended against the law. The real offenders," he insisted, "who ought to be on trial are these two men Hudson and Arnold. The clergyman who went from Newport to Washington to protest against this outrageous proceeding was entirely right; it was a menace to public morals."[18]

Judge Brown then began his charge to the jury. In a criminal case such as this, he pointed out, the jury was "the sole judge of the facts." "You are to test the facts and you are to try the facts, gentlemen, upon the evidence which has been presented before you in this court." This procedure by which citizens rather than government officials determine an accused's guilt or innocence, he explained, "is one of the safeguards of our republican form of government." In this situation, there were seven alleged offences; each one was to be considered separate, and jurors should not be "prejudiced by the fact that there are many charges."

This case was being tried in a federal court under a "war statute" passed under the "war powers" provisions of the constitution. The legitimacy of the law itself was incontrovertible since the U.S. Supreme Court had validated it. The statute protected servicemen against intoxicating liquors, venereal disease, and moral "contamination" by establishing zones ten miles around military installations. Specifically, it prohibited prostitution, the establishment or maintenance of "a house of ill fame, brothel or bawdy house," or the reception of a person "for the purpose of lewdness, assignation or prostitution into any vehicle, conveyance, place, structure or building.'' Thus the prosecution had to prove in each instance that ''some person was received for the purpose of lewdness into some place or building within this district and within the zone.''

Judge Brown emphasized that Kent was innocent until proven guilty ''beyond a reasonable doubt.'' No easy definition of ''reasonable'' existed, although certain general guidelines were possible. ''You are not to try the case, gentlemen,'' he implored, ''on imagination or supposition, or conjectures, as to what has happened outside.'' Jurors should be limited to evidence presented and ''such just and reasonable inferences as common sense men can draw from what is said and what is proven.'' Both sides had presented evidence related to each charge; the jury's ultimate responsibility was measuring credibility. ''Who do you believe?'' they must ask. ''What, as reasonable men, must you believe from the testimony?''

He explained how the testimony of witnesses not directly associated with charges against Kent ought to be evaluated. ''The only use that you can make of that other testimony,'' he instructed, is ''to aid you in arriving at the conclusion as to whether the defendant is to be believed. That reputation testimony,'' he went on, ''is for you to weigh. . . .'' As to whether or not to believe the operators, the ''consistency of their statements'' became all important. ''You are entitled,'' he told the jurors, ''to apply the principle that if a man is detected in a falsehood, and that is the necessary result of a contradiction, in one matter, he is to be discredited on other matters.'' The vital question became ''whether or not it was a natural and probable thing that the defendant would have indulged in such conduct under the circumstances alleged. . . .''

The fact that so many witnesses had been, as the judge characterized them, ''detectives,'' ''operators,'' and ''sleuths'' created other problems. Frequently, Brown explained, such men could collect evidence that was otherwise unavailable. On the other hand, they might be suspected of ''color[ing] the testimony.'' Under U.S. law no one could have been compelled to ''subject his person to indignity,'' so it must be assumed that the operators performed their duties either ''voluntar[i]ly or under unlawful compulsion.'' The jurors must, therefore, determine whether the ''voluntary assumption of a duty of this kind'' affected the witness' credibility.

''So then gentlemen,'' he continued,

you have a very important duty. It is a serious case. The statute is a statute designed for a meritorious purpose. We must obey it, and if you are satisfied beyond a reasonable doubt that this defendant is proven guilty to your satisfaction on any count in this indictment, it is your duty to find him guilty. If, on the other hand, you have a reasonable doubt concerning the contradiction in each case by a single individual, and the surrounding circumstances affecting that, the defendant under our law [is entitled] to the benefit of that doubt.

Following a brief, technical discussion related to the ten mile limit and the boat trip made by Kent and Dostalik, he concluded:

Now, gentlemen, take this case. This has been an illustration ·to you of the duty which may fall upon courts and citizens. Those duties are often disagreeable. In criminal cases, the duty is always a disagreeable one. This has been particularly so, but that does not change the laws of evidence in the slightest degree. No repulsion or feeling of disgust should be permitted to create prejudice. We should take this evidence as it occurred and apply, just as a doctor treats the most offensive and disagreeable case, just as a surgeon takes the most degraded person and treats him properly, so you are to take this case and consider it in the light of reason, judgement, common sense and justice.[19]

Judge Brown completed his half-hour presentation by 4:30 p.m., and the jury withdrew to deliberate the evidence it had heard over the previous four days. Three hours later, at 7:30, the foreman announced that Samuel Neal Kent had been found innocent of all charges. "Rev. Mr. Kent," noted the *Newport Herald* the next day, "was showered with congratulations by those who have stood with him in his trial, by attorneys, and others." He left immediately for Warwick and never again participated in the national controversy which soon arose over the scandal in which he figured so prominently.[20]

Daily coverage of the Kent trial by the *Providence Journal* brought the scandal to national attention.
Credit: *Providence Journal*.

CHAPTER 7

A National Gay Scandal

Publicity about the Newport scandal begun the day Kent went on trial accelerated following his acquittal; within days what had started as an attempt to prove a single man guilty of homosexuality was transformed into a broadscale attack on the navy. At the same time, a letter of complaint addressed to President Woodrow Wilson by a number of Rhode Island ministers brought the case to the attention of the highest officials in the U.S. government. Forwarded to the Navy Department, it stimulated the first of several official investigations. When these two prongs — newspaper publicity and official investigations — drew together, the sex investigation that could have been forgotten once Kent's trial ended grew into a scandal of national proportions.

I

More than anyone else, the person responsible for publicizing the anti-gay scandal was John R. Rathom, the Australian-born editor of the *Providence Journal*. A commanding figure standing over six feet tall and carrying in excess of 250 pounds, Rathom combined drive, showmanship, and a sense of the dramatic that increased the paper's circulation and income while boosting it to national prominence. As a recent history of the paper has asserted, "Even though he [Rathom] sat at the editor's desk of a newspaper in a small city, he became a national figure."[1]

Despite his journalistic success, Rathom was not above misrepresenting his own background and on occasion published what a sympathetic writer has termed "extravagant tales that strayed beyond the facts. . . ." At the time of the San Francisco earthquake, for example, the *Journal* published what claimed to be "exclusive" on-the-spot stories but really had been authored by Rathom in Providence using telegraphic accounts seasoned by his own familiarity with the city. Prior to United States entry into World War I, the *Journal* cooperated secretly with the British embassy in Washington to expose the presence of German spies in the United States. Rathom employed a brigade of half a dozen "counterspies" to seek evidence against the Germans and published details about what they found with great relish. Subsequent investigations, however, determined that many of these stories were entire fabrications, and nearly all elaborated greatly on the truth. Before the Justice Department finally forced the paper to suspend telling tales, Rathom earned the enmity of nearly everyone in the Wilson administration, not the least of whom were Navy Secretary Josephus Daniels and his assistant Franklin Roosevelt.[2]

The details of how and when Rathom became interested in the Newport gay scandal are not easily discernible. He was a friend of Bishop James D. Perry of Rhode Island who probably first acquainted him with the case of Rev. Kent. Perhaps, he learned more from another friend, Admiral William S. Sims, who had commanded U.S. Naval forces in Europe during the war. Following the armistice, Sims squabbled bitterly with Daniels and Roosevelt over who had been responsible for the poor state of the navy when war broke out. One biographer of Roosevelt has concluded: "That Sims aided and abetted Rathom in this enterprise seems almost certain, but Rathom was also soon motivated by his personal enmity toward the Assistant Secretary."[3] "The whole business was a long, complex and messy affair," concludes the *Journal* history, "and it's easy to see how John R. became involved." Indeed, Roosevelt partisans at the time and ever since have contended that Rathom was wholly responsible for generating a national controversy. As recently as 1981, an Assistant Director of the Franklin D. Roosevelt Library concluded that the *Journal* was "used by John R. Rathons [*sic*] as a vehicle to perpetuate the scandal."[4]

Reports the first day of the Kent trial were brief, objective, and relegated to the *Journal*'s back pages. The morning of January 9, however, a banner headline on page one trumpeted the chaplain's acquittal. "Lawyers in the case," the article noted, "declare it one of the hardest contested legal battles ever fought in the United States District Court" in Providence. The fact that "the character of a minister of the gospel had been attacked" increased its importance.[5]

Indicative of Rathom's growing interest in the case was an editorial titled "The Dirty Trail of Secretary Daniels." The verdict that vindicated Kent, it opened, had convicted the naval secretary, whom Rathom accused of having "deliberately employed every bestial and degrading scheme he could utilize to bring everlasting shame to an innocent man." Naval officials "acting under the personal authority of Secretary Daniels," the editorial continued, had been ordered to "get" the chaplain by using "degrading and vicious plots which shifty detective agents would have been sent to the penitentiary for resorting to." Kent had been tried once in Newport and found innocent, after which "men of the highest standing in the United States, familiar with Mr. Kent's life for many years," had protected "dishonorable practices." Daniels, nevertheless, decided to "seek revenge for having been defeated in his efforts," and "ordered" the second trial. Such activities aimed not only at Kent but at "further besmirch[ing] the good name of the city of Newport," which, as the *Journal* saw it, "seems to have become a mania with the present Secretary of the Navy." "It is this same Josephus Daniels," concluded the piece, "who has posed as the purifier of the Navy and a defender of its morals. Smug hypocrisy has never reached lower depths of degradation."[6]

Such language inevitably stimulated strong reaction. U.S. Attorney Harvey Baker—one of the prosecutors in the Kent case—denounced the editorial in a letter printed the next day. Accusations against Daniels were "absolutely false." Such "an unfounded attack," he argued, was "unworthy" of the paper and "casts an unjust reflection upon the efforts of public officers." Rathom's fury intensified as he defended what he apparently already accepted as a personal campaign against Daniels. "The *Journal*'s declaration," he replied, "is that the Navy Department has been besmirched and its honor tarnished by Secretary Daniels, who has permitted his 'blameless operatives' to weave a web of suggested infamy about a man who has been pronounced innocent after two jury trials."[7]

Nor were epithets limited to Baker. F. P. Garretson wrote the *Journal* from Newport to note that the town's "responsible citizens" were "gratified" that Kent had been acquitted of "the most abominable charges." "Never before," he noted, had "such charges, backed up by such witnesses, been brought forth in this free country" by any government agency. Even the idea of federally-employed "operators" was so "incredible" that few police courts would give their testimony "the slightest standing." "To

ferret out so-called crimes by employing witnesses to commit
crimes for evidence," concluded Garretson, "is beyond all human
comprehension." An editorial in the *Newport Mercury*, which the
Journal reprinted, also expressed relief at Kent's acquittal. It raised
the further question—soon added to the list of accusations—why
those sailors arrested nearly a year before and ordered by the Dunn
Court to stand trial had not yet been brought before courts-martial.[8]

A much different perspective came from Attorney Joseph C.
Cawley, who headed the prosecution team during Kent's trial. In a
letter addressed to Secretary Daniels the 12th of January and forwarded to him by Dr. Hudson, Cawley defended his action. The
evidence, in the attorney's view, had been carefully prepared and
was "amply sufficient" to warrant a verdict of guilty. Any more
evidence would have been "cumulative and superfluous." He characterized the defense witnesses as having known Kent "only by
meeting him casually or on infrequent occasions." Some had not
seen him for years. The chaplain himself admitted meeting the operators but "naturally denied the conduct attributed to him." Cawley admitted, nonetheless, that a juror had told him the initial ballot
had been nine for acquittal and three for conviction; the final vote
had been eight to four. "In my opinion," he concluded, "the jury's
verdict is contrary to the weight of evidence."[9]

II

The same day Baker's letter appeared in the *Journal*, a committee of Newport clergymen drafted a lengthy denunciation of the
navy's activities against alleged gays, affixed a special delivery
stamp to the typewritten envelope, and deposited it at the Newport
post office. It was addressed: "Hon. Woodrow Wilson, President
of the United States, The White House, Washington, D.C." The
acquittal of Kent by two separate courts, opened the petition,
prompted "those of us who have been associated in social and religious work among both army and navy" to call the President's
attention to "certain deleterious and vicious methods employed by
the Navy Department." Testimony during the trials, they continued, revealed that two men who claimed "the unusual power of
detecting sexual degeneracy at sight" had been given charge of
"over a score" of sailors. They had "instructed them in the details
of a nameless vice and sent them through the community to practice
the same in general and in particular to entrap certain designated

individuals." These activities had persisted for months despite "strong and continued protests" from "prominent citizens of Rhode Island."

"It must be evident to every thoughtful mind," explained the authors,

> that the use of such vile methods cannot fail to undermine the character and ruin the morals of the unfortunate youths detailed for this duty, render no citizen of the community safe from suspicion and calumny, bring the city into unwarranted reproach, and shake the faith of the people in the wisdom and integrity of the naval administration.

What was needed "at the earliest moment" was to "eliminate from the navy all officials, however highly placed, who are responsible for the employment of such execrable methods—contrary alike to the dictates of morality, patriotism, and religion." "The people of the United States," concluded the letter, "are entitled to the assurance that hereafter nobody who enlisted in the Navy will be consigned to a career of vice." Following were the signatures of fourteen clergymen, mostly from Newport, including Methodists, Episcopalians, Baptists, Presbyterians, and Congregationalists. The most prominent were Rev. Stanley C. Hughes and Bishop James D. Perry.[10]

President Wilson probably never saw the ministers' letter, for late in September of 1919, in the midst of a transcontinental tour promoting American ratification of the Versailles Treaty ending World War I and creating the League of Nations, he had become ill in Colorado. Back in Washington, October 2 a paralyzing stroke left him largely incapacitated and unable to conduct most business for the rest of his presidential term. Most routine work was conducted by Wilson's aides—especially Joseph Tumulty—or sometimes by Mrs. Wilson. As a result, the letter that reached the White House January 11 was forwarded to Navy Secretary Josephus Daniels himself.[11]

Thus the man accused of masterminding the Newport sex investigation received the ministers' complaint and determined how to act upon it. According to date stamps on the envelope and letter—the original of which is among Daniels' private papers in the Library of Congress—the envelope mailed Saturday the 10th did not arrive at the Navy Department until the following Wednesday, January 14. Even earlier, apparently based on a press report describing the contents of the message, Monday the 12th Daniels announced that he would appoint a naval board of inquiry to "investigate the charges" made by the Newport clergymen. It would, he added, "have the authority to make such recommendations for further action as may be necessary." The story, carried nationally by the Associated Press, first brought the navy's anti-gay campaign to the attention of Americans outside Rhode Island.[12]

Not until the 17th, however, did the secretary reply to the ministers' request. A letter addressed to Bishop Perry in Newport (he resided in Providence) acknowledged receipt of the petition sent to Wilson and announced that a naval court would soon inquire into the "methods" and "scope" of the anti-gay investigation, "covering all pertinent matters leading up to, surrounding and growing out of the investigation." It would also recommend any further action that it "deems to be necessary."[13]

Even before any formal answer had been received to the petition, Bishop Perry denounced the way in which the petition had been handled. In a letter to Daniels, he accused the secretary of having assumed "official responsibility for the use of methods which no self-respecting community could submit to without protest." Enlisted men under his protection had been told by their superiors to "prostitute themselves and corrupt others." Daniels himself had approved these methods by authorizing the use of evidence in the Providence court. "I submit, sir," concluded Perry, "that this outrage done to the honor of the navy and to the public conscience is not a matter for an investigation directed by the one who was responsible for it."[14]

The credibility of Daniel's proposed investigation diminished further with the appointment to chair the court of Admiral Herbert O. Dunn. As Commander of the First Naval District, he was a friend and associate of many whom he was to investigate. He was especially close to Franklin Delano Roosevelt, with whom he had vacationed in the Azores during the summer of 1918. The month the inquiry began, Dunn secured Roosevelt's assistance in obtaining admission to the Annapolis Navel Academy for his wife's nephew.[15]

III

As might have been predicted, Daniels' actions inflamed Rathom's passion. In a lengthy editorial printed January 21, he criticized the secretary's actions as "the same sort of dust that he has been throwing in the public's eyes" for seven years, while all other navy men had been "rendered speechless under his autocratic censorship." Rathom then launched a personal attack on Daniels. He was "notoriously unfitted to speak for the Navy," having been appointed solely to reward service as publicist for the Democratic National Committee. Already there had been suggestions from "narrow-visioned" or "crassly partisan" congressmen that publicizing the Newport scandal would "sadly affect" the morale of the navy and "the public esteem which it enjoys." Such concerns were groundless, argued the *Journal*, for the "professional personnel" in the service would not be affected. "Officers and men," Rathom continued, "will rejoice to have the light turned on." In fact, the navy's essential sturdiness" was evidenced by having survived seven years of Daniels' administration "without suffering any impairment of its soul. . . ." "What is being exposed," the editorial added, "are the weak, vicious and dishonorable methods of those civilians who have exercised political control over its affairs. Never," argued Rathom, "in all its history has the Navy been subjected to such a reckless administration as has been imposed on it during the Daniels period." Now was the time for a full and impartial airing of the facts about the anti-homosexual campaign. "Let us have the story now," he demanded, "instead of relying on some inquisitive historian to delve into a camouflaged record and reveal it to posterity."[16]

In addition to such public criticisms, Rathom moved aggressively to procure a hearing before a more objective tribunal. January 18 he sent lengthy telegrams to each member of the U.S. Senate Committee on Naval Affairs. "Disclosures in the Providence Journal within the last week," he opened, "prove[d] beyond any doubt" that conditions in the navy were "rotten beyond conception." The secretary was fully cognizant that seamen "had been used for the most vile and nameless practices" to entrap innocent men. Daniels and Roosevelt were aware that a "secret division of Naval Intelligence [had] operated and [been] maintained for this purpose." Moreover, numerous sailors jailed since April of 1919 were "innocent of any crime or misdemeanor." All efforts to secure their releases had failed. Other men "dragged out of hospitals in serious condition" had been "compelled after hours of the third degree" to commit perjury against innocent people.

As a result of these perverse activities, Rathom charged that the morale of the navy was "being rapidly destroyed." The blame for the situation, he argued, "stands at the door of Mr. Daniels and nobody else." "Mr. Daniels with full knowledge of these degrading and vicious plots," insisted Rathom, had "personally attempted to cover with infamy the names of innocent men who have sought to expose the acts of his subordinates in the matters above mentioned." What was mandatory, he insisted, was a full scale-investigation by a Congressional committee "armed with full powers to ascertain the truth."

Rathom then introduced seven specific allegations against the navy which became the basis for most later discussions of the Newport case. First, he charged, "young men, many of them boys," in the navy had been ordered "to commit vile and nameless acts on the persons of others in the Navy service, or have suggested these to be practiced on themselves." Second, "victims" who were entrapped had been "picked out in every case" by Hudson and Arnold, "both of whom have declared that they were able to recognize degenerates by the way they walk along the streets." In all, argued the third allegation, twenty men had committed offences "of the character outlined" with persons "selected for this persecution."

The remainder of Rathom's charges focused on the official sanction of these activities within the navy. Both Daniels and Roosevelt, he asserted, had "known of these methods for several months." Not only had they been deaf to the appeals to terminate activities, but they had directly or indirectly approved citations for the men. The telegrams also quoted from the ministers' January 10 letter in charging that the anti-gay activities had persisted despite protests from "prominent citizens of Rhode Island." Sixth, Rathom charged the existence within naval intelligence of a secret "Section A, O.A.S.N.," the purpose of which was "to compel confessions of nameless vice." A naval intelligence representative had reportedly admitted its existence but declined to reveal details "with regard to its power or its methods."

Rathom also raises once more the issue of what had happened to sailors confined by the Foster Court of Inquiry. He complained that they had been jailed for months without trial despite "continual pleadings" from friends and relatives. Even Training Station Commander Edward Campbell revealed that he had made "official requests" every ten days for action in the cases.[17]

Several days after Rathom despatched these telegrams, on January 21, the ministers addressed a telegram of their own to Chairman Carroll S. Page of the Senate Naval Affairs Committee. "Ministers' Union urgently requests that the fullest possible examination of naval abuses at Newport be included in your investigation," they appealed. "We agree with Bishop Perry that the man responsible for the conditions should not appoint investigating committee."[18]

Next day, the clergymen supplemented their telegram with a letter to Senator Page. Although Daniels had already appointed a "committee of naval officers," to look into the case, appearance before such a body by the ministers was improper because the same man who appointed the investigators and to whom they would report was the subject of the clergymen's "chief and most important charge." As for the anti-gay investigation itself, sailors under the command of a young doctor had been "sent through the city, day and night, for months with orders to engage in unnatural acts." Such activities "degraded the unfortunate youths" ordered to this duty at the same time it "constituted an indignity [to the] people of Newport." "Our people," explained the clergymen,

> opened their homes to the young men of the navy, entertained them, introduced them to their sons and daughters, did so gladly as a friendly aid to navy morale. And now we find that some — a good many — of these youths were acting by orders which seem to have proceeded from the Navy Department itself in a way that should exclude them from every home in the land. What are we to think of such proceedings? What recourse have we? What recourse has any innocent citizen accused by these depraved persons?

More significant than these parochial questions were the larger public policy issues generated by the Newport scandal. How, for example, could the navy explain its policy to the parents of operators who took part in the investigation? They had "entrusted [their sons] to the navy for the defense of the country and then [they had been] sent out to [commit] acts of shame[.]" So serious were these concerns that they fell beyond the jurisdiction of the department responsible for the investigation itself. Ultimately, the ministers demanded to know who was responsible for such a sad state of affairs. "We do not intend to let the matter rest until this point is settled," concluded the ministers, "and till it is definitely established whether the American people are content to leave in charge of young men enlisted in the navy any official guilty of the employment of such methods."[19]

Senator Page took prompt and vigorous action to initiate and organize the kind of investigation Rathom and the ministers demanded. The day after receiving the newspaperman's telegram, the full Naval Affairs Committee voted to appoint a small group to conduct a preliminary investigation and recommend action. Two days later Page announced his nominations. The two Republicans, representing the Senate majority, were to be Lewis H. Ball of Delaware and Henry W. Keyes of Vermont. Not coincidentally, Ball, a physician known for his geniality and breadth of interests, and Keyes, a railroad man and banker, were simultaneously investigating charges against Daniels leveled by Admiral William S. Sims. Sims claimed the navy had been inadequately prepared at the outbreak of World War I and blamed the secretary for having bungled subsequent rebuilding and reorganization efforts. Especially because of Sims' long association with the Naval War College at Newport and friendship with Rathom, many supporters of Daniels interpreted the controversial sex scandal as an extension of the larger attack on the Secretary. The ultimate objective of both was to discredit the Wilson administration.[20]

To represent the Democrats, Page initially recommended Rhode Island Senator Peter G. Gerry, the party whip. A Newport resident, he had served for many years on the Naval Affairs Committee and was widely credited with securing major naval installations for his state. In addition to his political activities, Gerry had become interested in the newspaper business, and in 1921 purchased the *Providence News*, the principal competitor of Rathom's *Journal*. Undoubtedly recognizing the precarious position in which service on the subcommittee would place him, Gerry declined. In his place, Page named William H. King, a conservative Utah Mormon who later became one of the New Deal's severest critics.[21]

IV

In the midst of these events, criticism turned to yet another navy official who previously had maintained silence regarding the Newport scandal, Assistant Secretary Franklin D. Roosevelt. In a formal statement included in Associated Press dispatches dated January 22, FDR characterized Rathom's accusations "in view of the circumstances a deliberate and malicious effort to create trouble, in addition to being false." A month ago, Roosevelt continued, apparently referring to Bishop Perry or Rev. Stanley Hughes, Rathom had sent a representative to Washington. He was told that the matter had been transferred to the Department of Justice and assured that "the very moment" the Kent trial ended, the Navy Department would investigate allegations of "highly improper" methods. Only ten days having passed since Kent's acquittal, he continued—apparently ignoring the obvious impact of the clergymen's letter to Wilson—the navy had "proceeded to carry out its intention of conducting an investigation." Indeed, on January 17 a Court of Inquiry with "full powers to go into this question" had been appointed. "In view of the fact that Mr. Rathom knew the above circumstances," concluded the Assistant Secretary, "and that the department was proceeding in this case, in entire good faith, his statement can only be considered a maliciously vicious, dishonest and dishonorable attack on the United States Navy."[22]

Roosevelt's statement interjected him into the dispute while spurring Rathom to intensify his criticism. Thus a prolonged debate over the anti-gay scandal would be aired in the nation's press for months to come. Rathom's immediate response was a page one story declaring FDR's charges "entirely false." The *JOurnal* had never attacked the navy nor claimed the "immoral conditions exist" in it. The paper had charged, however, and would prove to the U.S. Senate's special committee that navy officials had instructed more than twenty sailors "in the details of a nameless vice" and sent them throughout Newport to "practice the same in general" and "entrap certain designated individuals."

Rathom challenged the accuracy of Roosevelt's account: The Navy Department, he insisted, transferred the Kent case to Justice when he and Daniels had "full and complete knowledge of the almost inconceivable practices" used to collect evidence. Nonetheless, uniformed sailors, "made perverts by official order," continued their work. Even more serious, Daniels had either ordered directly or agreed to grant these men citations for "their interest and zeal in the work." "Innocent boys," Rathom further claimed, had been held for months without trial while requests for their speedy release were ignored by Daniels and Roosevelt.

"The Providence Journal has no interest whatever" in those who had been accused, concluded the article. It knew none of them and did not care if they were guilty or innocent. The paper's only goal was the maintenance of honorable and decent conditions in the United States navy and of its morale, the protection of tens of thousands of honorable officers and enlisted men in the navy, and the punishment of the brute beasts responsible for the present conditions and of those who have permitted such conditions to exist.

Roosevelt's accusations, the article ended, were "absolutely false in every respect." "We stand by the evidence and witnesses. We are ready to prove the truth of every charge we have made."[23]

An editorial the same day used even sharper language to criticize Roosevelt. The Assistant Secretary's statement was a "wild and clumsy" effort "to answer facts with invective." Loyalty to his "pussy-footing chief" had led FDR into a "bog of falsehood and unfairness." The only explanation for such overreaction was that administration leaders considered themselves "so immune from criticisms that all they have to do in their own defense is shout 'Liar.'" Despite such efforts, Rathom predicted: "this is the beginning of the end for Josephus Daniels and he begins to realize it."[24]

The *Journal* also reprinted a telegram Rathom had sent to Roosevelt. It denounced the Assistant Secretary's "amazing attack" and defended the paper's actions as "a public duty for the protection of the honor of the United States" against "the most bestial and dishonorable methods known to men." Sailors, the editor insisted, had "been forced into the position of moral perverts by specific orders" from naval officers with the knowledge of Daniels and Roosevelt. "We resent your unwarranted and false charges against us," concluded Rathom, "and intend to prove, by evidence which we have not sought or inspired, the truth of every statement we have made."[25]

In a calculated effort to extend knowledge of the Newport scandal from Rhode Island throughout the United States, the night of January 22—the date Roosevelt's attack and the *Journal*'s response had been published—Rathom prepared a lengthy presentation of the case which he distributed nationwide via telegram to "leading newspapers." The only motivation of the *Journal*, opened Rathom's version of the controversy, was "to maintain honorable and decent conditions" in the navy for current sailors and to provide incentives for future enlistment. Millions of dollars had been spent trying to recruit men into the navy since the armistice, explained Rathom, and hundreds of officers had devoted time to such efforts. Little had been accomplished, however, perhaps in part because of events such as had occurred in Newport. The telegrams denied any suggestion of widespread immorality among the naval personnel. "This is not true." He then spelled out the seven allegations previously presented to the Senate Committee. Two more noted that the only two civilians accused of misconduct (Kent and Brown) had been acquitted, the former on two different occasions. Rathom also claimed that when the navy's "'spotter' witnesses" appeared in court, Judge Brown had ruled that since no legal order could compel them to have undertaken such activities, they must have worked "either voluntarily or under unlawful compulsion." In the case of jailed sailors, Rathom added, the government had failed "to produce testimony of any character whatever against men who had been confined without trial for many months." He attached a list of thirty-five witnesses who could confirm this evidence.[26]

The resulting national publicity made Roosevelt angrier than ever. He protested to newspapers that printed Rathom's version of the Newport scandal and sent copies of stories to the Senate Committee with suggestions that for the sake of the navy Rathom be prevented from issuing such statements. "Any mother reading the headlines," he argued, "would very properly hesitate before allowing her son to enlist in the Naval Service." "In fact," he continued, the average person who read Rathom's report would likely conclude "that the Navy as a whole is a pretty rotten institution, and that it is not a proper place, either on its ships or in its training camps, for young Americans to be."[27]

Within less than two weeks a local scandal focused on a single obscure chaplain had become a national controversy involving some of the highest appointed officials in the government and publicized by leading newspapers. The careers of men like Roosevelt and Daniels now seemed to be in almost as much jeopardy as Samuel Neal Kent's had been. John R. Rathom had found a story as titillating as German espionage on which to focus his journalistic attention. Already hearings before the Dunn Court of Inquiry were scheduled to begin, and soon the Newport scandal would be a topic for discussion within the committee rooms of the U.S. Senate.

The Newport case received little news coverage until the day after the acquittal of Rev. Kent, the *Providence Journal* featured news of his trial on page one.

Credit: *Providence Journal* copy from UMI

John R. Rathom, controversial publisher of the *Providence Journal* is often accused of using his journalistic power to magnify the importance of the Newport scandal.
Credit: *Providence Journal*.

Assistant Navy Secretary Franklin D. Roosevelt attacked John Rathom and the Rhode Island clergymen for their criticism of the Newport anti-gay crusade.

Credit: *Newport Recruit*, U.S. Naval Historical Center.

CHAPTER 8

Defending the Right of Petition

The naval court of inquiry convening at Newport the third week in January 1920 had been assigned to investigate the government's pursuit of homosexuals and alleviate growing public concern about the Rhode Island sex scandal. Prompted by a letter of complaint addressed to the President of the United States, it had been called into existence by Secretary of the Navy Josephus Daniels. Here was the chance for the navy to demonstrate seriousness about getting to the bottom of the controversy and punishing anyone responsible for wrongdoing.

Almost from the moment the court opened, the proceedings intensified rather than reduced concerns over U.S. government behavior. Members of the court were friends, colleagues, or subordinates of those implicated in the scandal; throughout the hearings they demonstrated undeniable partiality. The system of military justice was skillfully manipulated to protect military officers and enlisted men while placing civilians who questioned the government's conduct in awkward, defensive positions, made worse by the aggressiveness of the judge advocate and their attorney's ignorance of naval procedures. Furthermore, coverage given the hearings by the *Providence Journal* and less fully by the Associated Press (and thus by newspapers everywhere) kept the case in the headlines for months.

I

A wire from Secretary Daniels to Admiral Herbert O. Dunn on January 17, 1920, appointed members and spelled out the charge of the board. In addition to Dunn, the evidence would be heard by Captains John F. Hines and David E. Theleen. The judge advocate—theoretically the man responsible for ascertaining the truth, really the person defending the navy against its critics—was Ensign Henry I. Hyneman. The court was to "inquire into the methods employed" by Hudson, Arnold and their operators "in investigating moral and other conditions" in the navy. Furthermore, it was to "ascertain and inquire into the scope of and authority for said investigation and for the methods employed in conducting the same" as well as "all pertinent and material matters leading up to, surrounding, and growing out of" the investigation. As required by navy procedures, Hudson, Arnold and their men would be considered "interested parties" and afforded legal rights. The final report would provide a "full statement of the facts," opinions based on those facts, and recommendations for "further proceedings." Sessions were to begin at 10:00 a.m., the 22nd of January at Newport, with needed clerical support provided by the Training Station commander.[1]

With such short notice, the hearings got started slowly. Finally at 10:30 a.m. on the 23rd, with Dr. Hudson having arrived late, the business of the court began. He challenged none of the court members, but learned that he—unlike civilian participants—could have an attorney, call and cross examine witnesses, and present evidence.[2]

As the first witness took the stand, the navy's strategy became apparent. The Rev. Aaron Theopolus Peters introduced himself as minister of Newport's Union Congregational Church, the oldest Negro church in the United States. As Peters identified his signature on the January 10 letter to President Wilson, the court changed his status from a "witness" to a "complainant." Judge Advocate Hyneman wasted no time putting Peters on the defensive. The witness denied knowing everyone who served on the committee that drafted the letter, whereupon Hyneman challenged him: What did he know about the case that enabled him to sign such a letter? Peters explained that a "number of men, some colored" had been "taken up" and brought to trial in district court. The "most prominent" was Rev. Kent. At these trials, the "evidence . . . given by the prosecution had brought out a number of alarming facts" which led him to sign the letter. But what evidence, demanded Hyneman, had he to back up these generalities? Peters had not attended any trials, but he had read "a copy of the proceedings" from Newport.

"Do you know of your own knowledge," the questioner persisted, "any particular incident of vice connected with men in the Naval service?"

"What do you mean," inquired the clergymen, "if I have come in personal contact or whether I know in an indirect way?"

"I mean this," repeated the Judge Advocate: "Can you give in this court the names of any officers or men in the U.S. Navy whom you know of your own knowledge to have committed any immoral acts?"

Peters still did not understand. "Do you mean by coming in practical contact with men who were operating on others," he queried, "or do you wish to know if I had knowledge from my own parishioners?"

The court could call parishioners as witnesses, replied Hyneman; he did not want to have hearsay, "what anyone else told you." The court wanted "any facts or names within your own personal knowledge."

"I have no facts in that way," he replied.

The attorney for Peters, as for all the ministers, was the same Frank Nolan who had represented Neils Johnson before the Foster court of inquiry. He was so inadequately prepared, intimidated by the military court, and naive about the direction of questioning that he asked only a single, inconsequential question before allowing Dr. Hudson to interrogate his client. If much of his information came from members of the ministers' committee, it was vital to know exactly who had told him what based on what evidence. "Do you mean to tell this court, sir," he continued in heightened rhetoric, "that you cannot remember the name of any man who gave you that information . . . ?"

"I do," he replied. "It is not that I am trying to withhold any information from the court. It is simply that I cannot be positive, and I would [rather] not suggest any names at all." With that he stepped down.[3]

II

The navy's strategy became clearer as other clergy were called to the stand. First came W. J. Lucas, from Mount Olivet Baptist Church, then Charles P. Christopher of the Second Baptist Church, and John Deming of St. George's Episcopal Church. Episcopal clergyman Everett Smith from Portsmouth was even less knowledgeable than most.⁴ In each case, witnesses were required to admit that they had little or no personal evidence on which to base their charges and were badgered by Hyneman as to why they had signed a letter containing charges about which they knew so little.

More important testimony came from William Safford Jones, minister of the Channing Memorial Church since 1904 and the self-proclaimed "dean of the clergy" in Newport. Hyneman demanded to know if Jones had any personal knowledge about the case.

"I thank heaven no," he replied. "I should feel disgraced if I had known a single operator in that squad, or anyone who directed those operations."

The judge advocate began to ask about the "official" character and completeness of the Newport transcript. In language stronger than any of his colleagues, Jones insisted that such detail was irrelevant. "What we did was protest in the name of decency and good morals and good citizenship," he insisted, and ". . . against the method pursued by the Navy Department in gathering evidence of sexual perversion . . . in the city of Newport." Whether the transcript was eighty percent complete or seventy-five percent or even twenty-five percent, "after wading through the mass of filthy detail, any man who had any moral sense whatsoever would say, 'This thing is rotten, and this thing cannot go on.'" In the same way, he concluded, "the people of the United States, when they know the facts, will rise up and say it must stop."

Nonetheless, Hyneman wanted details about the subcommittee the ministers had organized to investigate vice. This had not been its purpose, responded Jones; it was to "draw up a statement of the concensus of opinion" in the Union. "Our function," he went on, "was to put in writing the strong moral indignation felt by every man there" and ask the President to investigate. Before the letter was sent, Rev. Hughes had telephoned Bishop Perry to read the draft. ". . . we asked him clause by clause," explained Jones, "whether or not we were justified in making these statements." The bishop not only approved the wording but authorized the addition of his signature. Rev. Hughes mailed it and, almost at the same time, gave it to the Associated Press through the *Newport Herald*.

Jones also criticized the court itself. He and the other ministers "felt strongly," he argued, that the navy convening a court of inquiry to investigate its own methods was "to us, at least, rather a doubtful question," in fact "a manifest impropriety." Admiral Dunn interrupted to note that the court could investigate "everything in connection with the matter" by calling "any person in the United States." It had "full jurisdiction and full powers to inquire and settle everything." Jones admitted his opinion might change, although he wanted the secretary and assistant secretary of the navy to be called. "This is the point we feel to be very important," added the clergyman, for the most important question was "the source of authority in this matter; who gave the power to any man to institute investigations along this line. We want to know," he concluded, "and the people of the United States want to know."

"That," answered Admiral Dunn, "is what the court is trying to find out."

Jones reported for the first time that "careful sociological studies of moral conditions" in Newport had found "practically" no evidence of homosexuality. Therefore it seemed logical to "question very seriously the wisdom, not to say the decency, of the Navy sending men over into Newport for the purpose of securing evidence. . . ." He also reminded the court that earlier in the war when Secretary Daniels had asked the people to help make Newport "cleaner and better," the ministers union had pledged full cooperation and done everything possible. "And now that a[n objectionable] method [is] being used," he concluded, "(mark the words) with the sanction of the head of the Navy Department, we feel it equally to be our duty to protest as strongly as we can."[5]

III

Every other Newport minister who appeared before the court of inquiry paled in importance to Rev. Stanley C. Hughes, Rector of Trinity Church. He had collected most of the background information related to the anti-gay crusade, personally visited Washington to protest naval activities, and drafted the letters and telegrams sent by the Ministers' Union. Several witnesses identified him as the person who influenced them to sign documents. Except for Bishop Perry, no clergyman had been more significant in bringing the incident to public attention. Thus Hughes' appearance before the Dunn Court of Inquiry stimulated major interest on the part of the other ministers, the judge advocate, the court members, and the press. During two and a half days, he responded to more than 1,300 questions, the transcript of which fills 166 typewritten pages.

Hughes' antagonism to the navy in general and Admiral Dunn's court in particular became evident at once. No sooner had he been introduced, identified his signature on the letter to Wilson, and been made a complainant, than he began questioning the court itself. Could he be assured, he asked, that the court would "make a full, complete and impartial inquiry" into the activities of Hudson and his subordinates and the authority for their activities? And, if so, would the ministers be provided a copy of the transcript? The hearings would be complete, responded Dunn. No regulation, however, entitled complainants to a copy of the transcript, although the clergymen could attend sessions to learn what occurred.

Further testimony revealed new details about earlier studies of immorality in Newport. A man named Aronovici, reported Hughes, had investigated Connecticut and Pittsburg before being employed by Newport organizations to "come incognito to look over the whole town thoroughly." Later, private detective Ralph Kneeland, who had surveyed Providence, received $1,000 to study "vice and other conditions" in Newport. Both men found gambling and prostitution, although there were fewer "places of ill resort" than expected. Neither study, emphasized Hughes, "found any trace of homo-sectual [sic] vice." Furthermore, since the employment of Chief of Police John Tobin, conditions had become "pretty good," although "things creep[ed] in now and then." Hyneman questioned how a clergyman would know how many prostitutes or perverts populated Newport. Attorney Frank Nolan protested such hypothetical questions, but Hyneman insisted that he was only probing the churchman's assessment. When Admiral Dunn overruled the objection, Hughes protested. The Ministers' Union had clarified its charges against the navy. Unless these complaints were proven false or "in some way impugned," it was a waste of time and great impropriety" to interrogate the ministers about subjects with which they were unfamiliar. "We stand upon what the Navy read into its own record in this trial," he went on, "and I do not think that it [a question about other matters] is fair." "The court," interrupted Admiral Dunn, "wants to find out what you do know." Questions such as Hyneman had posed were "being asked because they are relevant to the matter under investigation by the court."

When did Hughes first learn that there were homosexuals in Newport? At first he characterized the arrest of Kent "as a thunderbolt out of a clear sky." Under close questioning, however, he recalled that in July 1919 he visited George Collins, a Providence boy charged with "gross immorality with sailors." The jailer had told him that the navy had been "making a very broad investigation" and that eight men had already been arrested. Like Rev. Deming, Hughes first learned that Kent was suspected of being gay while selecting the new director of the Seamen's Institute. A naval officer on the selection committee had described the chaplain as "one of the men under surveillance." Following his arrest at the end of July, Hughes came to the chaplain's defense. He and retired Judge Darius Baker, explained Rev. Hughes, represented Newport on the Episcopal Church War Commission which sponsored Kent's work. As soon as they learned of his arrest, Hughes wrote Kent "that the church would stand by him and that we would do all that we could." Later attorney William Harvey read him the specific charges. Hughes and Harvey found character witnesses to testify on Kent's behalf and agreed to have a transcript of the trial prepared "on account of the horrible things going on in Newport." Because he had been the last witness in the Newport trial, Hughes had not heard the operators' presentations. From what he knew, however, their testimony was suspect "because it was contradictory and it dealt with things no one would believe a good man would do."

Early September had found Hughes and Hamilton Fish Webster in the office of Franklin D. Roosevelt. As soon as they reported "the dreadful things going on in Newport," the Assistant Secretary remarked that if their report was true, "somebody must swing for it." He added, however, that Newport had "always been a very bad or immoral place." Little credence could be placed on kent's acquittal, FDR argued, because Newport courts were "corrupt and untrustworthy." The judge who acquitted Kent was reputed to "give his decisions for political reasons." Webster responded that he had known Judge Baker for years and knew him to be "of the highest rectitude and character and . . . thoroughly straight and reliable." Roosevelt told the visitors he "hadn't time to go into this matter" thoroughly, gave them a note of introduction to Captain Richard Leigh on his staff, and ushered them out of his office.

Hughes and Webster had taken the transcript of the Newport trial to Washington, showed it briefly to Roosevelt, and left it with Leigh. It had never been returned. Hyneman wanted Hughes to tell him how much of the transcript had been shown to Roosevelt, whereupon Nolan demanded that the government return the papers.

"I am entitled to test this witness' memory in any way that is legal and proper," retorted the judge advocate. The court sided with Hyneman, who indicated that he had no intention of producing the purloined document.

"I respectfully ask," responded Nolan, "that this court cause to be subpoenaed, Mr. Franklin D. Roosevelt, Assistant Secretary of the Navy, and Captain Richard Leigh and have them produce the notes of testimony left with them." Dunn never answered.

Questioning, however, persisted. Could Roosevelt from the portions he saw have "formed a fair, complete, and unbiased judgment" about the case? Hughes was unable to say, though he was certain anyone ignorant of the matter could have made up his mind about the case from having read half to a third of the document. Had Roosevelt been given the testimony of operator Charles McKinney? "My impression is that we did, but I cannot say" was Hughes' best answer.

Further questions attempted to undermine the transcript's reliability and value. Hughes admitted it was neither complete nor official.

"You do know," argued Hyneman, that "this is not worth the paper it is written on as an official document of the court?"

"You mean to say," countered the clergyman, "that a document [that] is not official is not worth anything as an official document . . . ?" Hughes argued that because the witnesses had perjured themselves, their testimony was "not worthy of belief."

Then how could he use that same testimony to prove the government had sanctioned improprieties? demanded Hyneman.

"The Navy Department had accepted that as the ground on which they would blacken the reputation and ruin a man," responded Hughes. ". . . and either the Navy Department regarded that as the truth and therefore must stand upon the record they accepted or they must say that they are willing to know it to be false and say that the testimony was given in order to ruin this man."

Hyneman had the last word. Citing an admission during the Providence trial that the transcript did "not purport to be a full record," he concluded: "It was that same transcript upon which you twenty four hours later, and the Ministers' Union based a portion of the facts in the letter to the President of the United States under date of January 10!"[6]

Hyneman's later interrogation focused on why the ministers had waited so long to send their letter and what specific evidence substantiated their charges. Hughes explained the cumulative impact of continuing Navy Department activity and argued that by failing to drop the Kent case and repudiate the methods utilized the navy had endorsed the entire affair. "We knew that the same men were em-

ployed to dog him and to pursue him even to Warwick, Pa.,"
Hughes explained, "and to tell his parishioners that he was a criminal and wanted for many crimes." Because such arguments presumed the on-going nature of the investigation, Hyneman demanded to know "the last date on which these nameless vices were
practiced by anyone in the naval service." Hughes pleaded ignorance. "Our complaint," he argued, "is based on the use of these
men for rotten purposes and to ruin the reputation of innocent citizens."

What evidence was there to prove that sailors had been instructed
"in the details of a nameless vice?" demanded Hyneman. Their
own testimony, answered Hughes, given in public court. If these
men were perjurers, rebutted the judge advocate, how could they be
believed? He read long excerpts from the testimony of McKinney,
securing admission that nowhere did he confess to receiving instructions in immorality. He had Hughes read Crawford's testimony, then Young's. What did this evidence show to have been
their orders? asked Hyneman shortly before court recessed. ". . . to
submit to immoral relations with men, and [t]he[y] did so."

As with previous witnesses, Hyneman turned to the alleged Newport transcript, which he now endeavored to place into evidence. "I
want to make myself perfectly clear," he argued, "that the seventy-
five pages were not an official document." It was not a "certified
copy of anything," not "anything official at all" but merely an
"incomplete memoranda." "I offer this in evidence," he continued, "for just what it is worth, as being a paper from which the
assertions of the Ministers' Union are largely based. That is all it is
worth." Nolan, perhaps unaware of how vital the transcript would
become in the government's attack on his clients, failed to object to
introducing the copy. His only complaint was that it belonged to
him and had been lent to Hyneman "for an hour or two." The
original would be returned, promised the judge advocate, as soon as
stenographers could transcribe it.

Hyneman next launched into an aggressive interrogation aimed at
forcing Rev. Hughes to admit that he and his colleagues had little
substantial evidence to prove allegations contained in letters to
President Wilson and Senator Page. They had charged the Secretary
of the Navy with employing "boys enlisted in the Navy to submit
their persons to improper acts."

"Are you prepared," he demanded, "to prove to this court that
the Secretary of the Navy is responsible for that?"

"I cannot," came the response.

"Then why did you say that in a public telegram?"

"That," continued Hughes, "is for the court to investigate and find." "You mean you averred things and scattered them broadcast to the press that you wanted a naval court to prove for you?" challenged Hyneman.

After all, replied Hughes, the Secretary of the Navy was "regarded" as the man responsible for everything that went on in his department. "Can you prove it? . . . Prove by legal evidence that the Secretary of the Navy is responsible for the activities of the Navy?"

Of course not, Hughes admitted. The ministers had not submitted proof but "a request for an investigation."

"Then your telegram, your open letter to the people of the United States, is not based on facts within your knowledge?"

It was, insisted the rector, based on facts, contained in the letter, the Newport transcript, and interview with knowledgeable people.

That must have been the admission Hyneman was awaiting, for he accused the ministers of having "upon the incomplete unofficial transcript, rumor, opinion, and what you had heard from others, . . . broadcast throughout the United States a statement which you are not prepared to prove by evidence other than what you have just said."

"It has been proved," replied Hughes.

Hyneman was not yet ready to abandon his word by word examination of the ministers' letters and telegrams. They referred in one place to "abuses committed under orders of the Navy Department" and in another to "naval abuses." Hughes contended that the former was merely "a more lengthy way of putting it," while Hyneman insisted that the substitution was "misleading." It should not be, jibed Hughes, "to an intelligent mind." The clergy were also criticized for having referred to "a committee of naval officers" to describe this court of inquiry. They had never been informed it was to be a court, insisted Hughes, and besides the difference was trivial.

"That statement we made is absolutely accurate," he argued, "and in no sense misleading. The report was correct."

"But you, sir," persisted the interrogation, "in your letter held out to the world that a committee of naval officers was coming up here to make a cursory investigation, when the fact is that the court is composed of a Rear Admiral and two captains. Is it not mislead-

ing to spread broadcast 'a committee' when it is a court of inquiry?'' All Hughes could do was reiterate his contention that nothing untrue had been said.

Hyneman was just as persistent in demanding to know what had
been meant by contentions that "we" had been "subjected to terrible abuses." Had the signers of the letter been abused, and if so,
who had suffered from what? Or was the reference more generally
to "the people of Newport?" Even without a plebescite, Hughes
was sure that it was "absolutely unanimous that this was a damnable outrage." "The people of Newport," he continued, "are entitled to go about the streets and not feel that they, their friends, and
their children are being spied upon and followed by men employed
to submit their persons to immoral practices, and paid to bring in
names of supposed victims." Like many other Newporters, Hughes
himself had five sailors living in his home, "exactly as guests, min-
gling with my family and my sons. . . ." Knowing what they now
did, every person who had offered hospitality had to question the
"propriety of allowing such intimate contact" unless assured that
"hereafter no such project as this—the instructing of enlisted men
in vicious practices and sending them through the town—is to be
permitted. . . ." "We said," concluded the clergyman, "exactly
what we meant as well as we could."

On and on went Hyneman's challenges to every phrase in the
ministers' public statements. It was inconsistent, Hyneman argued,
to complain that Hudson and Arnold were principle villains while at
the same time denouncing officials in Washington as ultimately responsible. The ministers' contention that a "number" of trials had
been held in Newport was misleading because only two could be
listed. The words "brought to court" could not be substituted for
"testify," contended the judge advocate, who also challenged the
contention that "a considerable number" of "boys" had been referred to when the clerics could not cite exact numbers or ages. The
ministers had described the investigation as having proceeded "day
and night for months" yet could not provide specific dates when it
began or ended. The only evidence that anyone had been ordered to
engage in sex came from the operators, whom the ministers themselves had labeled as "perjurers, liars, skunks, and unworthy of
belief." Use of the term "hired" provoked a long discussion in
which Hyneman explained that the operators had received nothing

more than their usual pay and subsistence; perhaps the ministers' ignorance about the meaning of "subsistence" had led to erroneous conclusions.

Hughes' contention that the investigation constituted an "indignity to Newport" provoked another confrontation. "Is it an indignity to the people of Newport," demanded Hyneman, "to clean up vice and immorality when the local police would not do it, and the local agent of the Department of Justice could not?" Nolan objected that such had been the case. "Tell this court then," persisted the navy lawyer, "the name of one son or daughter of Newport who has been degraded or harmed by the introduction of these men into the home of any man." "I think," replied Hughes, "the dignity and degradation is in [the] process." He knew, however, of "no individual who is a formal prey of these practices."[7]

Later criticism centered on whether the ministers' interest extended beyond the Kent case. "Do you mean to tell this court," Hyneman queried, "that that letter refers to anything in the world except the case of the Reverend Samuel Neal Kent?" "I do." Why then, Hyneman persisted, had the minister waited till after Kent's second acquittal before sending their letter to Wilson? The matter had been under discussion since mid-November, Hughes explained, and the intention had been to prepare a letter "as soon as . . . proper for us to do it." Obviously, however, "it would have been inappropriate to do anything as long as "the case was pending." Was it merely an accident that the letter had been sent so soon after the Providence trial? "Oh, no," insisted Hughes. "It was a prompted letter."

Next Hyneman questioned Hughes' authority for stating that Hudson and Arnold claimed "unusual powers" of identifying homosexuals. Like others, he cited Bishop Perry as the source of this information. Was it not misleading for every minister signing the letter to suggest first-hand knowledge of the pair's claims? Hughes denied it was even "a little bit misleading," while Nolan countered that every witness had verified his reliance on the bishop. The issue, insisted the judge advocate, was not whether the ministers believed Perry but whether "they phrased their letter as to carry an erroneous impression to the public." Nolan objected that the letter was accurate and could be proven, but Admiral Dunn overruled his objection to this line of questioning.

The President had also been told that twenty men had been "instructed in the details of a nameless vice." What were their names?

"You can get them from the record," responded Hughes.

Such arrogance further angered Hyneman. "I ask you to prove that statement," he insisted, "by giving me the names of the 20 men."

Hughes declined, insisting that he could prove his statement "otherwise" and that Wainwright had said there were about twenty.

Could he swear those were Wainwright's exact words?

No, conceded the rector, he could not.

Certain men had allegedly been "designated" against whom operators endeavored to collect evidence. Who were they?

Only Brown and Kent could be named, but Hughes was sure "a considerable" list could be obtained from the city attorney or mayor of Newport, including "men against whom this charge was particularly ridiculous."

Was it not reasonable, probed the judge advocate, for men in charge of the investigation to direct their energies against suspects? Furthermore, the letter implied that men were entrapped after protests had been made in Washington. "It is very misleading, isn't it?"

"It is as clear as day," replied Hughes; "It is the most clear and distinct language we could use." He also reasserted that "the activities of this stupid and malicious investigation proceeded in spite of the protests."

Who, demanded Hyneman, had been investigated for perversion after the protests? "Your question is misleading!" exclaimed the minister.

"Your letter is misleading."

"We stand on the letter," concluded Hughes, "not on false interpretation but on the letter."

"Do you think it is fair to the President of the United States," he persisted, "to state to him in a public letter that vicious methods were used despite protests" when no one who "used the method after the protests, or any person on whom such methods were used" could be named? "I do," answered Hughes. Nolan protested that such a question was unfair. No one had ever notified the ministers the investigation had stopped; in fact, officials in Washington had written letters which led them to assume continuation. The same operators, in fact, who had entrapped innocent victims had been employed to track down Kent in Pennsylvania. So the ministers had written their letter "in good faith." "The witness has made a statement," countered Hyneman. "He does not know the facts. He has no knowledge, nor had he any way of finding out whether the practices complained of ceased." Dunn closed the court briefly before asking Hyneman if he was prepared to prove that "no completed actions of operators" occurred after July 19, 1919. "I believe I am, sir," replied the naval lawyer. "If such be the fact then," continued Dunn, "this letter is or is not misleading?" "It is not misleading," insisted Hughes; "the letter is based on abundant facts."[8]

IV

Having completed his cross-examination of Hughes and nearly all the prominent Newport clergymen, Hyneman attempted a fatal strike against them for criticizing the navy. He listed twenty-six specific charges or "averments" made by the Ministers' Union and concluded that not one had been proven "by competent evidence." The clergy either demanded that the navy prove their charges or relied on "hearsay, rumor, and the incomplete memoranda of testimony." Because such baseless charges had been made against the government in time of war, he requested that the status of Hughes as well as William Safford Jones, John Howard Deming, W. J. Lucas, and Richard Silcox be changed from complainants to defendants, subject to trial before a naval court.

". . . to say that I am astounded at the statements of the judge advocate is putting it very mildly," retorted Nolan. These men, "in good faith" had complained of objectionable naval practices and had testified cooperative at hearings designed to initiate a "searching inquiry." Bring the operators forward, seek the truth from them, and the ministers' position would be vindicated. Only then would it be appropriate to consider status change. In a democracy, he added, men like Niblack, Wainwright, Leigh, Roosevelt, and Daniels were "only plain, humble citizens of the United States vested with a few hours of authority" and not immune from criticism. "We want an opportunity to have our day in court," he concluded, "and every one of these operators, instructors, civilians officials, and officers of the Navy summoned before the court." Admiral Dunn closed the court and when reopening it ruled that at least for the present the status of the ministers would remain unchanged. He then adjourned till the following Thursday, February 12, so the stenographer could prepare Hughes' voluminous testimony.[9]

Three more Newport clergymen—Frederick W. Coleman of the First Methodist Episcopal Church, Wilbur Nelson of the First Baptist Church and Charles W. Forster—who testified were not very knowledgeable about the case and provided brief and relatively minor testimony. Thereafter, Hyneman renewed his demand that these three men as well as others previously named become defendants. Dunn refused, whereupon Hyneman modified his argument. Because the United States had still technically been at war with Germany when the letter to Wilson was written, he argued that the ministers were guilty under Article 5 of the Act for the Government of the Navy. It prohibited anyone from spying, "delivering any letter from an enemy or rebel," or attempting to "corrupt any man in the Navy to betray his trust" in time of war. Penalties were death or any other punishment a military court might assess. Thus anyone who signed the letter could be "taken and tried by a court martial." "Frivolous," replied Nolan. If such were true, any of the "Senators and great personages" who had criticized the government could be similarly tried. "It is nonsensical and I know that the court is not going to put itself in that position." For once, he proved correct, for Dunn closed, then reopened the court, and he ruled that Article 5 did not apply to the ministers. They remained complainants.[10]

Admiral Herbert O. Dunn presided over the Naval Court of Inquiry regarding the Newport scandal. As a close friend of Daniels and Roosevelt, he was a Navy partisan who shielded the service from its detractors.

Credit: National Cyclopedia of American Biography.

CHAPTER 9

Rhode Island versus the U.S. Navy

Letters directed by the Newport Ministers' Union to President Wilson and Senator Page, as well as their testimony before the Dunn Court, were interpreted by naval defenders as the parochial protests of self-interested, small-town preachers. Thus the Dunn hearings changed significantly when Rhode Island's most prominent citizens added their voices to protest the government's crusade against homosexuals. With their influence and prestige added to the denunciations of the ministers who had testified previously, the investigation generated increased attention.

I

Few men better typified the kind of American who made Newport such a fashionable resort than Hamilton Fish Webster. He was a grandson of New York governor and U.S. Secretary of State Hamilton Fish; his father, Sidney Webster, a New York lawyer, had been private secretary to President Franklin Pierce; acquaintances characterized him as "brilliant [and] widely read." After graduation from Columbia University, Hamilton Fish Webster had married Lina Post, daughter of A. K. and Marie Post. The couple inherited such wealth that he never needed to engage in gainful employment. After 1901 the Websters resided at Pen Craig Cottage on Newport's fashionable Harrison Avenue and devoted their time to civic and philanthropic activities. At the time of his death in 1939, Mr. Webster left his widow a trust fund valued at $1,250,000.[1] At the outbreak of World War I, Webster had volunteered for Red Cross service in Europe. Upon his return, he and Mrs. Webster, together with the wife of Governor R. Livingston Beeckman, served on the Executive Committee of the Newport Red

Cross chapter. When the organization voted to emphasize assistance to local residents instead of servicemen, the couple resigned. Subsequently the Websters' energy and funds were channeled toward the Army and Navy Y.M.C.A., where they had met Chaplain Kent and from which sailors received frequent invitations to social events at Pen Craig Cottage. Mr. Webster also served as a board member of the Seamen's Institute; his wife helped establish a club for sailors at Coddington Point, in appreciation for which the navy awarded her a silver cup.[2]

Webster had accompanied Rev. Stanley C. Hughes to Washington to protest the navy's anti-gay activities to Assistant Secretary Roosevelt. They had presented him with portions of the Newport transcript, he explained in opening testimony before the Dunn Court, argued that sailors had been ordered to commit "immoral and illegal acts," and demanded an apology for Kent. Roosevelt responded that he knew of much vice and immorality in Newport, especially involving liquor, and reported that the arrest of men like Kent was probably necessary. He did seem surprised, however, that enlisted men had committed immoral acts and allegedly promised that anyone who had issued orders to do so would "swing for it." He also accused Hugh Baker of being a "political judge" whose innocent verdict was not necessarily definitive. Webster objected that he had known Baker for years and could be certain no "outside consideration" influenced him. Later Hughes and Webster had seen Captain Richard Leigh, with whom they left their evidence.

Back in Newport, Webster spoke with Captain Wainwright. Their conversation included assurances passed from Roosevelt that no sailor had been ordered to engage in homosexual sex and that "the acts of the men concerned in the Kent trial had been stopped."

Why, attorney Nolan asked, had Webster become so interested in the case?

First, he explained, no man found innocent by a court should "remain longer under a cloud." Something had to be done to restore Kent's reputation. Second, he feared the navy was being "greatly injured" by such activities and hoped to see morale improve by halting them.

Ensign Hyneman's attack on Webster, like those against the ministers, attempted to transform the accuser into the accused. He forced the witness to admit he had agreed to drop Kent's candidacy for directorship of the Seamen's Institute merely because of suspected homosexuality, and, furthermore, that he had talked to

Roosevelt without having read the entire Newport transcript. In a letter to the Assistant Secretary, he had indicated a willingness to bring charges against Kent had witnesses been "upright," "honest" and of "unimpeccable character." Collaboration would have also strengthened their veracity. "I do not believe," he explained, "that a man or a boy who is given to, or going about, performing these acts, can retain any proper sense of moral right and wrong." More directly, he added; "any person who goes about having his penis sucked loses all sense of moral right and wrong."

Just how, inquired Hyneman, should cases related to perversion be investigated? Surely it would be impossible to secure nonparticipating eyewitnesses. "I place very much more belief in a certainty," Webster answered without explanation. Would the same methods be appropriate for heterosexual as for homosexual cases? "I should not say necessarily," the witness responded, admitting that he had given the subject little thought and proposing no real alternative.

Just as the ministers had been closely questioned about their letter to Wilson, Hyneman queried Webster about a letter sent Secretary Daniels denouncing the navy's Newport activities. "At the time you wrote this letter," demanded the judge advocate, "did you have in your possession any facts upon which you based" it? No, he had none, admitted Webster. His purpose was merely to encourage the Secretary to "inquire into and investigate, to determine if the charges were true. I did not make them [charges] as truth," he added. "I merely handed them to him to be investigated by him."

Webster complained that Roosevelt knew of the entire affair and, in fact, had authorized the use of sailors to entrap suspects. Certainly, he argued, the Assistant Secretary did "not object very strenuously to such activities." He had not said that he knew of and sanctioned Hudson's procedures "in so many words," continued Webster, "but he gave me that impression." Hyneman condemned reliance on operators accused of perjury and argued that Webster's having issued a letter to the *Newport Herald* the same day the ministers wrote Wilson could not have been wholly coincidental. Webster denied collusion and blamed the navy for bringing Kent to trial a second time. Hyneman shifted responsibility to the Justice Department and asked why the federal trial should have been stopped if lawyers deemed the evidence sufficient to convict. Because of "the whole nature and character of the testimony given by the witnesses in the Newport trial," answered Webster. He explained further: "I don't think Mr. Daniels should have gone ahead in the matter if that evidence was collected . . . contrary to Navy regulations and procedures" or if "it was [not] given by credible witnesses."

Hyneman further objected to Webster's having "told the world" that sailors had "been ordered to commit immoral acts" without having also mentioned that they were "liars, perjurers, skunks, and unworthy of belief." The witness preferred deleting the word "skunks" and insisted that his statement was "absolutely truthful [and] fair." "It certainly is an incomplete statement, is it not?" persisted the military lawyer. "I think that it is a truthful statement," replied Webster, "without any attempt to give a wrongful impression." Could he prove the navy had sanctioned immorality? The acts had been committed, answered the witness; the navy had benefitted from the evidence; and that evidence had been used in court. Altogether the combination constituted sanction. "Acquiesence!" interjected Dunn, intimating some substantial difference between the two words. "The later use of that evidence," Webster continued, "sanctions the manner in which the evidence had been collected in the first place."

Hyneman also tried to demonstrate that a conspiracy existed among Webster, Bishop Perry, and John Rathom to publicize the case and embarrass senior naval administrators. Webster steadfastly denied under persistent questioning any such cooperative endeavors, however; and no substantial evidence of conspiracy emerged before court adjourned for the day just after 3:00 p.m.

Next morning Hyneman moved that Webster be made a defendant because he, like the Newport ministers, had leveled accusations against the navy which he was unable to prove except by "rumor – hearsay – [and] incomplete and unofficial memoranda." Nolan insisted no regulation allowed a civilian to be tried by a military court, to which Hyneman retorted that "any person, whether wearing a uniform of the United States navy or otherwise" could become a defendant. "This is a preposterous position," insisted the lawyer. The court had been convened to investigate the methods of Hudson and his associates, against whom evidence was to be presented. They, not the civilians who had brought the case to the attention of the government and the public, should be investigated.

"It is very plain from the precept what the duties of you gentlemen are," he lectured the court, "but the main interest of the judge advocate seems to be to make these witnesses defendants." "I do not think," he concluded, "that at any time you have the right or authority to make any of these people defendants."

Rather than back down, Hyneman expanded his demands, arguing that not only Webster but "everybody who had thus far been brought before this court certain averments and charges" be made defendants. Anyone, he persisted, who published charges "broadcast through the land . . . thereby making an attack upon the [Navy] Department and its officials in time of war" without adequate proof had broken the law and should stand trial. Dunn closed the court. When it reopened, he announced that Webster and the others would remain complainants. Hyneman had lost another round.

Not yet satisfied, he immediately moved that the status of the complainants be changed to "interested parties," a classification suggesting possible future prosecution. Nolan again argued that civilians "could not be involved in any way that would give this court jurisdiction over" them.

He also challenged the judge advocate's motives in attempting to intimidate witnesses. "Does it come from Headquarters?" he asked. "I am warranted in feeling that some sinister purpose was back of that attempt of the Judge Advocate to brand this man and make him a defendant. . . ."

Hyneman demanded a "public apology," and Nolan complied, although his closing appeal revealed how frustrated he had become at the course of events. "We came here to try to give the court all the information we can in regard to the practices adopted and the alleged methods and abuses," he complained, "but we do not seem to have much of a chance with the judge advocate's requesting a change of status every now and then." Soon after, Webster stepped down.[3]

II

If Webster epitomized the elite civilian population of Newport, no one better represented New England clergymen than James De-Wolfe Perry, Jr., Episcopal Bishop of Rhode Island. A native of Germantown, Pennsylvania and a distant relative of Commodore Oliver H. Perry, he was the son and grandson of Episcopal clergymen. After completing studies at Harvard University and the Episcopal Theological Seminary in Cambridge, he served churches at Springfield and Fitchburg, Massachusetts, and at New Haven, Connecticut before being named Bishop of Rhode Island in 1911. He served overseas as a chaplain during World War I and was active in the National Council of Bishops, which would elect him presiding bishop in 1930, giving him status akin as a *New York Times* obituary put it, to the archbishops of Canterbury or York.[4]

Perry's prominence within the Episcopal Church, his steadfast defense of Chaplain Kent, and his strenuous public denunciation of the navy accentuated the importance of his appearance before Dunn's court. He had known Kent "slightly" since 1911, the bishop reported early in his testimony, but he developed closer acquaintance while serving as chairman of the Episcopal War Commission which oversaw chaplains at Fort Adams, the Naval Training Station, and the Y.M.C.A. He had first learned of charges against Kent during August of 1919; only after the Newport trial had he become more familiar with the case.

Soon after Kent's acquittal, Hudson and Arnold had come to his Providence office to argue the cleric's guilt. The bishop became angry because of their assertions and argued that they, not Kent, were "guilty in this matter. The people of the United States," he continued, "will not tolerate such methods." Hudson claimed that he "personally represented" Secretary of the Navy Daniels and boasted abilities to "recognize a sexual pervert when he met him on the street by his manner and bearing." Arnold supported this contention by insisting that "experts" like themselves could "detect a sexual pervert by watching him on the street as to his walk, manner, and bearing." Perry was particularly disturbed that such activities had been sanctioned in Washington, as a result of which he told Hudson he would raise the matter with Secretary Daniels himself.

The more Perry learned about the case the angrier he became. He had not attended the Newport trial but heard oral reports of what occurred and examined the transcript. The methods had been "very vicious and were absolutely to be condemned," he reported, and could "not have the sanction of the people of the United States," or naval authorities. When he and Rev. Hughes had expressed their concerns at the Training Station, Captain Campbell denied any responsibility for the anti-gay investigation and "seemed to assent" to their visiting Washington.

September 22 the bishop arrived at the Navy Department. He had not expected to see Daniels, whom he believed to be on a western trip, but learned that the return of the secretary that morning made a brief appointment possible. He reviewed the case concisely before Daniels and argued that since a mistake had been made, the navy owed Kent exoneration. Daniels referred him to Admiral Niblack, Chief of Naval Intelligence, with whom a much longer discussion occurred. Niblack seemed thoroughly familiar with the case, agreeing that an investigation of the investigators was appropriate; "the whole proceeding" should end. Perry was pleased with this response "as far as it went," but he argued it was "only fair that a statement should be made acknowledging the wrong done and exonerating Mr. Kent." Any hope for easy resolution vanished when Perry received a September 27 letter from Daniels refusing to apologize and insinuating that the navy planned further prosecution of Kent.

The recess of hearings until March 1, 1920, in no way muted the judge advocate's cross-examination of Perry. Again he emphasized the unofficial nature of the transcript the bishop had seen and criticized him for basing decisions on an informal document and the testimony of perjurers. Hyneman interrogated Perry extensively regarding his meeting with Hudson and Arnold. Over and over he demanded recall of exact words. He made much of Hudson's claimed ability to detect gays "at sight" and what those words meant; no less vital was whether men in Section A had been ordered "to have immoral relations with men" or had merely put themselves in positions where perverts could "act upon" them. Perry seemed disinterested in such distinctions. "Having immoral relations with men," he concluded, "is an immoral act."

Hyneman further complained of Perry's attempts to obtain an "apology" for Kent. "When," he demanded, "did you first determine upon a publicity campaign to extract an apology from the Secretary of the Navy?"

"I never," replied the bishop, "referred to an apology, or requested an apology. I never determined upon a publicity campaign." All he requested was a "statement acknowledging the wrong done, which would exonerate Kent."

What then, was his major concern. Hyneman pushed, getting Kent "exonerated" or stopping improper activities within the navy?

Perry argued the two issues were inseparable, and intense grilling by the judge advocate failed to produce admission that his primary concern was Kent.

Was he just as concerned about the use of "rotten methods" against a Negro butler as against Kent? "Yes." "I am interested in violations done to the honor of the Navy, and I think I have reason to be." But why was it necessary to bring the controversy to public attention? Was he merely angry that the navy refused his request for an apology and went ahead with the second trial? "Absolutely not!" interjected the clergyman. "I felt we were doing an injustice to have possession of these facts and not to bring them to the attention of anyone." Had Daniels acknowledged "the wrong that had been done" and "given his stamp of disapproval upon the methods that had been used," that might have "closed the whole matter." His refusal to do so required that the methods "come to light."

Later interrogation focused on Perry's brief interview with Secretary Daniels. According to the bishop, the navy head characterized his revelations as "horrible" and promised that Admiral Niblack would "hear his story from him." Thus when Daniels later wrote he had taken "all the evidence under examination" and yet decided to pursue the case, Perry presumed this statement approved the methods used. Hyneman demanded "the most minute details" of the conversation, to which Perry responded that few details were possible during a four- or five-minute meeting. "I told him that I considered the proceeding altogether wrong. . . . I requested an acknowledgement of the mistakes which would exonerate Mr. Kent. It was as simple as that." The naval lawyer called on Perry to prove that he had given Daniels enough facts upon which to take action, but the bishop protested the position into which he was being driven.

"I am appearing as complainant," he argued, "and the basis of my complaint as it refers to the Secretary is" that after having been told the facts, he had "refused to make an acknowledgement of wrong done" and said the navy was "to take further action."

But what "facts," demanded Hyneman, had he given Daniels?

"When men of administration approach men of administration," explained Perry, "they know how to talk to each other, and I was talking to the head of a great department as an administrator myself."

Could he prove that Daniels had sufficient information?

"I knew," came the reply, "that the whole matter was a subject of record, and that these records were accessible. I cannot make it clearer than that."[5]

Hyneman also interrogated Perry about January 10 letter to President Wilson. What followed were the usual demands that words be explained and proof provided for each allegation. Perry, like the others, was bombarded with questions about how he could denounce the operators for perjury and at the same time cite their testimony to prove his arguments. Either all testimony was equally credible or none of it could be used. Perry tried in vain to explain that while he did not believe the operators had committed the acts they claimed with Kent, he believed they had operated under orders which left the navy guilty of encouraging immorality.

At the end Hyneman demanded to know if "the average American reading public" would understand the letter as the ministers intended it. "The average American would have been outraged by every condition of fact to which I have referred," retorted Perry, "and I could add also, that the American public has been outraged." The letter had been written, he added, "to protect the liberties or the liberty of American citizens, and the moral standards for which I felt the President would hold himself responsible." Was it not true, persisted the navy attorney, that the letter had been made "more forceful" to "gain quicker action"? ". . . this was the most immediate and strongest means" which the ministers could use to "call for action," replied Perry. "It was," he concluded, "as an American citizen that I signed the letter."[6]

III

If it might have been anticipated that civilians like Webster or Bishop Perry would have objected to the navy's anti-gay campaign and defended Chaplain Kent, it was less predictable and, therefore, more forceful to have civil and police authorities join in criticism of the military.

The strongest complaints came from Newport Chief of Police John S. Tobin who traced his association with the sex hunt to a visit from Justice Department representative J. J. Daly in March of 1919. He had shown the chief a collection of evidence about alleged homosexuals, but since nearly all those accused were sailors, the two concluded that the navy should handle the matter. Suggestions that immorality had occurred in rooms at 15 Whitfield Court led Tobin to speak to the owner of the house. He confirmed that some roomers dressed in "female attire" in preparing for a play at the Training Station. Tobin also visited the Army and Navy Y.M.C.A. where he saw two sailors "acting quite effeminately"; a retired seaman there reported the presence of several "fairies."

The afternoon of July 22 Tobin went to City Solicitor Jeremiah Sullivan's office where he found Arnold, a young man carrying a lawyer's briefcase, a navy chief, and two other sailors. Tobin urged caution in making arrests because what information he had seen would "never get a conviction of anybody locally" and was "all a sailor matter." Attorney Joseph Cawley was delayed coming from Providence, so Tobin returned to his office, leaving Sullivan with instructions to act as his "legal advisor." He promised to sign any arrest warrants that were recommended. That evening Arnold assured him that "two separate operations" proved the guilt of each man to be charged.

Tobin agreed to the navy's request for arrest warrants, and called the court clerk to draw them up. The accused included a New York actor, several servants, a Negro dishwasher, a Negro waiter and club attendant, a travelling salesman, and Chaplain Kent. Neither Duke Hawkins nor Eddie Harrington was included.

Did it matter, objected the judge advocate, that so many of the accused came from out of town? Yes, argued Nolan; with the navy complaining that conditions were too serious for local authorities to control, it was significant that only two Newport residents were involved.

Arrests began almost immediately. One man was apprehended as he was about to board a New York-bound boat; a sergeant and one of the operators found another on Thames Street. Tobin accompanied Arnold and several operators to Cliff Walk where they searched north and south of Forty Steps without success. When Kent could not be found at the Emmanuel Parish House, Arnold regretted losing "that 'God-damn' man." "You seem to be pretty hard on this man," remarked the chief. Arnold replied: "Kent is a mason, and I am a mason, but I want to get that 'son-of-a-bitch' because he is fucking those sailor boys."

As they drove along Annadale Road and up Narragansett Avenue, approaching Belleview, Arnold shouted: "There is one now." "Was it a man against whom a warrant had been issued? inquired the chief. "No," replied Arnold, "but I can tell him a mile off by his walk." Later Arnold accused half a dozen others pedestrians of being perverts. Tobin was shocked, for knowing several of those who had been pointed out "quite well," he was certain they were "respectable citizens." Later Arnold claimed to have spotted two more gays; given five minutes, he told Tobin, his operators could collect enough evidence to convict them. "Arnold," warned the policeman, "not with me will there be any frame-up here; if I catch any of your operators doing that, I will arrest them and lock them up." "I won't stand for it," protested the sailor. "You will stand for it, if I catch them," replied Tobin. In New York, Arnold boasted that Hudson was such close friends with the police commissioner that an operator who engaged in sex with a suspect always escaped when his partner was arrested. "We don't do that here," countered Tobin. Judge Advocate Hyneman objected to such testimony on grounds no one denied the complete cooperation of Tobin once his attention had been called to the situation. Dunn ruled, as a result, that further discussion fell "beyond the scope of the investigation."

The afternoon of July 27, a Sunday, Tobin had been called to Newport Beach, where operators had cornered a suspect. He and Palmer gathered the warrants, started up their car, and rushed to the spot where sailors brought forth a young man who was crying. They claimed he was a suspect named Annis against whom a warrant had been issued, but Tobin knew the boy as Robert F. Mahoney.

"What did this fellow do to you?" he asked operator James Coggins.

"He sucked my cock," responded the operator so loudly that Tobin tried to hush him so the large beach crowd nearby would not hear.

Evidence could be presented to Solicitor Sullivan with a request for a warrant, insisted Tobin, who refused to arrest the youngster.[7]

IV

Of all the Rhode Island leaders appearing before Admiral Dunn, the one who generated the most controversy had to be John R. Rathom, editor of the *Providence Journal*. He had become acquainted with the case long after nearly everyone else, and as it turned out, knew so little that his testimony had no practical value. Yet the power of the press was so great that Rathom stimulated continued discussion regarding the anti-homosexual campaign not only in Providence but through other newspapers on a nationwide basis. Ultimately, he rather than the navy or the ministers was responsible for transforming a minor local controversy into a national scandal.

Almost immediately when he appeared in Admiral Dunn's court, Rathom generated intense debate. He introduced as his counsel Claude Branch, only to have Admiral Dunn note that while complainants were entitled to representation, as a witness Rathom was not. Hyneman finally agreed to Branch's presence, but the journalist objected to his having been summoned to court at all. He knew nothing substantial about the case and had had no communication with Navy Department officials until after this court convened. Had any materials been sent to him about the case? inquired the navy lawyer. Branch explained that as a newspaperman his client received communications regarding the case but they did not "state any definite facts" and would be of no help to the court. When Hyneman demanded they be produced, Rathom protested violation of his constitutional rights. "These communications are of the most sacredly confidential character," he argued, "and so written, it is practically impossible for any newspaper man for one moment to produce such letters under the circumstances which they have been sent." Dunn ruled that the letters need not be provided, although he reserved the right to request them later "should they appear to be necessary."

Hyneman began to question Rathom about the nine charges against the navy he had sent the Senate Naval Affairs Committee and published in the *Journal*. Branch denied his client wished to make any accusations before this court, and Rathom argued that in printing materials his paper had merely performed "a public duty." Never had he initiated "some sort of conspiracy for publicity in this matter." In fact, he had "fought against publicity" for fear it would harm the navy. Only after the second Kent trial had his paper even reported the case. Moreover, everything Rathom knew about the case had been "good and complete information" acquired "in ordinary newspaper work." "We proceeded carefully," he explained, "upon evidence of men of high reputation and the official court records." The paper had no knowledge of "specific acts," no interest in protecting any individual, and no desire to "penalize or punish any person at all. That," he went on, "is not the part or function of the newspaper."

When court reopened the morning of March 12, Hyneman turned his focus to *Journal* editorials. Branch objected that they were "immaterial" to the court's purposes, but Dunn overruled him. The judge advocate introduced an Associated Press story that Rathom had sent a representative to the Navy Department. Then he presented accusatory letters between Roosevelt and Rathom exchanged after the Dunn Court had begun its sessions. He called upon Rathom to present to the court charges he had alluded to the previous day. The editor refused to deal with any of these questions, preferring to read "a statement with regard to the entire matter." Hyneman found that objectionable, insisting that either the charges previously sent to the Senate or new ones together with "the facts in support of them" must be provided. Branch reiterated his client's refusal to make charges. "We wish to make a statement in regard to the matters here," he continued, "if you care to have it. Otherwise we will not submit anything."

Hyneman denied questioning Rathom's "motives" in publicizing the case, but the editor noted for the record that the letter from Roosevelt "very seriously" impugned his "motives in the entire matter." As a result, he ought at least be able to show that he was "a complainant as to the methods rather than as to men. I am a newspaperman," he continued, "and working in my profession, and I cannot prosecute any individual. That is not my business." Rather than continue this needless argument, the judge advocate agreed to suspend questions, so Branch and his client could present "any points that Mr. Rathom desires to bring before the court."

Rathom's statement emphasized his concern about naval procedures. He could even sympathize with Hudson, noted the editor; he "had been drawn into the whirlpool of a damnable system" and was "bound to the wheel" in the matter. As a result, his zeal to do his duty had been "distorted into a sort of fetish in the glimmer of which all seems to have seemed proper, if only the end could be accomplished." Nothing would be gained through the "sap to justice" of punishing and disgracing a few men, especially in a case where the guilty operated from "a sense of duty, however distorted and twisted into evil." What needed change was a system which allowed people to do such things, "spurs them on, and teaches the triumph of disgrace and brings moral shipwreck" more to those carrying out acts than to those whom they seek to expose. "This," insisted Rathom, "is what must be torn out by the roots" if the navy and its men were to regain self-respect.

Once Rathom concluded his statement, Hyneman resumed his cross-examination. He started with a *Journal* editorial titled "the dirty trail of Mr. Daniels." When, he asked, did the "dirty trail" begin? "Just a minute," protested Branch, "does this bear on anything in this inquiry?" Rathom complained that he found it "embarrassing . . . to bring editorials from the Providence Journal to trial." They were opinions, he insisted, and it was far beyond the jurisdiction of the court to determine whether "Mr. Rathom has the right opinion or the right motives." For once Dunn sustained the objection.

"Mr. Rathom," he asked, "what was the moral or immoral condition of Newport" after the U.S. entered the war? After Branch's protest that his client claimed "no personal knowledge" had been overruled, the witness confirmed that two investigators sent to Newport in mid-1917 had found widespread evidence of vice. In this he and Secretary Daniels agreed. The pair's cordiality vanished, he continued, during the 1918 congressional campaign when Democratic house candidate Theodore F. Green had been given Rathom's telegrams reporting these conditions to Daniels and alleged that information about vice in Newport had been deliberately concealed to favor his opponent, Clark Burdick. "That was my first information," Rathom explained, "that the Secretary of the Navy was using personal knowledge in order to boon his own political party."

Hyneman began to review yet again the charges Rathom had made to the Senate, demanding explanations, details, and proof for each. "I don't think I ought to testify to that," the editor responded after the first set of inquiries, "because I have not sufficient . . . personal knowledge." The judge responded that having told the Senate he had "ample evidence," Rathom must "produce that evidence before this court." The memorandum, countered Branch, was perfectly sufficient in identifying witnesses whose testimony verified the charges. "What this witness has said he could prove to the Senate," repeated Hyneman, "is that same thing that this court wants proofs about, therefore I want to find out what this witness can prove to the Senate, and the nature of his proof."

Branch's objection having been overruled, questioning related to the Senate charges persisted. Rathom claimed there were twenty operators, but he now admitted that sixteen or twenty-five might have been equally correct. The number was "immaterial in view of the larger issue." Could he prove what Daniels knew, when he knew it, and what action he took upon his knowledge? Rathom admitted no first-hand information, but he argued that it was inconceivable that Roosevelt or Daniels had given "direct personal sanction" to the methods used or "originated the orders for such methods." The point, as he insisted, was that Daniels and Roosevelt had become responsible the moment they learned of the methods and could have taken "measures to stop them."

Was it not true, summarized the navy attorney, that all the *Journal*'s charges were based on "incomplete memoranda" of the Newport trial, testimony from the federal court, "a lot of rumors and statements" from clergymen and civilians, and the court martial transcript?" That was essentially correct, conceded Rathom but "unfairly put." In thirty years of newspaper work, he could recall no story where he felt "more justified in drawing a safer conclusion" based on the evidence. Aside from that, Rathom could provide the court with "absolutely no evidence and no testimony" other than "a lot of editorial dressing that you have added to the facts." "We have our editorial page and news columns," replied the journalist, "and we do not mix the two at all."[8]

Rev. Stanley C. Hughes, Rector of Trinity Church, Newport, and the leading Newport critic of the Navy's sex hunt.
Credit: Copy by the author of a portrait in Trinity Church.

James DeWolf Perry, Jr., Episcopal Bishop of Rhode Island.
Credit: Christian Century.

CHAPTER 10

Section A on Trial

Complaints against the navy from Newport ministers and Rhode Island leaders stimulated significant reaction, largely because of the way they had been treated on the stand; the testimony of men in Section A was also eagerly anticipated. Only they could reveal how the government's secret vice squad had operated. Hudson, Arnold, and the other officers and enlisted men who participated in the investigation could clear up remaining questions about who had authorized their work and who had known how much about procedures. Of still greater interest, especially to those seeking titillation, would be appearances by sailors who had moved through the streets, alleys, and bedrooms of Newport seeking gay sex. What kind of men would have participated in such activities? How would they defend their actions, and how much of what they had done would be revealed?

I

Observers expecting the activities of Section A to be quickly revealed found the first days during which navy officials appeared before the Dunn Court frustrating. Many were minor functionaries with limited roles who knew little about the case. Captain John Wainwright, for example, had been sent to Newport following complaints by Perry, Webster, and Hughes, to "investigate the investigators." The investigation lasted only a few days, and Wainwright remembered few details. Wainwright's report, introduced into evidence for the first time, concluded that the sailors "detecting moral perversion" had acted voluntarily under orders "not to solicit but to allow themselves to be approached."[1]

More valuable information came from Captain Edward H. Campbell, who had commanded the Naval Training Station throughout the investigation. Upon learning of Arnold's suspicions, he decided that "the situation [was] so bad that immediate steps" were needed to apprehend gays, court martial them, and "get rid of their influence." He discussed the situation with Admiral Oman and, subsequently, Daniels and Roosevelt, who had authorized action. Later he learned that Section A was being established under the Office of Naval Intelligence. He denied having followed the case closely, although Arnold came by his office occasionally "in an unofficial manner [to] drop remarks as to what was going on."

On March 18, 1919, Campbell had signed "camouflaged" orders reassigning Arnold's men to recruiting duty. The letter had been written on stationery of the First Naval District "by direction" of the commandant. Campbell admitted that no directive had been issued, and the commandant had not even been provided a copy. Claims that these orders had been verbally cancelled about 24 hours later and had never become operational stimulated close questioning as to why he had not put the revocation in writing or challenged the continued operation of the vice squad. Campbell assumed that between March 29, when his order was cancelled, and mid-April when Section A was formally established — a period during which substantial sexual activity occurred between operators and suspects — detective work had been authorized by either the Navy Department or the Department of Justice. Nevertheless, during this period Campbell received reports from Arnold about the investigation, signed subsistence vouchers, and learned that important new evidence had been collected for presentation to the Foster court. This information raised serious doubts whether the order of March 18 had ever been revoked or whether its cancellation had been transmitted to Arnold and his men. Campbell never relented, however: "I have testified twice this forenoon," he insisted, "that I knew Hudson and Arnold were engaged in some way in collecting evidence, presumably cooperating with the Department of Justice. It was not," he argued emphatically, "under my orders, and I had no supervision. . . ."[2]

Murphy J. Foster should have been in an excellent position to describe the activities of Section A, since he presided over the naval court recommending courts-martial for accused sailors. Foster provided considerable information about the origins of the case and described court sessions where Arnold presented "startling" evidence of immorality. Foster anticipated that the matter would be transferred to the Justice Department and his court would never reconvene. He was surprised, therefore, to receive orders to proceed using available evidence.

Extended questioning related to the March 18 order assigning operators to duty under Drury. Foster admitted the court had intended the operators be transferred. Later when funds could not be found to pay subsistence, Campbell had "directed that all activities cease." Foster claimed he "carried" these oral commands to the court. From discussions with Drury, he felt sure Arnold had become "acquainted with the fact that these men were not to be officially ordered under his command." How then, inquired Hyneman, could he account for Drury's order nearly a month later "releasing these men from their special detail?" "I cannot," he replied, "account for that." Rather than assuming that operators fell under Justice Department jurisdiction, Foster believed their sleuthing had been carried out "on their liberties, still being attached to the station." "They were out there," he elaborated, "in their own interests in cleaning up Newport."

Suggesting for the first time the seriousness of his questions, Hyneman asked the court to inform Foster of his constitutional rights. The witness "need not answer any questions tending to incriminate him," advised Admiral Dunn. "By what authority," continued the judge advocate, "did the court of inquiry of which you were president, either officially or unofficially, directly or indirectly, detail men to Arnold, Drury, or anyone else to go out and get evidence?" At first Foster argued that no men "were actually detailed to go out and get evidence." Hyneman's persistence ultimately forced admission that the court "hoped to get" authorization from Campbell at some later time.

Hyneman repeated his intention of finding out who had sent operators out, by what authority, and why men admitting immoral behavior had been commended.

"I do not know," confessed Foster, "when they started and I do not know when they stopped."

"Did you ever question these men's authority for committing these immoral acts?"

"No."

"Did you ever question these men's authority to investigate?"

"No."

Why, if orders revoking the reassignment order were so well understood, continued Hyneman, had it been necessary to warn Drury repeatedly to make sure the men avoided immoral acts?

"I thought that the men might be laboring under a misapprehension in regard to their duties with reference to the good of the Navy," replied Foster, "and I thought that they might be overzealous, and I thought it was not right for them to go as far as they did. . . ."

"After the knowledge of the first completed act came to you," continued the naval lawyer, "as president of the court, what if anything did you do?"

"I did nothing."

"Did you consider that that was the proper way to get evidence?"

"That evidence had been submitted to the convening authorities," explained Foster, "and we were ordered to go ahead with the information before us."

Obviously unconvinced by Foster's testimony, Hyneman moved that "in view of the testimony just given by him," Foster be made a "party in interest." Admiral Dunn agreed, and the commander was read the precept, informed of his right to counsel, given an opportunity to object to court members, and advised that he need not answer incriminating questions.

Captain Campbell's cross-examination further undermined Foster's version of events surrounding the critical revocation order. Foster reiterated having told the court and Drury to make sure Arnold knew the transfer orders were not to be carried out. "Arnold wasn't there?" queried Campbell.

"I don't remember seeing Arnold there."

"Was Dr. Hudson there?"

"I think I delivered these verbal orders from you to the court while it was in session," he replied.[3]

Foster's credibility suffered still further during subsequent testimony. Hyneman argued that the date on which the March 18 order had been revoked was critical, for it could not have been passed to the court after recess on the 20th. Confronted with such logic, Foster retracted his earlier statement that he had reported the cancellation during a court session. Perhaps, he speculated, court members were getting their coats after meeting Campbell or walking along a drive toward their car. "I am quite sure," he argued, "the whole court was present." He was certain the operators themselves were fully aware that "they were not under the orders of this [Foster's] court in any way." Then why, Hyneman concluded, had the court record described witnesses as working "under the authority of the Commandant to assist the Judge Advocate?" "That is a well-garbled letter," responded Foster.[4]

II

If anyone could clear up the mystery of the revoked order, it ought to have been William H. Drury, the aide for information at the Training Station. He frequently discussed the case with senior naval officials and served as judge advocate during the Foster court. "I remember the court wondering how to gather the evidence which was to be presented," noted Drury, "and I believe Dr. Hudson suggested having the men who had been investigating more or less unofficially ordered to duty under me." The necessary order had been issued but was "countermanded a day or two later and the men were told to stop investigating." Not until April, however, had the retraction been put in writing. Meanwhile, Drury admitted discussing how to proceed. Both he and Arnold believed "some kind of investigation" would ultimately be authorized, and Arnold warned that if his operators "cut [off from] the suspected men entirely" suspicions would be aroused. "I don't care whether they continue their acquaintance with the suspected men," Drury reportedly told Arnold. "Don't allow any investigating to go on," he warned. "Don't allow them to get involved in anything." Thereafter, the men had no official relationship to him or to the court but were merely "working on their own interest . . . to help the Navy."

But "what was the status" of the men? inquired Hyneman.

"I don't know," replied Drury; "Dr. Hudson would know."

Drury's position became more precarious as he admitted having seen reports of operators "getting themselves involved" with suspects. "I warned them to stop doing it. I told them repeatedly not to do it." But he had never said anything to Hudson. "He was a senior lieutenant," explained Drury, "and I was an ensign." Nor had he notified the court or made any other effort to determine by whose authority the investigation was continuing. "Because the investigation was being carried on," he concluded, ". . . I supposed Dr. Hudson had the authority to carry it on." Drury also had difficulty explaining the notations recommended for the sailors' files. They had "worked with the best of intentions," he insisted, "were upright men," and "had the interest of the service at heart." Because they had testified "to these things" in court, something was needed in their service records "which would explain it."

Cross-examination revealed Drury's further participation in the work of Section A. The typewriter in the Red Cross office came from him, and he frequently visited the office, talked with the men, reviewed their reports, and witnessed the oaths of several sailors after he claimed the orders had been revoked. The arrest of the first sailor, Fred Hoage, on April 4 occurred on his recommendation. And when Drury moved his office to Boston, he handed out his telephone number to Hudson, Arnold, and the operators. He also conversed about the nature of homosexuality, arguing at one point that medical treatment rather than courts-martial would be more appropriate for gay servicemen. All Drury could do in light of such evidence was argue that other court members also knew what was going on, or that as a junior officer he had neither authority nor responsibility. "I didn't feel," he insisted, "I had any right to tell Dr. Hudson what he should do or what he shouldn't." Even when he saw reports showing "completed acts" between operators and sailors or civilians, Drury merely warned that such activities were "foolish."

Interest in Drury's testimony heightened as he was questioned by Ervin Arnold, upon whom the heaviest burden of responsibility seemed to have been thrust:

"Isn't it a fact," asked Arnold, "that if the [revocation] order had been given to you on March 18, 1919, verbally, that you forgot it and did not deliver it to me?"

"Not a chance."

"Why didn't I get it?"

"You did. . . . "

"Why was it seven days after March 18, 1919, that you notified me that the heads of departments had been notified to give these men certain privileges?" demanded Arnold. ". . . if that order was countermanded, why did you notify the departments and then tell me about seven days later, that it was all right to use these men?"

"You had permission to use the men," replied Drury, in what constituted a near retraction of his earlier testimony, "and go on as you had in the past, that is continue the associations, but not to allow completed acts."[5]

III

Another member of the Foster court was Lt. Commander Nelson W. Hibbs, whose testimony opened the Dunn inquiry the morning of March 19. Like those who preceded him, Hibbs endeavored to square his version of the operators' activities with what he and the other Foster court members had done. At first he thought Hudson and Arnold were investigating under Justice Department authorization. Now he believed that from late March until mid-April, operators had worked "entirely under their own initiative, and simply without adequate direction." When Hibbs admitted that the Red Cross office was "thoroughly organized" and provided with a telephone and other equipment, Hyneman queried:

"Did it occur to you to ask who was directing this?"

No, responded Hibbs; he assumed it must have been the Justice Department. Even when the reconvened court heard evidence of sex between operators and sailors, neither he nor anyone else questioned their authority.

Why the notations in the men's records?

"These men belonged to the Naval service," argued the witness, "and for the purpose of making it appear in our record that these particular men were witnesses [rather than suspects] and for future use in their records, that notation was made. . . ." No commendation of "the thing, one or two particular acts," had been intended.

By what authority had the court procured evidence? asked Hyneman.

It had none, admitted Hibbs, but when testimony became available, "the court would have been in error in not availing itself of such information."

Throughout this stage of the inquiry, attorney Frank Nolan played only a minor role, usually limiting his questions and failing to follow-up. As Hibbs concluded his testimony, however, Nolan asked if Roosevelt had signed the letter to Palmer based entirely on hearsay evidence "without any information at all" — a question paralleling dozens Hyneman asked the complainants. Now the navy lawyer launched into a tirade claiming that Nolan's only interest was "defend[ing] the fair name of Newport." "We are not investigating it [Newport] any more than necessary," he added, "and we are not attacking it at all." The question about Roosevelt was "nothing in law" because the assistant secretary had merely requested a thorough investigation. "I am only questioning how much information the Assistant Secretary had when he made this letter which alleges certain bad things."

"Ask that of the Assistant Secretary."

"Why get so sensitive," persisted Nolan, "when I mentioned the Assistant Secretary's name?"

Every navy man had been as thoroughly questioned as the Rhode Island clergymen, responded Hyneman, and "when I get Mr. Roosevelt and Mr. Daniels on the stand they are going to get the same kind of questioning."

"Don't," concluded Nolan before withdrawing his offensive question, "get so sensitive about the matter."[6]

IV

Having completed its work in Newport, the Dunn court reconvened the morning of April 6 at 116 West 77th Street in New York City in the headquarters for Section A. The first witnesses proved uninformative; the duties of operators John M. Rammond, Eilnut Fondon, Harold Cheney, and Frank Stafford included nothing beyond "shadowing" or clerking. August Bena, who accompanied Arnold to Reading in search of Kent, confirmed that while talking to a local journalist, Arnold had insisted nothing be published. Harry Brown had investigated immorality in Fall River and New York. Like many others, he had never been told to "take any initiative" with suspects but was merely "to find out what I could." He claimed no special qualifications and contended that "any man of ordinary intelligence" could have done the work. He had never engaged in sex with a suspect.[7]

More revealing testimony came from George P. Steck, an operator charged with tracking Kent to Warwick who had helped secure a picture of the chaplain.

"Do you know who obtained the picture of Mr. Kent?" asked Hyneman.

"Yes, sir."

"Do you know how it was obtained?"

"Yes, sir."

"Did Crawford [another operator in Warwick] obtain the picture?"

"I didn't see him obtain it."

"Did you obtain the picture?"

At first Steck avoided answering, but the judge advocate explained that since methods were not being suggested, self-incrimination was impossible. "Yes, sir," he then replied; "I obtained the picture."

"State to the court how you obtained the picture of Mr. Kent."

Informed of his constitutional right to silence, Steck declined on grounds his answer might be incriminating. The court agreed, and the questioning moved to another topic without a definitive reply. This operator could contribute little more, however, so court adjourned just after 2:00 p.m. to await the appearance of a star witness the following morning.[8]

Ervin Arnold, forty-three at the time he took the stand, had served nearly fifteen years in the navy. Before enlisting, he spent nine years as a state detective in Connecticut doing "anything connected with any criminal offenses;" he also "ran down perverts." His language was nearly identical to that given the Foster court as he described his discovery of gays among Newport hospital patients and staff and noted that once while walking along Thames Street a civilian had "slid his hand from his pocket to where my penis was near my pocket." Otherwise, Arnold merely repeated gossip or personal observations of "fairies' behavior." His own marital status, sexual preference, and experiences with gays were never discussed. Arnold did, however, reveal considerable knowledge of gay lifestyles. "One fairy," he reported, "will know another by signals, and if you get in and acquainted with a fairy he will be able to pick out for you very nearly every time what are called fairies." This became possible because of "signals or actions . . . posted by them."

He described in detail how he passed on information to navy officers in Newport and Washington. All had been surprised to learn how many perverts there were, gratified for his having come forward, and eager to suppress vice. Placing investigators in positions where they could be solicited constituted the only means by which adequate evidence could be collected. Once needed authorization had been obtained from Daniels and Roosevelt and the transfer orders had been issued, the investigation got underway. Both Isaacson and Hudson had told Arnold "it would be a good idea to keep my ears and eyes open and learn anything I could. . . ." His task had simply been to "inform the proper authorities about what I had seen and learned." Arnold also chronicled how he had selected operators, their first meetings, and the administration of Naval Intelligence oaths to them. But had not the order of March 18 been revoked? asked Hyneman. "It was not revoked to me," insisted Arnold. "It was not revoked to me at that time and was not revoked to me until either the night of April 16, 1919, or the morning of April 17, 1919." Support for this argument cited numerous instances in which Hudson, Drury, and other officers helped inaugurate the investigation and assisted the operators.

What instructions, asked Hyneman, had been given the operators about how they were to behave? It was unwise in such circumstances, argued Arnold, for someone distant from a situation to provide detailed guidance. "You people will be on the field of operations," he recalled having told his men. "You will have to use your own judgment whether or not a full act is completed. If that being the fact, it might lead to something greater. . . . You have got to form that judgment at the time you are on the field with that party." Arnold admitted because conditions in Newport were so "rotten," he could "hardly see how an operator could keep from a completed act."

Like others, Arnold emphasized the personal endorsement of his activities by senior naval officials. During one meeting, he had been praised as the only chief petty officer on base "with nerve enough to report the conditions existing." Roosevelt had led him to believe Hudson had direct authority over the investigation. Otherwise, Arnold revealed surprisingly few details of the work in which he had been engaged, and he stepped from the stand without ever having been asked probing questions by either Hyneman or Nolan.[9]

V

Arnold's appearance served as a preliminary to the testimony of the individual who by all accounts had primary responsibility for the Newport sex-hunt, Dr. Erastus M. Hudson. Thirty-two years old, married and the father of two, he had graduated from Harvard and the New York College of Physicians and Surgeons. Hudson joined the navy in 1917 and served aboard the U.S.S. *Leviathan* before coming to Newport. For a time in England and New York he studied finger print identification, earning sufficient renown to provoke rumors that he worked for Scotland Yard. This training initiated a lifelong interest in the subject which years later led him to testify in the Lindbergh kidnapping trial.[10]

Hudson first suspected a vice problem in Newport while investigating the suicide of a sailor who had frequented a house of ill-repute on Tewas Place where a mulatto woman "was in the habit of performing unnatural acts on certain enlisted men" for whom she provided whiskey. Evidence of cocaine use among hospital employees and patients also came to his attention.

Late in February, 1919, Arnold alerted him to homosexuals in and around the Naval Training Station. Convinced that the "situation [was] very serious," he discussed his findings with Ensign Isaacson and Admiral Oman, under whom he had served aboard the *Leviathan*. The admiral sent him to Captain Campbell, who suggested that alleged perverts be discharged as undesirable. "I disagreed with him," testified Hudson, "as I felt if these suspects were given undesirable discharges that the conditions would go on just the same." Civilians were also "breaking in recruits" by getting them drunk and threatening to expose anyone who declined sexual advances. Further dangers included drug addiction and venereal disease. "Taking all these things together," Hudson told Campbell, "I thought these civilians were breaking down the morality of the men at the Training Station." Campbell was reluctant to act on his own but agreed to meet with Oman, Wood, Roosevelt, and Daniels to discuss the situation. Ultimately, Campbell received permission "to do whatever he desired to remedy these conditions in Newport."

Meanwhile, Arnold and other volunteers frequented gay hangouts, made friends with suspects, and wrote down what they learned. According to Hudson, Isaacson had approved these activities. Evidence presented at the Foster court demonstrated the need for further investigation as the result of which Campbell issued the letter reassigning sailors to Arnold through Ensign Drury while Hudson arranged for the men to be notified and sworn in using a navy intelligence oath. The next day, as the true extent of drug use, liquor traffic, and "homosectual [*sic*] practices" became evident, the court drafted a letter encouraging Justice Department involvement.

Hudson participated in the organization of the operators, including acquisition of a Red Cross room. He had told Hall "in so many words that it was to be used by the Naval Intelligence," he confessed, "but I did not exactly tell him so."

Despite the accomplishments of the Foster court, Hudson had grown increasingly exasperated over the persistence of homosexuality in Newport. One evening at his house, a discussion of the subject developed among him, Arnold, Drury, and Stewart Davis, who had recently retired from naval intelligence work. Hudson had heard Greeks were "working quite a practice of sodomy in Newport, in breaking in young men by getting them so drunk they didn't know what they were doing." Hudson believed civilians were primarily responsible for the perversion of sailors. Moreover, Newport police had proven "practically powerless to do anything" about such activities. Davis, "quite an intimate, personal friend" of Roosevelt, proposed informing the Assistant Secretary of the situation. As a result, by April Red Cross director Hall had been urged to contact FDR through Governor Beeckman, initiating events which led to the creation of Section A.

Hudson's appearance provided a singular opportunity to expostulate general views of homosexuality. He explained that "of course, sodomy, or pederasty as it is known when the intercourse is between human beings, sodomy being the more common term as applied to lower animals" was "a very common practice among the Greeks." Captain Williams once told him that an ancient Greek general had "fifteen or twenty boys on his staff for this purpose." Despite the passage of thousands of years, Hudson had not been surprised to "find the Greeks in Newport indulging in the same practice, of having sexual intercourse with boys through the rectum."

A still more curious analysis of homosexuality came as Hudson continued his testimony on April 16. "I know from a medical viewpoint, a phyciatrical [*sic*] standpoint," he told the court, that "perverts" fall into three categories: "a congenital pervert where it is inherited, a retarded pervert where it is inherited but crops out later. Another class of pervert is in the case of an old man leading a pretty high life, and the only way he can get sexual pleasure is by resorting to sodomy." In addition, "a great many" "normal people" submitted to "acts of perversion." They did "not become perverts themselves" because their only motivation was fear of "contracting disease through sexual intercourse in the normal manner." Sodomy was also common, he observed, in lumber camps and army posts where men lived together "isolated from ordinary life." Hudson was obviously worried about how exposing operators to gays might affect them; perhaps the practice was contagious or once a man savored such pleasures he could never enjoy relations with women. Nowhere, however, did the literature mention "any man in the status of an investigator or spotter."

Hudson, of course, denied the orders signed March 18 by Captain Campbell had ever been revoked, insisted that Drury commanded the operators until the creation of Section A, and denied that upon discovering "completed acts, his duty had been to "go over Mr. Drury's head and report it to anyone." Captain Williams disapproved of the entire operation, he reported, and refused to issue naval intelligence cards; he never explained where those the men carried came from.

Informed by Leigh and Hall of Bishop Perry's interest in the case, Hudson visited the clergyman with Arnold. His recollection of the event differed in nearly every particular from the bishop's. Hudson claimed to have made an appointment; perry said he arrived unannounced. The doctor said he presented convincing evidence of Kent's guilt. "I told him that it was common knowledge . . . that he [the chaplain] was a man of that type," recalled Hudson, noting that he personally had seen Kent "feel up certain boys." Only because government witnesses had been disallowed during the Providence trial had Kent been acquitted. Perry claimed no substantial evidence had ever been presented him. Hudson denied accusing the Newport judge of being "corrupt," as Perry reported, although the bishop might have "inferred" such from the use of other words. The doctor also denied having claimed the ability to detect perverts by casual observation; immediately, however, he launched into a monologue which claimed exactly that: "It was common knowledge," he explained,

> that if a man was walking along the street in an effeminate manner, with his lips rouged, his face powdered, and his eyebrows pencilled, that in the majority of cases you could form a pretty good opinion of what kind of man he was, and that in the majority of cases a man would be right in forming the opinion that that man was a 'fairy.'

"Didn't you tell the Bishop," asked Hyneman, "that you could detect a degenerate at sight, at a glance, and that if you saw a man, walking along, and observed his actions, not hastily, that you could tell pretty well whether that man was a 'fairy.'"

"That," replied Hudson, "is common knowledge." In fact, the only way to "detect this degeneracy" was by observation, which might include measuring skull size, watching the "uranist or sexual pervert," or by "catching him in the act." Keen observers could spot men who had an "effeminate manner," used cosmetics, had a peculiar manner of speech, or wore women's clothing.

Discussions about retrying Kent in federal court, explained Hudson, included the impact of publicity on naval recruitment. Leigh worried that sailors testifying in public court about homosexual relations could "not only hurt recruiting, but that it would not look well if people wanted to make an issue of it from a moral standpoint." Admiral Niblack, on the other hand, argued that the "right methods" had been used and should continue.

"Did Mr. Daniels understand that the men had committed immoral acts?" probed a member of the court.

"Yes, sir," replied Hudson. "He knew about it all, and I explained to him all about the different acts, from sodomy down." Finally Daniels had authorized Hudson to "go ahead and leave no stone unturned to bring those men to justice."

Hudson first learned from a newspaper that his activities as commander of Section A were being investigated. Never had he been notified of the charges against him, as required by naval regulations, or provided an opportunity to respond to them in writing. In fact, because the Ministers' Union rather than the military had alleged misdeeds, he did not even know how to respond or to whom. He had been told repeatedly that his men were immune from prosecution for what they had done, but that now seemed uncertain. Everyone from the Secretary of the Navy to the local commander sanctioned his activities, but now the extent of his authority was being challenged. Hudson argued that he would like to be able "to state everything that happened, what every man did, and have every man state that . . . ," but in view of questions about immunity, he refused to answer any further queries "regarding the exact operations of those operators" on grounds that they might be incriminating. He hinted the men of Section A would take the same position.

What seemed like the best opportunity for a full airing of Section A's activities suddenly disappeared. The court changed Hudson's status to defendant, allowing him still wider discretion in answering questions.

The doctor's attorney, Cawley, reported his client would discontinue testifying because of the "extremely difficult position" in which he had been placed. "He would be compelled . . . to subject himself to cross-examination," explained the lawyer, "and to defend possibly the conduct of high officials in the Navy Department, so that he has been compelled to go from high to low, from great to small, and to run the gamut of accusations. . . ." Only if Hudson were informed "with accuracy and detail [of] the nature of the charges against him" would he be willing to testify further.[11]

Discussion of Hudson's status continued the next day. Attorney Nolan, representing the complainants, asked whether he would ever have an opportunity to examine Hudson. "I have quite a lot of material I would like to clear up."

"That rests with Hudson himself," replied Admiral Dunn, "whether he goes on the stand again."

"It seems to me that is rather unusual," noted Nolan, adding that having changed Hudson's status once, the court could reverse its action.

"The court won't change it." Dunn replied. "The court has made him a defendant."

But that meant that the doctor's lengthy testimony would go "uncontradicted" with no questioning, complained Nolan. "I don't believe [that] is the purpose of the court, [which is] to get all the evidence we can."

Judge Advocate Hyneman supported Hudson's contention that his rights had been denied because no specific charges had been made against him by complainants "Hamilton Fish Webster, John Rathom, and Bishop Perry."

"Mr. Rathom," corrected Nolan, "is not a complainant but a witness."

With most important witnesses having been made defendants and similar status possible for the operators, Hyneman continued, the complainants might be left with only one person who could prove their allegations. "You can put Mr. Kent on the stand," he insisted, "and have him tell us whether he was entrapped." The judge advocate even volunteered to issue a subpoena for the chaplain and, if desired, Arthur Leslie Green as well.

"I have no authority [to represent] Mr. Kent," announced Nolan; "I have never met the gentlemen in my life or Mr. Green either." The judge advocate could subpoena Kent if he wished but such was neither the responsibility nor the intent of his clients.

Nolan persisted, however, in his desire to cross-examine Hudson. Because numerous statements, especially those related to Bishop Perry, directly contradicted earlier testimony, surely he ought to have an opportunity to challenge these statements. "He goes on and makes certain statements under oath and then his status is changed to defendant and that is the end of it," protested Nolan.

"To the ends of justice that doesn't seem right. I have never heard of such a thing of that kind in my life."

"I would like to ask Mr. Hudson if he is willing to be cross-examined," interjected Nolan.

"It is improper," rebuffed Hyneman. Such a question might "have been for publicity or effect," sniped Hudson's attorney, "but has no proper place here."

"Mr. Cawley, you know very well I am not looking for publicity," responded Nolan. "What I want. . . ."

Before he could finish, Cawley interrupted to apologize for "casting any reflection on my brother. I am simply abiding by the rules." Hudson had the right to refuse testimony, and he intended to see that the regulations were enforced.[12]

VI

The appearance of sailors from Section A was a high point in the Dunn Inquiry, not merely because of what they could reveal about their activities but also because of the mystique that now surrounded them.

The first operator to have been actively engaged in pursuing gays was 30-year-old Dudley J. Marriott, who had joined Section A in June 1919 and supervised investigators out of Fall River. At first he refused even to confirm that he had investigated perversion; all his answers were vague. His orders had been to "investigate general conditions" and to "report" any attempted immorality. The decision about how to proceed had been left "up to the man's discretion to a certain extent."

Was it true that he had been ordered to "go the limit, if necessary, or if it would lead to higher game?" asked Hyneman.

"I was never informed that, that I can remember," he replied, noting that he had been told his actions were sanctioned by the navy and that he was "legally protected."

Marriott had been selected by Arnold, with whom he had been a shipmate in Charleston, South Carolina. He enjoyed investigating and volunteered without knowing exactly what the work entailed. Had he tried to secure release once he found out?

"No, sir," answered the sailor, ". . . I thought it was the proper thing to do to eliminate such conditions that existed where thousands of young boys were. . . ."

Marriott participated in the search for Kent in Providence and later visited an Episcopal mission in New York where he told a secretary he wanted to see the chaplain "very badly" but "did not explain my mission." The young lady handed him a paper bearing Kent's address, then "snatched it" back telling him he would have to go through a Rev. Nichols at the Newport Torpedo Station. From this episode, he deduced that the church was covering up Kent's trail. He also accompanied Arnold to Battle Creek to arrest the chaplain and had gone to Adrian, West Virginia, to interview a former sailor about Kent. "I knew they would get him sooner or later," the youngster had told him. He told how Kent had embraced him, touched his penis through his pants, and tried to unbutton his fly. Another former sailor interviewed in Brooklyn apparently provided similar evidence, although Nolan's protests prevented the account from being introduced.

Adopting his characteristic approach in interviewing operators, Hyneman introduced a report by Marriott describing sex with a Newport artist. The sailor agreed to answer questions so long as the report itself was kept out of the public record.

Had his morals been "corrupted, undermined or ruined" by his actions? asked Hyneman.

"No, sir, I should say not," replied the operator. "If anything they were strengthened, because it put me on guard against people who otherwise I would not have had suspicions against."

Why had he allowed this artist to do such things to him?

The navy, explained Marriott, promised the parents of recruits that their sons' morals would be protected and that they would not be assigned to a "nest hole of vice." Many recruits were mere "high school boys, clean physically and morally," often from the "middle section of the West" where nothing was known "of this vice proposition." In places like Newport, however, such youngsters could be "solicited by some men that are worse than beasts, do things beasts won't do." Even a "welfare officer" to whom such a boy might talk could "attempt an immoral action upon him." "Before I am assured that this question has been entirely eliminated," concluded Marriott, "I would not give my consent to anyone that is near and dear to me to be sent up to any Navy rendezvous where those conditions are upheld."

"Why did you permit this artist to do what he did?" repeated Hyneman.

"Just to save such boys as that from having their morals destroyed, and also to uphold the morale of the Navy, and to eliminate men lower than beasts from a rendezvous where young boys 17 years of age are stationed." "I didn't go into this investigation to satisfy any sexual passion," he assured the court. "I went in for the uplift of the Navy, and the Navy as I know it."

From his association with Police Chief Tobin, Marriott ascertained that Newport lawmen were negligent or incompetent. One night while pursuing suspects, he had "zigzagged all through the streets" yet never been "picked up as a suspicious character." The evening of the mass arrests, Tobin refused to take in a pair of men who approached them "in a very lady-like manner" on grounds he lacked authority; next day, one was arrested on a warrant for having sex with an operator. Tobin seemed unaware of the active night life near Forty Steps and ignored the presence of whiskey and gambling throughout town. After the raids, the lawbreakers left, showing how valuable the investigation had been. "I never saw such a clean city," Marriott concluded. "Every pervert took a train to San Francisco, or distant parts, I believe."[13]

Senior operator Clyde L. Rudy, age thirty, had begun work with Arnold March 19 upon receipt of orders to report to the X-ray room. Later he supervised operators in New York. For the first time, he responded to the ministers' charges that "third degree" methods had been used to interrogate sailors. After taps, he questioned Harrison Rideout with Arnold and McCormick. The prisoner was naturally "quite nervous and excited," refusing at first to answer any queries about his sexual preferences. He ultimately agreed to "tell the truth," confessing that stories of having lived in San Francisco and elsewhere were lies. After coming to Newport, he now claimed, a Greek had gotten him drunk and "while I was intoxicated this Greek performed an act of sodomy on me." Thereafter, Rideout claimed "that it was a weakness that he could not control. He said," according to Rudy, "he could not control it and would rather be dead." No compulsion had been used to gain this confession, and none of the information obtained had been used against Rideout.

The testimony quickly shifted to Rudy's sexual relations. The operator insisted on describing how repulsive the situation was at the Y.M.C.A. especially as younger, less sophisticated sailors enlisted after the armistice. Older, "strong, able bodied men" on occasion denounced the "cesspool of perversion" the "fairies" had created there. No sooner did the youngsters "who had been at home running wild while their older brothers were at war" enter the building than "one of these fairies would be making some kind of overture on them." "We fellows decided to clean that up," he declared, "as embarrassing as it often was."

One night, for example, a sailor named Kreisberg began squeezing his hand and invited him to a room where operator McCormick watched. Soon "his funny work began." "There was no erection and consequently no emission," he explained, "and the whole thing to me was a joke because I knew that McCormick was watching, and I could hardly keep from laughing. . . ." As soon as he could, Rudy broke off the lovemaking and left. "Of course, I couldn't tell him that I was doing that so as to rid the community of his kind," explained the operator. "I had to act politely and in a friendly manner so as to keep him from tipping the other fellows off."

Under close examination Rudy admitted that while he objected to Kreisberg's "mushing" him up, "if he wanted to go down there and start his real business, it was all right."

"He could not excite your passion?" asked Hyneman.

"No, because I am a man, and I have more respect for the other fellows. . . . The thing was so horrible in my sight that naturally I would not become passionate and there was no erection. . . ."

"You said your reason for not doing it was because you were a man?" continued the judge advocate. "Weren't they men too? The other operators [who allowed completed acts]?"

"Well, I am not here to defend the other operators."[14]

Operator John Phillips, 25 and unmarried, had verified the presence of whiskey, gambling, prostitution, and homosexuality in Newport during his brief career with Section A. Once he had learned from a woman he followed to the Colonial Theatre that she, her child, and her mother were all illegitimate. Another occasion he had seen women pick up navy officers at the beach and take them to a house on Thames Street. A waiter at the Tokio Restaurant offered to arrange dates with girls for five dollars, while a Greek at the Ideal Restaurant rented rooms. He had the telephone number of a lady at 249 Prospect Hill who arranged for prostitutes. Newporters even hauled sacks filled with whiskey bottles into town, and drunks openly consumed liquor on streetcorners.

While Phillips willingly discussed prostitutes and liquor, he and his attorney protested every question about his pursuit of gays. Persistent interrogation elicited claims that he had never "performed an immoral act upon anyone" or permitted any sailors to "commit immoral acts'' upon him. The introduction of a series of reports, however, revealed four separate incidents when civilians engaged in homosexual relations with Phillips. He refused to answer any questions regarding these reports on grounds that his reply might incriminate or degrade him.[15]

Much the same pattern emerged during the testimony of Preston Paul, a twenty-six-year-old bachelor who had begun investigating March 25. He traced the organization of the operators' squad, efforts to collect evidence at the Y.M.C.A., and subsequent activities in Newport, Pawtucket, and New York. This work, he argued, had "materially strengthened" his morals. "In the future," he explained, "I would be able to take these things a whole lot easier and keep away from them." Before, he was "not absolutely certain about the character of different fellows"; now he knew how "to read the character of different men, being associated with the class of fellows."

When Hyneman introduced reports revealing sex between Paul and sailors, civilian gays, and women, the witness could not recall the incidents, refused to identify documents, or declined to answer on grounds of potential incrimination or degradation. The court made no effort to encourage responses. Once, for example, Paul seemed ready to answer queries about the night he and another man spent with two yeowomen, when Admiral Dunn cautioned him about replying. "Do I understand that if he asks me about that house on Second Street," inquired Paul, "that I can be cross-examined on that, on every report that I have taken down?" "If you answer the question on that particular house," replied Admiral Dunn. "I refuse to answer the question."[16]

Twenty-five-year-old Millard Haynes had first been recruited by Arnold to type reports describing gay activities and continued his work only until April 17. He refused to answer questions about a sexual tryst with Frank Dye, nor could he be cross-examined about testimony before the Foster Court of Inquiry. "Every one of these witnesses comes in here with a stereotypical phrase," complained a frustrated Frank Nolan when he was prohibited from reading testimony from the previous court into the record, ". . . and I want to show some of their conduct." He was never able to examine the witness, who was soon excused from further testimony.[17]

Charles McKinney, still only 23 in 1920, had served with Hudson and Arnold longer than nearly anyone else and led one of the more active sex lives. Like others, he described how he had been recruited into Section A and swore it was left to his discretion how far to go with suspects. Why had he testified in the first Kent trial that he had been instructed to allow himself to be masturbated? He was so tired, nervous, excited, and confused, admitted the witness, that "I permitted myself to be led into questions that did not express my true statements." At Providence, "vicious cross-examination" accounted for similarly erroneous testimony.

With the introduction of reports showing repeated sexual involvement with Newport civilians, McKinney refused to answer any questions. Attorney Nolan attempted to cross-examine him about testimony to Captain Wainwright, but Hyneman's protests were sustained by the court.

No less successful were efforts to determine exactly what he had meant to say during the Newport and Providence trials.

"I cannot even remember now what I testified to in Newport," was McKinney's typical answer.

Just how far did he feel he had to let a suspect go for conviction? asked Nolan.

If "I should go out with a man and only let him play with it, and I could not get away immediately, such as at his house," the sailor responded, "and I wanted to get away without having an act, he would probably become suspicious and jump the country . . . and in such cases it is sometimes necessary to let them go the limit."[18]

Henry Dostalik, a Texan born of Bohemian immigrant parents, was another operator whose testimony the ministers and Rathom frequently cited to support their charges. Yet when asked, for example, whether he had volunteered or been ordered to serve, what instructions he had received, or from whom he had received them, he could not remember or was unsure. His excuse was that having grown up speaking Bohemian, his English was poor.

"You seem to be able to use as good language as any of us here," observed Hyneman. "Is there any question that I have asked you that you don't know the meaning of?"

No response.

Later questions produced emphatic denials that specific orders about how much evidence to collect had never been given. The sailor admitted, however, having been told to collect evidence against "Duke" Hawkins and to associate and make friends with other suspects.

"Was any man's name mentioned to you?" inquired Nolan.

"I do not know."

"Wasn't Kent's name mentioned to you to look out for?"

"I do not remember."

Introduction of reports describing relations between the witness and several civilians, including Kent, stimulated retreat behind the fifth amendment; Dostalik left the stand without ever having answered specific questions about his anti-gay sleuthing.[19]

VII

Perhaps because he had left the navy to resume studies at the University of Michigan and thus had not been prepared like the other operators, operator Charles B. Zipf's testimony was both the frankest and the most damaging. His only concern was that nothing he said get into the newspapers.

Zipf revealed how as a hospital operating room attendant, he had begun frequenting the Y.M.C.A. and collecting evidence of perversion on a voluntary basis. He had also been told never to "take the initiative in an immoral act" but otherwise exercised near total discretion. He generally allowed a man to approach him, went along with him and followed his suggestions until certain "that the man was or was not a pervert." "A great deal of that," he explained, "was involuntary in as much as the man placing his hand on my penis would cause an erection and subsequent emission. That was uncontrolled on my part."

Alone among the operators, Zipf answered questions about reports he submitted and discussed sexual encounters with such Newport sailors as Harold Trubshaw, Frank Dye, David Goldstein, and Harrison Rideout. "I put my penis in his mouth and he sucked thereon until there was an emission," he testified in one case. "Went upstairs and went to bed, and Dye committed the immoral act on me," he reported later.

"What did he do?" probed Hyneman.

"He put my penis in his mouth and sucked until there was an emission." Allowing such actions, explained Zipf, was the only means of discerning "absolutely whether a man was a pervert."

"Did you like this work?"

"Not the actual work; no."

"Every try to get out of it?"

"No. I liked the principle involved too much."

"What do you mean by that?"

"I mean I went into this work because there were a great many young fellows going into the Navy," explained the former detective, "and harbored in and about Newport there were these social perverts, and it seemed to me it was for the good of the service to get rid of them whatever the method may have been."

Zipf's testimony at Newport having been cited by the ministers as proof that men had been "ordered" to entrap victims, considerable discussion focused on the earlier case. The ex-operator insisted problems stemmed from testifying before civilians who used the words "ordered" and "advised" interchangeably without understanding the narrow military usage of the former.

Had he been ordered to have his penis handled until he "had an erection and an emission?" asked Hyneman.

"No, sir," replied Zipf, "my orders never were to allow the handling of my penis. I never received any orders."

"But the Bishop of Rhode Island says that you were compelled under specific orders to allow yourself to be handled."

"Frankly, I don't see where he gets it."

As his testimony continued, however, Zipf admitted both that he had said otherwise during the trial and that he had been "told" to allow his "instrument to be sucked if necessary." "We did not consider 'telling' in the Navy," he explained, "or at least I do not, as an order."

Zipf's testimony regarding other instructions from Arnold was no more precise. He admitted having been told to "get evidence on Kent if it was there to get" but claimed the instructions applied equally "to every member of the community." How did he know the amount and kind of evidence necessary to convict if no one told him? asked Hyneman.

"My father is a lawyer" was the best answer mustered.

"Well," continued the judge advocate, "you want this court to understand that on your own free-will, and for the benefit of the service, you would go around and do the things you have done without advice?"

Cawley objected to such a question as "confusing."

"You want to know whether he did it in the line of duty or not?" interrupted a court member.

"I want to know if he made reports to his superior officer of what he was doing," explained Nolan.

"No one would ever know that from the question," observed Hyneman cynically.

Cawley also complained about questions centering on the accuracy of Zipf's reports and the differences between his Newport and Providence testimony as "absolutely unfair."

Nolan took advantage of his lone opportunity to cross-examine an operator about his reports of homosexual activity. He demanded to know who had unbuttoned whose pants, how long oral sex had lasted, and, particularly, why it was necessary to ejaculate with every suspect.

"That was involuntary," protested Zipf. "Probably I would have had it [an emission] when I got back in bed anyhow." He denied ever having committed buggery, insisting that during the trial he had thought the word referred to both "taking it in the mouth and putting it in a man's rectum."

"I got the words all 'balled up,'" explained the last witness from Section A at the end of his testimony.[20]

Charles B. Zipf, the only "operator" of whom a photograph has been found, from his medical school yearbook from the University of Michigan.
Credit: University of Michigan Libraries.

Erastus M. Hudson, M.D., commanded the original anti-gay squad at Newport as well as "Section A., O.A.S.N." He later gained fame as an expert witness on fingerprints during the Lindbergh kidnapping trial.

Credit: *Literary Digest*.

CHAPTER 11

Defending the U.S. Navy

By the time Admiral Dunn and his associates reopened hearings in Washington May 8, 1920, the anti-homosexual crusade begun in Newport had achieved widespread notoriety. In part, interest in the case stemmed from its famous locale and the lurid nature of the evidence. To a greater extent, however, the scandal stimulated public interest because of the role played by the most prominent members of Woodrow Wilson's administration, especially Secretary of the Navy Josephus Daniels and Assistant Secretary Franklin D. Roosevelt. Not only would their testimony shed additional light on the origins and administration of Section A, but once the court had rendered its opinions, many of these same senior naval officials would review the recommendations and implement or reject them.

I

Commander C. B. Mayo, head of the Bureau of Navigation, had been closely associated with the anti-gay campaign almost from its inception. His recollection of the first young officer, Lt. Commander Hibbs, who came to Washington was "very dim." Later Arnold and Hudson had told him of a "great deal of moral perversion" infecting the Newport area. Mayo argued that "no matter how well meaning" the pair, close supervision of their activities was mandatory. The debate within the department, he explained, had been over which section should take responsibility for the investigation. He understood that despite objections, Captain Williams from Naval Intelligence had agreed to supervise Section A. Mayo had occasionally seen Hudson and Arnold later: "I was always sympathetic with them," he reported, "and believed that they

were honest and only conducted the investigation for the good of
the young men and the station.''

"You want the court to understand," asked judge advocate
Hyneman, ". . . that Captain Leigh and Mr. Roosevelt . . . about
the first of May [knew] that Naval operators were out working obtaining evidence? Is that your testimony?''

"Yes," responded Mayo. "If you call voluntary work Navy operators. The whole things was quite unofficial."

"I mean men in Naval uniform passively submitting to immoral
acts."

"No . . . '' explained the navigation chief.

> My understanding of the procedure was this: that they watched
> men under suspicion and sometimes went to a room with
> them, and these men under suspicion would, at times, make
> indecent proposals to them and then they would leave without
> actually having any indecent act performed upon them.[1]

II

When the next witness, Admiral Albert P. Niblack, took charge
of the office of Naval Intelligence the first of May, 1919, he found
that action had already been taken to restrict domestic surveillance.
Such work had been one of the bureau's "recognized function[s]"
during the war but conflicted with its primary work collecting technical intelligence data from overseas. As a result, he objected to
Roosevelt's May 5 memorandum giving responsibility for the Newport investigation to his office. He also favored the use of professional detectives over amateur sailor-sleuths and had even employed a private firm to "determine the lay of the land in
Newport." He anticipated that Intelligence participation in the investigation would "soon cease."

Perhaps because of his background, Niblack tolerated the operators' methods better than most of his colleagues. It was impossible
to prove perversion, he argued, "except by experience." "I do not
think you can handle 'pitch,'" he added, "without getting some of
it on your hands." His only criticisms involved utilizing amateurs
"in a case that required the best professional expertise, because
they were going up against expert criminals."

Hyneman inferred from Niblack's response that he had disobeyed
or at least complied unenthusiastically with Roosevelt's orders. "I

seem to have given the impression that the order of the Assistant Secretary did not receive the loyal support of the office,'' admitted Niblack. He argued, however, that it had been "carried out in every respect." Use of civilian investigators constituted an additional activity neither required nor prohibited by the order. He had, however, refused to issue Naval Intelligence cards until Roosevelt personally ordered them made available to Hudson and Arnold. Next day, Section A had been formally transferred to FDR's office.

Niblack's subsequent association with the case had been limited to meeting Bishop Perry after he called on Daniels to demand an apology for Kent and generally to complain about the anti-gay campaign. The admiral, having not kept current with the case, was unaware of the methods being used or the evidence collected against Kent. As a result, he promised only that the matter would be thoroughly investigated; Perry would receive a response from the secretary. Subsequent discussions with Arnold and Hudson having convinced him that ample evidence against the chaplain existed, Niblack had recommended against an apology.

Later, during a Newport trip to lecture at the War College, Niblack telephoned Rev. Hughes to warn him that defending Kent put "himself in a very bad position." During a more extended conversation, he informed Hughes that Kent could only be innocent if operators had committed perjury. "I insisted," he testified, "that there was no occasion for the Reverend Mr. Kent to receive an apology because it was up to the church to not put itself in the position of allowing a minister of the gospel to rest under any suspicion." The best way to remove the cloud, he argued, was to bring him to trial again. Only if acquittal resulted would he admit "there must be something criminally wrong with the evidence." In rebuttal, Hughes described his knowledge of Kent and defended him "in the highest praise," insisting that these "stories could not be true." He deemed certain operators had perjured themselves and "ridiculed' the affair as "irresponsible." "We arrived at no very definite understanding," concluded Niblack, "as you may well imagine."[2]

Hyneman interrupted to raise yet again the question of hailing Kent and Green before the court. This time he asked Nolan whether Rev. Hughes had obtained their addresses. Nolan claimed ignorance but insisted there was a larger question:

"Do you really want Mr. Kent here?"

"I should think you would. . . ." replied Hyneman.

"I am conducting this side of the case," replied Nolan, repeating that he did not represent Kent.

"I also understand that you are representing the complainants."

"Of which Mr. Kent is not one."

"No; he is not, but he is one of those entrapped, so your clients say."

"Well, what of it?"

"Well, the man to prove that he was entrapped and wronged, is the man who was entrapped and wronged."

"What are you getting at," demanded Nolan, "asking me if I have his address for you when you don't want to get him here? Do you want to summon him here?"

"Yes," concluded Hyneman, "I think I will, unless it will generate into a third trial of Kent."[3]

As the testimony resumed, Niblack responded to Hyneman's suggestion that in proceeding with the second trial, the military was "sanctioning the objectionable methods by which the evidence had been obtained." The admiral had not considered that question at all and still deemed it insignificant. Far more important than any methods used was the need of "protecting the Navy and the Y.M.C.A." "You cannot," he explained, "stop to consider all the methods when you are after a rattlesnake."

The letter signed by Daniels, explained Hyneman, suggested that the Secretary had gone "carefully over the evidence in the case." What did that mean? he asked Niblack. At a conference attended by Hudson, he explained, the secretary's attention had been called "to page after page" of documents demonstrating Kent's guilt. "He explained every detail of it," the admiral went on, "from his knowledge of sexual perversion, from his education in a medical school, and from his knowledge of all the symptoms and methods."[4]

The session gained added interest as Franklin Roosevelt rose to cross-examine Niblack. His questions revealed that the May 5 letter had actually been prepared by Mayo in the Bureau of Navigation and that Niblack had never formally protested to Roosevelt about it. "I demurred on several occasions to the office getting mixed up in this matter," he replied, "although I can't recall any specific incidents in which I made any form of protest." Had he consulted with Roosevelt before employing a private detective? asked the Assistant Secretary. "No."[5]

III

Assistant Secretary of the Navy Franklin Delano Roosevelt appeared before the Dunn Court at a time when his political career seemed about to catapult him into national prominence. The son of one of New York's most prominent families, he was a relative of President Theodore Roosevelt. Handsome, well educated, articulate, and politically astute, Roosevelt had been appointed Assistant Secretary of the Navy and benefited from political tutorage of Josephus Daniels, a veteran Democratic stronghorse. Marriage to a distant cousin, Anna Eleanor Roosevelt, enhanced his political potential; none but the most intimate family members realized, however, that Franklin's affections had increasingly focused on a lively young secretary named Lucy Mercer, with whom he had engaged in a torrid affair. Discovery of incriminating letters from her husband to the woman in 1919 prompted a family quarrel, as a result of which marital relations between Franklin and Eleanor ended. Nevertheless, by the time he appeared before the Dunn court, FDR was actively mentioned as a Democratic candidate for Vice President in the upcoming election.[6]

Roosevelt's testimony revealed his long and intimate association with the anti-homosexual crusade. Before leaving on a European trip in mid-March, Daniels had asked him to "keep in touch with the situation." As a result, when the recommendations of the Foster court reached his desk, Roosevelt had not hesitated to sign a letter requesting Justice Department assistance. In fact, he noted having personally scribbled "confidential" on the corner of the envelope.

Roosevelt had paid little attention to the details of the investigation. He did not recall, for example, if the letter to Palmer had been answered and was uncertain whether illegal liquor sales had been discussed. He claimed to have heard nothing more about the case until the end of April and to know "absolutely nothing about the [Foster] court or its methods or its personnel." Hyneman questioned Roosevelt about what he knew until Admiral Dunn, in an attempt to shield the Assistant Secretary against aggressive interrogation, ruled that "a general statement" without detail would suffice. FDR insisted that with dozens of different cases each day, he would need ten lives to be knowledgeable about the details of each.

"Do you mean to tell this court," inquired the judge advocate, "that if there was a court of inquiry investigating vice at Newport that the Assistant Secretary of the Navy wouldn't know about it?"

"Not necessarily," replied Roosevelt, "and certainly not about its details."

FDR's association became more intense following a call from Governor Beeckman, "a very old friend," who asked him to see Charles Hall. During a meeting on April 25th Hall told him about the Foster court and the failure of the Justice Department to follow through with requested assistance. Hall suggested a "new investigation" using navy men who could operate surreptitiously, while Hudson was a "thoroughly trust-worthy" [sic] person to be in charge. The physician had been summoned to Washington, where Roosevelt remembered seeing a paper with names listed in one column and offences beside. Hudson had, as the Assistant Secretary recalled, opposed continuing the investigation in its present form because his operators were too well known. AFter careful consideration as to how an expanded inquiry could be administered, FDR ruled that despite a general policy to the contrary, Naval Intelligence was best "able to go ahead with it." After issuing orders to this effect to Captain Williams, his association with the case ceased except for "signing of certain perfunctory orders."

Amidst these discussions, someone had mentioned possible participation by Stewart Davis, a boyhood friend of FDR's who had recently retired from wartime intelligence duties. "My idea was not to make Mr. Davis an investigator by any means," recalled the Assistant Secretary, "but I thought it advisable . . . that . . . a line officer [have] general charge of the whole thing."

Following introduction of Roosevelt's May 5 letter transferring Hudson to New York, attorney Claude Branch asked to see the exhibit. He identified himself as counsel for Perry, Rathom, and Webster. Judge Advocate Hyneman used this request as an excuse to launch into yet another attack on the complainants. "As you represent the complainants," he added, "perhaps you can tell me the address of the Reverend Samuel Neal Kent and Mr. Arthur Leslie Green." Branch could not, so Hyneman demanded to know where Rathom was. Branch pleaded ignorance, although suggesting he could be located through the *Providence Journal*.

Attorney Frank Nolan intervened.

"Mr. Hyneman," he asked, "will you kindly tell me what day you want Mr. Kent? You knew that Mr. Green was in Newport," he persisted, "and you had an opportunity to summon him, and now you are continually asking about Mr. Kent."

"Any time you can inform me where he is," replied the navy lawyer, "we can get him."

Roosevelt described his surprise when Stewart Davis called in late May or early June to report that the investigation had never gotten underway. Questions to subordinates revealed a "general crossing of wires" as a result of which the necessary orders had never been issued. Another meeting including Hudson resulted in the attachment of Section A to his office. The only reason for this administrative arrangement, FDR insisted, was "to keep the investigation out of the files, the routine files, or the Department, and to prevent publicity." Roosevelt also predated a letter to May 15 so Hudson could prove to his superior that he was "not a liar." Didn't he send letters to Hudson and Arnold which gave them "considerable scope and authority, for which you might personally be ultimately held responsible?" inquired Hyneman. "I did," replied Roosevelt, "and the ultimate result justified my giving them the letters, and the fact that they have not misused them in any way still remains."

Roosevelt's personal association with the case received more probing examination during the next session. He denigrated the importance of Section A's association with his office by arguing that the arrangement had been ordered simply so routine activities could be taken care of and expenses paid from the secretary's budget. Costs had been paid from a contingency account established for "just such a purpose." Suggestions that Section A administered the third degree to prisoners were "ridiculous," and he denied knowledge of the vice squad's investigating methods. "I knew nothing of any methods either [for] obtaining evidence against acts of perversion," he added, "or the other evidence which I supposed was being obtained" regarding drug sales, prostitution, or other kinds of vice. His disinterest seemed to stem not from a moral standard but from his intense interest "in getting results." "I was not concerned any more in finding out about the methods than I am concerned in finding out how the commanding officer of a fleet takes the fleet from New York to Newport." What mattered was getting the ships to their destination. All he sought to learn from Hudson was "whether his investigation was proceeding satisfactorily or not."

Following Kent's Newport trial, Hudson had come to Roosevelt's office "very much disappointed." "I happened to be an Episcopalian," noted the young Democrat, "and was rather glad, personally, knowing very little about the case, that the Reverend

Mr. Kent had been acquitted. . . ." Hudson replied, however, that if Kent was guilty, an innocent verdict constituted "a miscarriage of justice." This was not a court of record but the equivalent of a New York magistrate's court where a prosecutor could not always "get the kind of a proper trial that he would get in a court of record." In this case, a "political appointee" had "balked the prosecuting attorney at every point" to inhibit satisfactory presentations. Had he labeled the judge corrupt? Roosevelt avoided a direct answer by replying that he considered the Newport judge "one of the types of magistrates (I don't like to call them even judges), . . . a political appointee who knows very little about law, and before whom it is very difficult to obtain the proper kind of justice, especially from the point of view of the government or the state."

To further questions regarding Judge Baker of Newport, Roosevelt admitted that he considered him "incompetent," which was very different from "crookedness or unfairness." Was that a serious charge to make with only limited evidence? "No," replied FDR, "now I don't consider it a serious thing," He had made it clear that he was only repeating what he had been told by the "man who has had more or less charge of these cases" – Dr. Hudson. Dunn indicated the court was "not particularly interested in Judge Baker." The attack on a man's reputation had "affected him seriously," protested Branch, so the basis of that criticism should be "cleared up at this time." Roosevelt claimed never to have heard the man's name mentioned and argued that he had no desire to "reflect [personally] on Judge Baker." Nevertheless, he reiterated his conclusion that the trial "had been conducted in rather an incompetent and informal way."

Branch endeavored to learn Roosevelt's attitude toward the methods used during the anti-gay investigation. "Mr. Roosevelt," he demanded, "would you sanction the method of having enlisted men in the Navy submit their bodies to unnatural vices to obtain evidence[?]"

"As a matter of information, of course, no," replied the Assistant Secretary.

"If you knew that was being done," probed the complainant's counsel, "what would your attitude be in regard to it?"

"Stop it."

"You would consider it extremely improper."

"As stated by me," repeated Roosevelt, "yes."

If Roosevelt knew the investigation was proceeding, and if he knew that sodomy was being investigated, should he not also have realized how "evidence of such a claim could be obtained."

"As a lawyer," replied FDR, "I had no idea. That is not within the average lawyer's education."

But had Roosevelt given "that matter any thought whatever?"

"Of course not any more than how they were going to close whore houses or [stop] the sale of drugs."

"Did you realize as a lawyer or as a man of intelligence," continued Branch, "that the investigation of such matters, very often has led to improper actions on the part of the investigator?" "I never had such an idea," replied the witness. "Never entered my head."

FDR declined to answer questions about Hudson's detection abilities and claimed not to have known that the name used to identify the investigators (Section A, O.A.S.N.) referred to his office until he "found somebody else had wished them" on him. He did not know Red Cross rooms were being used and could not adequately explain why a New York headquarters had been necessary. Branch endeavored to get Roosevelt to indicate whether homosexuals should be allowed to remain in the navy, but Admiral Dunn upheld the judge advocate's objection on grounds such policies were set by the Bureau of Navigation. "The court doesn't wish to hear from me in regard to that?" protested Branch. "I think it is an important question." "The court doesn't" came Dunn's curt reply.

After the noon recess, Branch challenged Roosevelt's contention that he was unaware of the contents of orders bearing his signature. Was it possible, he asked, that an Assistant Secretary signed orders without reading them? Cawley objected to so general a question, whereupon Branch specified the all-important letter of June 11 establishing Section A under FDR's office. "Whoever brought it into my office," explained Roosevelt, "stated the general purpose and tenor of the letter and I glanced over it in all probability not reading it word for word, and probably only reading a couple of lines of each paragraph."

Roosevelt then interjected an elaborate explanation of why private detectives could not have been used at Newport. Every time the Navy Department had gone to Congress requesting funds for "police and detective work," he explained, the appropriation had been denied. During the war, Naval Intelligence had been permitted to conduct domestic surveillance, but this authority ended with the armistice. The only alternative was using naval personnel for "police work." In Newport neither local navy officials nor the police could have accomplished the needed objectives. As a result, "it became necessary to resort to this absolutely authorized power, which we had, to investigate through Navy personnel."

Roosevelt also described his visit with Rev. Hughes and Mr. Webster. Early in the conversation, the pair introduced "some papers" identified as a transcript of Kent's Newport trial. Having previously learned from Hudson that this had not been a "court of record," he was surprised, although saying nothing "because I had too much official business to attend to that day to read the testimony. . . ." Instead, he referred the pair to Captain Leigh. He admitted, however, having said that anyone who had ordered sailors to commit immoral acts "ought to swing for it," promised to stop any on-going offences, and pledged to see that "nothing like this occurs again." Later Leigh had briefed him on the meeting, indicating his own horror at the allegations. As a result, Hudson had been summoned to his office and ordered verbally to cease operations. "Dr. Hudson," FDR recalled, "said that it was not true that he had ordered any methods of that kind, and that of course they would never occur in the future."

"Did you ask him whether without his orders, that thing had gone on?"

"No."

"Why didn't you ask him that?"

"Why should I?" protested the Assistant Secretary, whereupon Ensign Hyneman protested that no evidence "before the court" showed that "any operator at any time, while attached to Section A, committed an immoral act." Dunn sustained the objection.

Perhaps, continued Branch, Roosevelt was "not sufficiently interested" to ask more probing questions.

"I was sufficiently interested," replied the assistant secretary, "but perhaps you will realize that it is not the province and duty of the Acting Secretary to go into the evidence of a court martial in person, and he has to delegate that to other persons."

When testimony resumed the morning of May 22, Roosevelt failed to recall details and persisted in placing full responsibility for decisions on the shoulders of subordinates. In the case of having recommended federal prosecution of Kent, for example, he argued that "every person who read over the testimony" concurred that a retrial was needed.

He had not, he added, complied with Rev. Hughes' request for an apology because he considered the demand part of "a very natural, very mistaken campaign. . . ." Even now Roosevelt refused to admit any error in the way the case had proceeded, acknowledging only that "a man is naturally injured by being tried on a charge of this character." Would the navy be willing to admit the chaplain's exoneration and "express regret for the arrest and trial?" asked the complainant's attorney. "I don't know what the future may bring in regard to the Navy Department," Roosevelt responded; "it is not customary, usual or necessary," he added, "for a prosecuting attorney . . . to make a public apology to a man who has been indicted, tried, and [not] convicted. The acquittal carries with it vindication."

Turning to larger policy considerations, Hyneman asked whether utilizing sailors for such investigations could result in their being "consigned to a career of vice." Roosevelt replied that the navy had done no such thing; the chances of corrupting men engaged in police work of this kind were no greater than in any other criminal investigation.

Even more serious, Newport clerics accused civilian authorities within the navy of having "authorized these terrible abuses." "What have you to say to that?" queried Hyneman.

"The whole testimony which I have given," replied Roosevelt, "absolutely disproves that."

Roosevelt claimed that he had stopped the investigation in early September, after which no perversion cases had been investigated. "Does not the fact that this organization is in existence today," asked Branch, "prove conclusively that you, at least, have been deaf to all appeals to break up these practices?" FDR denied any connection between the cessation of anti-gay activities and the continuation of Section A. "Neither does the court," piped in Admiral Dunn in yet another demonstration of partisanship.

Claude Branch's cross-examination was neither adequately prepared nor sufficiently detailed, focusing almost entirely—perhaps because he was paid by Rathom—on Roosevelt's meeting with Arthur Fairbrother of the *Journal*. The minister's attorney, Frank Nolan, tried to ask about the repayment of money borrowed from the Red Cross, but Roosevelt claimed to know nothing of "any financial transaction between the operators and Mr. Hall." Nor could he recall whether or not he had read the Wainwright report. He did, however, ask that Rathom be recalled for further questions about his charges to the U.S. Senate. With that request, Roosevelt withdrew from the stand.[7]

IV

The much anticipated appearance of Secretary of the Navy Josephus Daniels began after the noon recess. Considered by many one of the true heroes of World War I, he was without doubt one of the most influential Democratic leaders and Wilson cabinet members. Assignment of Assistant Secretary Roosevelt as his counsel further dramatized his presentation. But much as the testimony of the operators, Hudson, and Arnold had been disappointing, so, too, Daniels proved less informative than expected. In part, this resulted from the strategy adopted by Hyneman and Roosevelt; instead of reviewing with their witness his association with the Newport case, they turned the proceedings immediately over to attorney Claude Branch, whose poor preparation, lack of familiarity with the case, absence from earlier sessions, and inability to phrase proper questions seriously deterred his effectiveness.

Daniels claimed only general knowledge of the affair and admitted no responsibility for what had occurred. Whenever potentially embarrassing issues were raised, Dunn sustained objections by Judge Advocate Hyneman. For instance, Branch asked if Daniels approved of naval men "submit[ting] their persons to such immoral acts." Cawley complained that his language was insufficiently detailed. A change to "sexual perversion" brought complaints that an opinion, not a fact, was called for. Hyneman argued that the question called for "the convening authority to express an opinion upon the subject which this court is to ultimately determine." Daniels was thus heavily protected in the kind of question he need answer. Branch objected to his being treated differently than other witnesses just because he had convened the court, to which Hyneman and Cawley noted that military procedures had to be followed regardless of impact.

Some subjects were, nevertheless, still open to discussion. Daniels described the visit to his office by Bishop Perry, claiming it was the first time he knew the navy was investigating "civilian miscreants." "If I had heard it [before]," he added, "it had escaped my memory." Later he had expressed shock over the affair to Captain Leigh, who told him operations had been suspended. Not the navy, he argued, but the Department of Justice decided to press federal charges. "When a matter is turned over to the Department of Justice," he explained, "it is their affair."

In what was perhaps the most incriminating document, Daniels had written Bishop Perry that he had "gone carefully over the evidence." Yet he now claimed ignorance of any details. The secretary admitted not "having read every line of evidence." "I carefully went over some of these affidavits," he continued, "and the officers there whose business it was to have studied the question, explained to me that this evidence was very damaging and very compelling, and having this information, I wrote this letter. . . ."

Branch endeavored to find out if Daniels had sanctioned the use of perjured testimony in the second trial, but Roosevelt protested that since the entire trial was a Justice Department responsibility, the question became immaterial. Branch countered by citing FDR's earlier admission that navy suggestions "would have had some influence" at Justice. At that point, Cawley lectured Branch that "it is very improper to make use of statements of a man in one capacity" to counter an argument he made in another. The objection was sustained, and testimony moved ahead.

Daniels claimed to have seen evidence "which showed Kent guilty," but when challenged to produce it refused "on the grounds that they were signed affidavits by men other than operators who had never testified in court." This tantalizing suggestion coupled with Daniels' persistent refusal to produce documents infuriated the complainant's lawyers, but there was nothing they could do to counter rulings that documents need not be produced. And when Branch asked Daniels to identify an operators' report as one he had seen, the secretary feigned forgetfulness. "Mr. Secretary," asked Nolan, "would you consider that the official to whom that report was made. . . ." Before he could finish, Hyneman lectured him: "You know better than ask the Secretary of the Navy the question you are going to ask him." Because the objection was again sustained, the question was never completed.

"I am sorry that we are in a position of that kind," Nolan added in total frustration, "that the Secretary is a witness here, and we can only use his testimony to a certain limited extent." As a result, continuing examination was useless. Roosevelt argued that the problems stemmed from the fact that Nolan's questions had "no bearing on the question at issue before this court." Nolan's final query was whether, as charged by Rathom, Daniels had been "deaf to all appeals for the breaking up of such [investigating practices]?"

"That is absolutely false," insisted Daniels. "Not a scintilla of truth in it." Then he stepped down.[8]

V

Just how far the Dunn court had strayed from the original investigation demanded by Newport ministers became clear when the court reconvened at Westerly, Rhode Island, to hear yet again from the witness who knew almost nothing about the anti-gay investigation and yet who now had become its central figure — John R. Rathom of the *Providence Journal*.

Judge Advocate Hyneman interrogated the witness more aggressively than before. He demanded, for example, proof to support the "charges" and "averments" against the navy published in his newspaper. Rathom's response that his articles had been designed to stimulate an investigation and that he personally had "no knowledge whatsoever" provoked renewed and more antagonistic interrogation. "Is it your policy and that of the papers under your direction," he demanded, "to make charges to a Department of the Government and against government officials during a state of war based upon what is told you by others?" Ultimately the question was withdrawn when Branch objected. Next he accused the *Journal* of printing statements containing false information. Branch objected that such a question served no conceivable purpose but "to make an inference of degradation" against his client, and for once the court sustained him.

Hyneman demanded to know what witnesses not already heard by the court could substantiate Rathom's charges. When Branch claimed not to know everyone who had testified, the judge advocate denounced him for not having been present for the entire proceeding. Furthermore, he endeavored to debate the accuracy of *Journal* reports on the daily proceedings of the Dunn court. Branch objected that such information was irrelevant, but Admiral Dunn upheld the naval lawyer's contention that he could prove Rathom had attempted "to try this case in his newspaper and his attempt to attack an officer and enlisted man in the navy as well as the Secretary and Assistant Secretary" using "proofs" which readers never saw. "I think," he added, "it is proper to show whether his purpose was honest or ignorant in labeling these things proof." Such language prompted Branch to worry that evidence was being accumulated for a planned law suit. Rathom argued that nothing more than daily news stories had been printed, admitting that he had used the word "proof" journalistically without legal advice. "The *Providence Journal* is an honorable newspaper," argued its publisher, "and under my direction and . . . that of my predecessor, it has never been guilty of an improper act in its publication." Statements to the contrary, he insisted, were "simply attempts to carry out threats made by interested parties in this case which have no bearing on this case and are an insult to the court itself." Had the *Journal* published statements which "turned out to be false fact?" demanded Hyneman. "We have very many times," Rathom freely admitted "as every newspaper in the world has done. . . ."

As if his questioning had not already strayed far enough off track, Hyneman interjected questions about the stories of German spies for which the *Journal* had been castigated during the war. Branch complained that the issue was irrelevant, asking "what possible issue can that have with the matter embraced in the precept of this court . . . ?" Not so, rebutted Hyneman. Rathom's having previously published stories "about or against a Department of Government or claimed to unearth scandalous stories when no such things existed in fact" demonstrated a "policy" that applied here as well. He offered Rathom the opportunity of taking the fifth amendment if answering questions incriminated or degraded him. Branch objected that raising this issue unfairly attacked his client's reputation. "Nobody," answered Hyneman, "is attacking Mr. Rathom's character." "I don't know what you would call it," replied Branch, at which point Dunn overruled the objection and ordered the journalist to answer. Rathom, whose replies to earlier antagonistic questions had been marked by restraint, erupted: "That statement," he charged, "is a willful, malicious, deliberate falsehood in everything it states and implies. . . ." It had only been asked so it would appear in the record and could be further disseminated.

Hyneman next introduced a letter from Rathom to the Justice Department that presumably admitted wrongdoing in relation to the German spy stories. The *Journal* publisher objected on the grounds that he and the Attorney General had pledged the document would "never be used or shown, to any other living person, except one person." Hyneman demanded that Rathom identify the letter, and Admiral Dunn refused to accept any explanation for refusing except a claim of degradation or incrimination. Branch contended that the contents of a confidential letter need not be revealed, to which the judge advocate argued that much other evidence of a confidential nature had been introduced without objection. "I asked him," he repeated, "whether he wrote the letter and whether the signature was his."

"It is immaterial and I object," responded Branch, with rare aggressiveness.

"You have acted improperly before and are acting improperly now, Mr. Hyneman," he lectured. "I will certainly say you are acting improperly now, if not before.

"I demand that you apologize for that statement right now," shouted the navy lawyer.

"I will not apologize."

Ensign Hyneman further queried Rathom about his role in publicizing the Newport case. Rathom insisted that far stronger evidence "fortified" his stories on the sex scandal than any incident he had previously encountered. Sending telegrams about the incident to twenty or thirty newspapers was merely "in the ordinary course of our work." His only regret was accusing Roosevelt and Daniels of never having "contemplated" establishing a court of inquiry. To Hyneman's question of what else could be done to prove his allegations, Rathom conceded that at this point the issue centered not on evidence but on "a matter of judgment." "I don't know," the journalist concluded, "of any method you could employ other than what you have already employed, very successfully." With that and only a few more inconsequential queries, the Dunn Court of Inquiry adjourned.[9]

VI

The court devoted nearly a month in closed session to discussing evidence and preparing a statement of facts, opinions, and recommendations filling 135 typewritten pages. The findings were remarkably candid. After rehearsing the events leading up to their having been convened, the court addressed specific questions. They argued, first, that operators were immune from prosecution for their sexual activities in the process of gathering evidence and should not face courts-martial for "scandalous conduct." Second, the court condemned the use of sailors in sleuthing work of this kind. It had been "unfortunate and ill-advised" that Assistant Secretary Roosevelt had "either directed or permitted the use of enlisted personnel to investigate perversion."

Third, the report condemned nearly everyone outside Washington for participation in the Newport investigation. Letters of censure were recommended for Lt. Commander Foster and Ensign Drury as members of the original Newport court of inquiry. Dunn commended Dr. Hudson for "conferring from time to time" with Navy Department officials, but condemned him for "extremely bad judgment" in not making certain that senior naval officials were "fully cognizant of the details of the methods which were being employed by the organization under his command." The use of "immoral methods" by members of Section A was "in direct contravention of the traditions of the Naval Service." Arnold was similarly censured for having used "enlisted men . . . to obtain evidence in the investigation of perversion . . . which are contrary and repugnant to the traditions of the service. . . ." No courts-martial were recommended for anyone, however, and no punitive action whatsoever was suggested for Roosevelt, Daniels or other senior naval officials.[10]

Long delays in transcribing and organizing the testimony postponed further review. The passage of nearly three months without the records and exhibits having yet been prepared led Admiral Dunn to write the Judge Advocate General complaining that there was "no excuse for such an unusual delay." He ordered Hyneman to deliver the materials to Washington for completion. Hyneman presented a long list of excuses, principally that five copies of 4,750 pages had to be typed and corrected.[11]

Concern about this delay among senior navy officials was minor compared to that expressed by principals in the case. Those members of Section A whose status had become "interested parties" or "defendants" in the course of Dunn's proceedings had been retained in the service pending the outcome of the court. Once the findings were complete, however, on October 14, 1920, the Judge Advocate General notified the Bureau of Navigation that "no disciplinary action was now pending" against those operators not "interested parties." By early November Hudson had received authorization to issue honorable discharges to all "interested parties" whose enlistments had expired. The next month "duration of the war" men were also given honorable separation. On December 10 sailor George Steck, who had more than two years left to serve, was discharged by special order of Daniels.[12]

This left only defendants Hudson, Arnold, and Drury remaining from Section A. Hudson requested permission to resign his commission and resume his medical career. A first letter of resignation dated November 24, 1920, having been rejected, in mid-December he addressed a detailed plea to Secretary Daniels. He asserted that no charge made by the Newport ministers had been "substantiated by facts" and that the men under his command "gave uncontradicted testimony to the effect of refuting all charges made by the complainants." In view of the court's findings and the release of the other men, he argued that "in tendering my resignation I am doing nothing except that which is just and proper under the conditions."[13]

Daniels worried that a release might be "very unwise," but he passed on the letter to Roosevelt, who had resigned public office to campaign for the vice presidency and after the election was living at his Hyde Park, New York, estate: "You know more about this case than I do," he wrote, "and I would like to have your view about it."[14] Roosevelt concurred with the secretary, although his reasoning related primarily to the public outcry that could result. "If his resignation were accepted now," FDR concluded, "it would merely cause another howl from people who are trying to cause trouble and pay off grudges." "Good policy" required delaying acceptance of the doctor's resignation for another six weeks until just before the inauguration. Perhaps a personal letter from the secretary would placate Hudson during the interim.[15] Daniels agreed and hurried off a note to Hudson.[16]

The nearer the end of the Wilson administration, the more nervous Dr. Hudson became and the harder he pressured Roosevelt to get him out of the navy. "I have had a talk with Dr. Hudson, and, as you know, he is very anxious to get out of the service," FDR wrote Daniels in mid-January. The doctor knew the length of the Dunn testimony and worried that transcription could not be completed until after a new administration took office in March. Who knew how Republicans might act with regard to the controversial case! Would it be possible to set a specific date for the doctor's release whether or not the review had been completed? asked Roosevelt, suggesting February 27 as a possibility.[17] Daniels declined to act until he had seen the testimony, so Roosevelt suggested a new strategy: Since this had not been a "regular legal court-martial," Daniels could do "anything . . . [he] want[ed] to," including the rendering of a decision before full transcripts became available.[18]

In the meantime, on Roosevelt's suggestion, Daniels immediately contacted Judge Advocate Hyneman, who was completing the transcription in Philadelphia. The navy lawyer promised that he would have the work complete in ample time for review by March 4, at which point Hudson could resign; "it will be better for him and for everybody."[19]

"I hate to bother you again about this same matter," FDR wrote Daniels again the beginning of February, "but for each time that I write you our friend Dr. Hudson comes in to see me or telephones to me at least a score of times."

Hudson was now convinced that it would be April—long after President Harding's inauguration—before the transcript would be ready. What could be done? Roosevelt suggested that since the findings were complete, Hyneman could file them with the Judge Advocate General. The secretary could then review the document, ascertain that no courts-martial were being recommended, and sign a discharge for Hudson.[20] Daniels was still reluctant to circumvent procedure, so he promised to do everything possible to "pass" on the Newport matter and accept Hudson's resignation. "I don't think there is any doubt about this," he assured FDR.[21]

Not until February 25, 1921, had Judge Advocate General Clark obtained the complete transcript, evaluated the court's recommendations, and prepared the first endorsement. He commended the court's handling of the case and characterized its opinions as "sound," "deliberate," and logical. He disagreed regarding the immunity of operators and their liability to prosecution and contended that exemption from liability did not extend to persons who "actually commit, as principals of the first degree, acts of sexual perversion. . . ." Members of Section A (like their sex partners) were, therefore, subject to trial for "scandalous conduct" or other appropriate charges.[22]

Final consideration of the case moved to the office of Secretary Josephus Daniels. Before rendering a decision, the navy head consulted trusted aids, including former Assistant Secretary Franklin Roosevelt, now engaged in private law practice in New York. Roosevelt's five-and-a-half-page single spaced analysis of the case was submitted to Daniels on March 1.

FDR's principal interest was the court's conclusion that his having directed Section A was "unfortunate and ill-advised." "That is a grossly unfair assertion," he complained, justifying his action on the basis that so many navy officers, "more conversant with the facts" than he, had "thoroughly approved" of the action. Daniels' report, he urged, must make the responsibility of these officers clear. "Frankly, I must decline to be made in anyway the scapegoat for things which had their inception among the regular navy officers concerned."

Roosevelt also addressed the issue of whether sailors who had sex with suspects in Newport were subject to prosecution. He noted that while the court had ruled that no criminal action was possible, the Judge Advocate General had argued to the contrary. If Daniels accepted the latter position, FDR reminded the Secretary, he would have to recommend courts-martial for many of those who had worked under Hudson. Roosevelt argued that since no lawbreaking was intended, prosecution was inappropriate; but he advised Daniels to consult the U.S. Attorney General for a definitive opinion.

Finally, Roosevelt turned to the "big question" of issuing letters of "censure and condemnation" to Hudson, Drury, and Arnold. If the navy approved such letters, individuals who were "after your [Daniels'] scalp at any cost" would accuse him of making "scapegoats out of a couple of reservists and an enlisted man." Sympathizers would accuse him of being "pretty rough" on men who "were under very difficult circumstances trying to do their duty in the way they thought to be best." The preferred approach, he suggested, was to rule that the men's conduct had been "contrary and repugnant to the traditions of the service," but since Hudson and Drury were reserve officers only temporarily in the service, "they did not know and had no opportunity of becoming inculcated with Navy traditions" against such activities. Arnold had merely followed the lead of men to whom he reported.

To facilitate implementation of his opinions, Roosevelt drafted a "suggested method of handling the case" for Daniels. Nearly half the document focused on criticism of Roosevelt while condemning those senior navy officers who had endorsed the creation of Section A. The actions of Leigh, Williams, Mayo, and others, Roosevelt concluded, were "at least more unfortunate and ill-advised" because high-ranking officers "should be supposed to know naval traditions." Hudson, Drury, and Arnold should be spared censure because violations of navy traditions consisted "solely of a bona fide mistake in judgement." And because sailor-sleuths had neither criminal intent nor had actively solicited others to commit crimes, they should not be prosecuted.[23]

As soon as he received FDR's letter, on March 2, Daniels had Ensign Hyneman personally deliver a letter to U.S. Attorney General A. Mitchell Palmer requesting an opinion on whether sailors should be prosecuted as Roosevelt had suggested.

Palmer, who—like Daniels—was preparing to leave office, moved swiftly, returning a 3-page response to the Navy Department the next day. A review of case law convinced him that a person feigning "participation in a criminal offense for the purpose of enforcing, not violating, the law" was not an accomplice because "criminal intent" was lacking. The Judge Advocate General had argued that this rule excluded cases of sexual perversion that were "*mala in se*" [bad in themselves] and did not "require any specific intent." The Justice Department disagreed: no authority "supported this distinction," and the only one which dealt with it supported a contrary opinion "so far as it goes." "The reason why a feigned accomplice is not considered a real accomplice," Palmer argued,

> is because he lacks criminal intent, an absolutely necessary element in every crime, except where the legislature provides otherwise. His intent is not evil but meritorious, since it is in aid, not in obstruction, of justice. This principal, being general and all embracing, applies to unnatural sexual crimes as well as to others. The abhorrent disgust which such crimes excite may make the burden heavier upon the apparent accomplice to show that his true intent was not criminal, but it does not deprive him of the right to justify himself by showing he acted as an agent of the Government, under the orders of his superior officers, in order to detect and punish crimes against the Government.[24]

Having received the last advice he needed, Daniels prepared his endorsement March 3, 1921, the day before he and the entire Wilson administration left office. Not until 7:30 p.m. on the evening of the 4th were the documents signed and ready for return to the Bureau of Navigation. "I have been sweating blood over the Newport case," the navy secretary wrote Roosevelt that day, promising that Hyneman would send him a copy of the opinion. "It was not easy." He had discussed the case "in all its phases" with as many people as possible. "I believe the conclusion reached is just to all concerned."[25]

Accepting the recommendations of the Attorney General, Daniels concluded that operators such as those employed against gays were immune from prosecution. The secretary also disapproved Admiral Dunn's recommendations that naval personnel be excluded from investigating such matters and "regretting the action of the Department and its officials in permitting such an investigation."

Daniels appended a long discussion of his repeated efforts to clean up Newport, undoubtedly prepared long before he saw the Dunn transcript or the court recommendations and focusing entirely on attempts during the war to have prostitutes arrested and liquor sales suspended. Roosevelt helped prepare the document, for a version edited in his handwriting is in the Roosevelt Library.[26] Possibly FDR prepared the document for Daniels; more likely, Daniels sent him a copy for review and modification.

The document demonstrated beyond any doubt the degree to which the Navy Secretary misunderstood the Newport case and the complaints of the Rhode Island clerics. The unwillingness of Newport officials to cooperate demonstrated that local authorities accepted immoral conditions that had "existed in a greater or less degree for many years" and refused to eliminate them for fear of "wide publicity and the consequent general spreading of ill repute throughout the country." Such a tendency, he insisted, was especially prevalent, "in those communities dependent upon summer visitors for their prosperity." This attitude was unimportant in peacetime but in time of war when large numbers of young men were assigned to a locality, it became a "matter of very grave moment" for those charged with managing the navy "to see that they were protected from evil influences in every possible way."

"I have always held that the mothers of the boys enlisted in the navy," he continued, "should be justified in feeling that the Naval authorities assumed responsibility for more than their physical health and well being." Every sailor, he contended, should leave the service "better fitted, not only in his education and in his physical condition but with a very high standard of personal morality and honor" as well. To forestall criticism from the *Providence Journal*, he quoted a letter Rathom had sent him in June of 1917 confirming that Newport maintained "houses of prostitution of the lowest type" under the patronage of city officials with police officers detailed to keep visitors in order." The letter concluded: "The people of Rhode Island owe you a debt of gratitude for your timely exposure." Later Governor Beeckman commended the navy's activities and assured him that Newport would "remain as safe a place for young sailors as any in the country."

This narrative, although wholly unrelated to the detection of homosexuals in Newport, justified Daniels' belief that he had "exhausted every one of the regular channels in an effort to clean up" the town. "Not until failure after failure," he continued in what constitutes a clear misrepresentation of the facts, had he become "convinced that in cooperation with the Department of Justice, the Navy itself must take steps to secure a wholesome environment for youths sent to Newport for training."

Contrary to Roosevelt's suggestion, Daniels approved letters of censure for Hudson, Arnold, Drury, and Foster; presumably they were released from the navy soon after, although documentation to this effect has not been located. Only general letters were issued Drury and Foster; Arnold's commanding officer was instructed to censure him for authorizing methods and permitting the use of enlisted men "which are contrary and repugnant to the traditions of the service." The long detailed letter to Hudson condemned him for "extremely poor judgement"; at Roosevelt's suggestion, a clause explained that "by reason of your short term of service you could not have had an extended knowledge of naval tradition." Hudson was reminded "to avoid a repetition of this delinquency" and asked to acknowledge receipt of the letter, "at which time the Department will consider the matter closed." Daniels failed to exonerate Roosevelt, although he overruled the condemnatory language recommended by the Dunn court.

In concluding his opinion, Daniels reiterated his conviction that the "methods used in this investigation" were "contrary and repugnant to the traditions of the naval service irrespective of their legality. . . ." As soon as he had heard of them, he had ordered them stopped. Future military commanders should maintain similar vigilance "to see that nothing of this kind occurs" again.[27]

As soon as Daniels signed the report, the "Navy News Bureau" issued a press release making the decision public. The Navy's official interpretation was that with only a few minor exceptions the Dunn Court had found that charges lodged against the Department from Perry, the Newport ministers, and Rathom "were either disproved or not proved, in whole or in part." Even the charge that sailors had been held for months without trial was "in a measure excusable."[28]

Although Daniels' endorsement completed the two-year review of the anti-homosexual campaign, it was August 6, 1921, before Ensign Hyneman recommended that the Court of Inquiry be formally dissolved; telegrams to Admiral Dunn and his colleagues released them from duty.[29]

Secretary of the Navy Josephus Daniels. The inscription reads: "To the youths of Newport Training Station upon whom the Republic confidently depends."
Credit: *Newport Recruit* from the U.S. Naval Historical Center.

CHAPTER 12

Before the Senate of the United States

Frustrations stemming from the conduct of the Dunn Court of Inquiry were partially tempered by the fact that one more tribunal had yet to investigate the navy's anti-homosexual campaign. The navy might manipulate procedures to protect itself, but U.S. Senators ought to be able to uncover the truth and be unafraid to criticize where justified. Moreover, no Senate finding would be subject to review by the very men accused of malfeasance. Perhaps Senate recommendations or publicity resulting from the deliberations could prevent the repetition of such incidents.

I

With charges from both John R. Rathom and the Newport ministers before them, Senators Lewis H. Ball (Republican of Delaware), Henry W. Keyes (Republican of Vermont), and William H. King (Democrat of Utah) began collecting evidence late in January of 1920. At a meeting Saturday the 25th they decided to conduct initial hearings in secret, so details of most presentations are unavailable. The first witness was Bishop Perry, who had come to the capital several days earlier as guest of the Bishop of Washington. Then Arthur L. Fairbrother, representing the *Providence Journal*, read a prepared statement describing the evolution of the scandal and levelled seven specific allegations against the government. They condemned the immoral activities of Section A, denounced the claimed abilities of Hudson and Arnold to spot gays, accused the Navy Department of authorizing these activities, and protested the ill-treatment of sailors accused of homosexual offences. Fairbrother also provided the committee with evidence the *Journal* had collected and a list of witnesses who could provide further information.[1]

The committee also heard from such Navy Department witnesses as Captain Leigh, Admiral Niblack, and Assistant Secretary Roosevelt. They presented what FDR later characterized as "an informal preliminary outline of the general actions of the Department." Because details were omitted, Roosevelt sought assurance that the Navy would be given ample opportunity to "see the evidence and correct or add to any questions which in our judgment were not clear" before the investigation ended. The committee agreed.[2]

The evidence presented apparently proved sufficient, for on March 2, Senator Ball recommended to the full committee that a thorough inquiry of the naval vice operation be initiated. He argued, as Senator Page recalled, "with all possible force and emphasis," the need to get to the bottom of the matter. No one objected, so authorization for the three-man subcommittee to continue its probe "when, where, and as it" saw fit was quickly approved.[3]

The collection of evidence occupied the Senators intermittently throughout the spring and summer of 1920. Mid-April found Keyes and Ball in Newport to interview Captain Campbell, who had left command of the Training Station to pursue advanced study at the Naval War College. They also met with Lt. Commander Murphy J. Foster, who had presided over the court of inquiry that investigated homosexuality among soldiers and civilians. Both men insisted that they had revoked the orders authorizing Hudson to investigate immorality and bore no responsibility for the anti-gay campaign.[4]

Four months later the Senators returned to Newport for more extensive hearings at the city's Hilltop Inn. The first witness appearing the morning of August 11 was Rev. Stanley C. Hughes. He declared that "commercialized vice" had been eliminated from Newport in 1917 and denounced the operators for having used "execrable methods" which "spread immorality rather than check it." Reiterating complaints made to President Wilson, Hughes maintained that evidence collected during the ensuing months had "abundantly proved" the ministers' charges. Still unclear was the identity of specific persons "who originated and were responsible" for the use of "objectionable methods."

John R. Rathom urged the Senators to devote specific attention to operators who had been spared from effective cross-examination during the Dunn inquiry. Despite promises to the contrary, no opportunity had been provided to interrogate Hudson. Furthermore,

Rathom accused Roosevelt of "incomprehensible assertions" in denying he knew what methods operators had used. He insisted that in prosecuting Kent a second time, after having become aware of how evidence had been collected, both Roosevelt and Daniels had tacitly approved these methods and endorsed the truthfulness of the operators' testimony.

Both Hudson and Arnold claimed that Ensign Drury had supervised the first phase of the investigation, but Drury himself repeatedly argued that he had cancelled the order authorizing the transfer of operators and denied ever having been in charge of the sailors or knowing how they were collecting evidence. "Did you as judge advocate approve of those methods?" asked Senator Ball. "We all disapproved of the methods used," he replied; "we thought they were disgusting and rotten. . . ." The men had gone too far, he concluded, only "through inexperience and [a] desire . . . to benefit the service." Drury was particularly angry that he had never been provided an opportunity to rebut the statements of Hudson and Arnold and thanked the Senators for giving him a forum. Drury must have been persuasive, for according to the *Journal* Senator Ball "expressed satisfaction" with his "apparent innocence." The Senators also interviewed James Esleek, a Newport policeman who described conversations in which Arnold boasted of his ability to spot gays and of his close association with FDR. A visit to the Training Station enabled them to inspect the brig where sailors awaiting trial had been confined.[5]

First in April and again in August, the subcommittee visited Portsmouth, New Hampshire to interview convicted gay sailors in the naval prison. Frank Dye, Frederick Hoage, Samuel Rogers, Albert Viehl, Harold Trubshaw, and David Goldstein were serving sentences of two to ten years. Contrary to the official record, the convicts claimed they had requested legal representation but had been told that the court could not wait for them to obtain counsel. They were assured that Ensign Drury, as judge advocate, would protect their interests, but he had never cross-examined a single witness from Arnold's vice squad. When courts-martial had finally been held, most witnesses had not even appeared in person. Their earlier statements were merely read into the record, allowing no opportunity for cross-examination.

Several prisoners told how they had been mistreated. Frank Dye complained that evidence against him had been "created" by Arnold's men; neither he nor his lawyer had an opportunity to challenge the truth of their testimony. He also complained of having been held in solitary confinement from his April 8 arrest until his court martial October 13. Dye and several others accused Lt. Brown, commander of the provost's guard, of dragging them from bed in the middle of the night to "ply them with questions" to exact confessions. Fred Hoage charged that Hudson had taken him into a stateroom aboard the U.S.S. *Constellation* and threatened to "make it hard" for his friend Albert Viehl unless he confessed to having had sex with Kent and Green. Several characterized the interrogation of Harrison Rideout as "the third degree," while Rogers told how he had been "coached" to confess before the court. Both Trubshaw and Goldstein accused operators of lying about sex with them, insisted that they had been denied adequate counsel, and complained that opportunities to interrogate their accusers had never been provided.[6]

From Portsmouth, the subcommittee moved to New York for meetings with Dr. Hudson and Chief Machinist's Mate Arnold. Close interrogation of the physician concentrated on his claim that the first phase of the investigation had been authorized and supervised by Drury. Both men denied they had been notified that the order authorizing their activities had been revoked. The only new information came from Arnold, who now argued that by approving the report of the Foster Court of Inquiry, the Navy Department had authorized the use of "spotters" in such investigations.

The Senators also interviewed thirteen members of Section A. Once more, however, the operators declined to detail their sexual activities or identify those persons with whom they "had gone the limit." Such testimony was deemed unnecessary, according to the subcommittee, since written reports in their possession revealed exactly who had done what with whom. No doubt, too, the lawmakers felt as uncomfortable as the sailors in public discussion of homosexual activities.[7]

II

The anti-homosexual scandal received added attention because 1920 was an election year, and many of those associated with the investigation were active in the campaign. Interest increased when the Democratic National Convention in San Francisco chose Assistant Secretary of the Navy Franklin D. Roosevelt as his party's vice presidential standard bearer. As might have been expected, the

Newport episode was a source of considerable embarrassment for
Roosevelt, and no Republican-dominated investigating committee
could be expected to dispose of such a spicy case quickly or quietly
in the midst of an election campaign.

Given his demonstrated antagonism to FDR, John R. Rathom's
vehement criticism of the vice presidential nominee was hardly surprising. The day after the nomination, the *New York Times* lauded
Roosevelt for his "frankness and manliness." Rathom responded
next day that the Democratic nominee was "utterly lacking" in
either characteristic. "His deliberate attempts to cover up the true
conditions existing in the navy Department," continued the *Journal*, "and the lengths to which he has gone in this direction, have
shocked hundreds of naval officers who know the truth." Roosevelt
might attempt to portray himself as a "fine-fibered young man in
public office," but the record was so clear that "neither he nor his
chief [Daniels] dares to take any steps that will bring the facts to
light."[8]

In addition to having authorized the Newport investigation,
Roosevelt was accused of wrong-doing at the Portsmouth Naval
Prison, where several sailors convicted of homosexual offences had
been jailed. The Portsmouth and Newport cases were viewed as
parallel examples of Roosevelt's having endeavored to undermine
attempts by regular navy officers to strengthen discipline. The issue
first surfaced during the summer of 1920 when the *Army and Navy
Journal* printed documents bearing FDR's signature permitting an
allegedly gay Portsmouth "graduate" named Parker to return to
active duty in the navy. Saturday evening, October 23 – just over a
week before the election – Roosevelt was campaigning at Newburg,
New York, when Arthur L. Fairbrother of the *Journal* staff handed
him a letter from Rathom accusing him of reinstating Parker, of
threatening subordinates who were reluctant to follow his orders,
and of having "destroyed or sequestered navy records" to cover up
his action. Copies of the letter were mailed to Republican newspapers nationwide in envelopes bearing the return address of the Republican National Committee. That night Roosevelt contacted the
Journal's Washington bureau chief, Sevellon Brown, to warn that
unless the letter was "killed," Rathom himself would soon see embarrassing materials in the papers he would not like.[9]

Rathom's refusal to back down initiated a series of retaliatory
actions by Democrats. Angry at the carefully planned, politically-
motivated attack, FDR asked the U.S. Attorney for the Southern

District of New York, Francis G. Caffey, to file a libel suit against the Providence publisher. "In view of the fact that the circulation of charges of this character would obviously blacken my character as a candidate for the office of Vice President of the United States," he argued, "I believe that they are not merely libelous but criminally so." "It is almost needless to assure you," he added, "that they are wholly untrue."[10]

Caffey delayed his response until November 5, three days after the national election. After consulting with an associate who specialized in such matters, he concluded that Rathom's letter constituted "no violation of federal law." The only possible violation of a federal statute, he argued, related to the transmission of libelous material, and that law applied only when the material appeared on the outside of a mailed article. Such not having been the case, prosecution was impossible.[11]

Meanwhile, Roosevelt sought other means of counteracting any damage that Rathom's attack might have generated. He notified newspapers across the country that false reports were being circulated about him, described his plans to initiate law suits, and warned that any paper printing the Rathom letter would "do so on its own responsibility."[12] At a Sunday evening meeting with advisors, *Louisville Times* editor Arthur Krock suggested filing charges against the Publicity Bureau of the Republican National Committee. No one expected to win the case, but the suit itself would "demonstrate to the public anew the careless way in which that Committee spread calumny against us."[13] On October 28 Roosevelt announced that he was filing a $500,000 damage suit against Rathom and Republican Party publicists Edward Clark and S. C. Bone for "circulating false and defamatory libel."[14]

Nor was Roosevelt content with legal action. At his behest, U.S. Attorney Caffey made public Rathom's 1918 letter to the Justice Department regarding wartime stories about German spies. This was the document that Ensign Hyneman had tried repeatedly to enter into the record of the Dunn inquiry. Obviously embarrassed by publication of correspondence admitting that tales of spy nests in the U.S. had been fabricated, Rathom accused FDR of attempting to divert attention from charges against himself to gain "some petty political advance on the eve of a presidential election." Caffey characterized the letter as a "confession," but Rathom insisted it had been written only to "protect hundreds of loyal citizens" who had given the *Journal* information about spies. The next day's paper devoted two full pages to demonstrating its patriotism in making known the presence of German espionage agents. Photographs of German officials who had denounced the *Journal* were captioned: "Three men who seemed to know what the Journal did in the war." An accompanying editorial denounced Roosevelt as "the possessor of an immature mind, a shallow thinker on subjects too deep for him, an amateur statesman — and a professional politician." [15]

How much impact these attacks and counter-attacks had on the election of 1920 would be difficult to measure. The Democrats considered the election a referendum on U.S. participation in the League of Nations. Vice Presidential candidates seldom affect elections one way or the other. Nevertheless, when Americans went to the polls on November 2, they favored Republicans Warren G. Harding and Calvin Coolidge by nearly two to one over Democrats Cox and Roosevelt. In the electoral college, the Democrats garnered only 127 votes to the GOP's 404. [16]

If national interest in the Rathom-Roosevelt controversy abated after the election, FDR's hatred of the Providence publisher intensified. Roosevelt employed his former Navy Department secretary, Charles H. McCarthy, to find evidence needed to force Rathom — in Roosevelt's words — to "crawl." A visit with Assistant Attorney General Stewart in early February convinced FDR that it was important to get copies of vital records before a less-sympathetic Republican administration controlled the files. FDR asked McCarthy to employ a stenographer to copy needed materials. "What we want are the main facts," he insisted, "showing that Rathom's life has been a thoroughly disreputable one in almost every part of the globe; that he has left a bad reputation behind him in every place, and that he is in no way to be believed." [17]

Meanwhile, the civil suit proceeded. Roosevelt filed formal documents accusing Rathom, Bone, and Clark of having "published of and concerning the plaintiff . . . false and defamatory libel" for charging that FDR had "prostituted his public office for personal and political advancement regardless of the public interest and had been guilty of falsehood, deception, and other dishonorable conduct." [18] Not even Roosevelt's confidants supported the suit against the Republican publicists, however. Krock pleaded that Bone and Clark be extricated from the case. Both were well-known, respected journalists whom Krock had known as colleagues for years; the Rathom letter had been circulated without their knowledge or consent. Perhaps the matter could be solved by their issuing a statement "disclaiming" the publicity, characterizing the accusations as "wholly unjustifiable," and admitting that their circulation had been "an offense against your [FDR's] standing as a citizen and a man." Roosevelt agreed, and asked the Democrat's chief publicist, Will Hays, to negotiate an acceptable statement with his Republican counterparts.[19]

Withdrawal of the case against Rathom could not even ben considered, however. Roosevelt employed former Judge Clarence Shearn from New York to represent him in the case and explained in a detailed 3-page letter his perspective on the case. Accusations that he had "destroyed or sequestered or removed" files from the Assistant Secretary's office were wholly untrue;' while some men convicted of "scandalous conduct" or even "moral turpitude" had been returned to duty, this had been done carefully, on a case-by-case basis, on the recommendation of responsible navy officers. The only practice changed under Daniels' administration was that youngsters convicted of minor charges were given "sufficient chance to make good." Roosevelt also found so many numerous "direct and veiled attacks" that the entire letter was "a libel in itself." Not merely a formal apology but a "complete retraction of everything said in the whole letter" would be necessary before the matter could be settled.[20]

As the case against Rathom proceeded, Roosevelt recognized the need for more detailed information on the Portsmouth case; through his trusted personal secretary and confidant, Louis Howe, he asked Charles McCarthy to review the Navy Department's records to identify every man whom Roosevelt had released from prison. Many of the 127 cases involved minor charges or non-sexual crimes like felony; those related to homosexuality revealed the degree to which sailors had engaged in same-sex activities not only at Newport but elsewhere in the Navy as well.

The most famous case raised by Rathom involved a Chief Petty Officer named Parker whom four men accused of suggesting, attempting, or performing sex with them. As in the Newport case, strong evidence was lacking: testimony was uncorroborated, months separated alleged incidents and accusations, and sailors charged with being gay had punished or "bawled out" their accusers. "I am positive," concluded McCarthy, "that Parker never could have been convicted in any Criminal Court where the evidence against the accused must be preponderant. . . ."[21]

Parker's case had come to the attention of the Navy Department through Commander Thomas Mott Osborne, a wealthy New York reformist politician who had led anti-Tammany Hall forces in the state. Because of his success as warden at New York's Sing Sing prison, Osborne had been appointed to run the Portsmouth facility over the objections of senior navy officers who preferred professional military direction. Osborne had based his activities on the premise that the war effort benefitted most when as many men as possible returned to the fleet rather than serve long sentences or face dishonorable discharge. Under his direction, two-thirds of Portsmouth's 6,000 convicts returned to active duty.[22] After reviewing Parker's case, Osborne concluded that the conviction was dubious and reported that in prison he had "shown himself to be most efficient and of excellent character." Clemency would allow him to contribute to the war effort. Roosevelt agreed, and signed the needed papers remitting the remaining portion of his sentence with the provision that his future conduct warrant continued retention in the navy.[23]

Such opinions were not, however, universal. The Parker file reaching Roosevelt included a letter from Captain Leigh (who had also encouraged Arnold and Hudson at Newport) "emphatically protesting against the restoration of a man convicted of moral turpitude."

Further investigation of the case proved difficult because McCarthy found Parker's personnel jacket missing and learned that it had been locked in the desk of Lt. Commander James Barry. What made this discovery important was that Barry's father, David, currently Sergeant of Arms in the U.S. Senate, had been the Washington representative of the *Providence Journal* and was the father-in-law of the *Journal*'s capitol reporter, Sevellon Brown. McCarthy suspected that the file would disappear until Rathom and his friends found it convenient to present it in court. Perhaps Roosevelt could ask Barry's superior, Commander Enochs, reportedly a good friend of the former Assistant Secretary, to retrieve the missing file for review.[24]

The ultimate disposition of the Rathom lawsuit is somewhat of a mystery. A review of legal documents by *Providence Journal* historians revealed that the suit never reached the calendar of the New York court in which it had been filed.[25] Rathom's attorneys "indicate[d] a disposition to discuss matters," but the paper never retracted its accusations, so an amicable settlement seems unlikely."[26] Most likely, Roosevelt's preoccupation with the Senate's forthcoming report on the Newport affair overrode his concerns about Portsmouth during the spring and early summer, after which serious illness diverted his attention from the entire matter.

III

Not until after the election, on February 20, 1921, were hearings resumed. Rhode Island state senator Max Levy's testimony revealed the intense political partisanship now associated with the investigation. He emphasized the injustice done sailors convicted with evidence previously presented to a court of inquiry, thus depriving them of any opportunity to confront and cross-examine accusers. ". . . the procedure which took place at Newport regarding the trials of these boys," Levy insisted, ". . . [seems] to be unfair and unjust, not only to them but to every American citizen. . . ." Moreover, why send boys to prison for acts that required medical attention? In one case, he noted, one of the "greatest authorities on mental diseases," after examining a gay sailor, recommended hospitalization. "That boy," he reported, "notwithstanding the testimony of the doctor, was sent away for 30 years." What was worse, according to the senator, sailors had not been allowed counsel when they requested it and had "made fool[ish] admissions" based on advice from the judge advocate. Several, including Stephen Brugs, had been subjected to "third degree" methods in attempts to force confessions. The entire investigation, he concluded, had been "wrong from beginning to end."

Senator King admitted that events at Newport together with cases in the army suggested the need to change the military justice system. He objected to having youngsters branded as criminal perverts "as some of these boys have been branded." King would not agree that evidence from a court of inquiry ought to be excluded at a court martial, however, and supported this position by citing precedents reaching back to English chancery law. Levy refused to relent in his contention, though, and as the *Journal* reported, "for 30 minutes the United States and the State Senators were at it hot and heavy." Finally, King picked up his hat, put on his coat, and left the hearing room "in a rather abrupt manner." On the way out, he denounced Levy's statements as unfair; the Rhode Islander replied with exactly the same words. Senator Ball adjourned the hearings until early March, noting as he did so that the committee had "stirred up something" and collected "a lot of facts."[27]

Meanwhile, Franklin Roosevelt maintained his interest in the naval scandal despite having departed from government service. The earliest reports of the Senate investigation indicated that he and Daniels would be given an opportunity to testify. In mid-July Edward Britton, the Washington correspondent for Daniels' *Raleigh News and Observer*, learned from Senator King that the subcommittee Republicans were about to issue a report making "libelous and scandalous statements" concerning the former Secretary and Assistant Secretary.[28] King needed help in preparing a rebuttal, but learned that FDR was vacationing at his retreat off the Maine coast. Telegrams flashed between Daniels in Raleigh, Howe in Washington, and Roosevelt urging immediate action. "Committee ready to report Monday on Newport[.]" warned Daniels, "Libelous report of majority . . . can you go [to] Washington at once."[29]

Roosevelt telegraphed Chairman Ball demanding a chance to testify before any report was issued on the basis that such an opportunity had been promised at the time of his informal appearance months before; he volunteered to come to Washington as soon as possible. Ball contended that Roosevelt had ample opportunity to explain his side of the matter to the Dunn Court of Inquiry; since the committee had a full transcript to consult, he "did not think it necessary to take further testimony." He could not recall any promise, but agreed to hear Roosevelt on Monday the 18th of July at 10:00 a.m. if he wished to appear. "Don't believe delay will be granted."[30]

When FDR appeared at the appointed hour, he recognized the impossibility of responding convincingly given the voluminous record before the committee. He had never been shown, for example, a transcript of his earlier February 12, preliminary testimony, "a courtesy usually extended to Assistant heads of Departments." Nor did he know what later witnesses had said, and he had never reviewed the full transcript from the Dunn court. He complained that the committee had taken 18 months to study the case, yet he was given only nine hours, until 8:00 that evening, to prepare a statement.[31] To make matters worse, at 4:00 that afternoon he learned that copies of the report had already been distributed to the press for release at 1:00 the next afternoon. Thus, he concluded, the committee's July 5 draft "would not be changed in any way no matter what my testimony might be."[32]

"I worked very hard up to 8 p.m.," Roosevelt wrote Eleanor, "then went before them with a statement covering every misstatement in their report and another statement of objections on the ground that they had twice used bad faith—also a request for 'various' findings all borne out by uncontradicted testimony."[33]

Roosevelt's defense in both a 13-page handwritten analysis of the committee report and in a typed, 17-point rebuttal rested almost entirely on claims that decisions regarding the Newport case had been made on the recommendation of or with the concurrence of senior navy officers. Captain Campbell, Admiral Oman, Commander Mayo, Admiral Clark, Admiral Wood, and Captain Leigh—not he—should be held responsible. He had not been informed of many activities and was never familiar with details. He had been shown records but never read them. "It never has been and never will be the proper duty of the Assistant Secretary of the Navy to read detailed files," he argued, "unless and until they come before him for final action." The only reason Section A had been placed under his office was because the Bureau of Navigation lacked funds and leaks were feared. "Any other construction of the order to keep the investigation confidential is a deliberate misrepresentation."

In sum, Roosevelt argued that he had never authorized the use of entrapment: "At the time I had not the slightest suspicion that improper methods had been or would be used," he argued

> and there is not the slightest evidence to show this. I willingly go on record as stating that knowing only what I knew then and having the recommendations of . . . [many senior navy officers], and believing, as we all did, that all other means had failed, I would of course do exactly the same thing again. So I believe would any of this subcommittee if you were anxious to protect American boys from the liquor, drug, and sexual evils that existed in Newport.[34]

IV

As Roosevelt anticipated, the report issued by the Republican majority (Ball and Keyes) contained the most detailed analysis of the Newport sex-squad's activities ever made public together with a strongly worded rebuke of nearly every navy official associated with it. It is still the only readily available account of the affair and, as such, is the standard source for information about the scandal. The thirty-seven page printed document approved by the full Naval

Affairs Committee and issued by the Senate July 19, 1921, provided a general background to the case, discussed each of John Rathom's seven charges, summarized the navy investigations, rendered conclusions about the case, and recommended ways to prevent recurrence of such events. An appendix listed each sailor convicted of homosexual activities and detailed the disposition of cases.

The arrival of so many young men at Newport during the war, the Senators observed, required that many seek lodging in unsupervised boarding houses off base. Recruits inevitably included, as the lawmakers put it, boys "whose moral character was not of the highest." Moreover, a navy town naturally attracted immoral people "plying their nefarious trades." Amidst such an environment Ervin Arnold, an "aggressive, uneducated" man "of the bulldog type," began investigating homosexuality; with the cooperation and endorsement of Dr. Hudson, Assistant Secretary Roosevelt, and Secretary Daniels, operators soon received instructions to "go forth into Newport and to allow immoral acts to be performed upon them, if in their judgment it was necessary for the purpose of running down and trapping certain specified alleged sexual perverts." While such conditions were a "menace to both the health and morale of sailors," sending "mere boys" into a city to practice immorality was, according to the committee, "utterly shocking to the American standard of morality. . . ." That any government official permitted such activities was "absolutely indefensible and to be most severely condemned."

The sailor-sleuths had suffered serious effects from such activities. Sexual encounters at which "seasoned veterans . . . shuddered" had been "practically forced upon boys who, because of their patriotism and the patriotism of their parents, had responded to the call of the country to defend their flag and their homes." Expecting such youngsters to show mature judgment and restraint in sexual matters "of this revolting character" was at least "questionable."

In pursuit of information about the investigations, Senators Ball and Keyes had visited Newport, Portsmouth, and New York in addition to hearing witnesses at Washington. Transcribed testimony from thirty men filled 650 pages.

Having reviewed testimony and exhibits provided by the Dunn inquiry, they raised especially serious questions about the conclusions of those who reviewed Admiral Dunn's findings. The inquiry had judged Roosevelt's actions "unfortunate and ill-advised," but Daniels had disapproved this interpretation and vindicated his aide. The Navy Secretary also reversed a recommendation that sailors never again be utilized to investigate immorality.

The committee's conclusions were far stronger than those of Admiral Dunn's court of inquiry. "Franklin D. Roosevelt's action was not only 'unfortunate and ill-advised,' but most reprehensible." Daniels' disapproval was "severely criticized." Furthermore, "naval officials who at any stage . . . even permitted or approved the use of enlisted personnel for such [immoral] purposes can not be too severely criticized and condemned from a moral standpoint."[35]

Because the seven allegations made by the *Providence Journal* covered most major issues raised in the course of the investigation, the committee evaluated them one at a time. First, sailors had been "compelled under specific orders . . . to commit vile and nameless acts" on other sailors or had "suggested these acts be practiced upon themselves." The Senators had learned that in all 41 sailors had been involved; ten were aged 16 to 19, the remainder (except Arnold) between 21 and 32. After having been issued Naval Intelligence identification cards, the men had been ordered to special duty in Newport, where they had "permitted the basest of vile acts" to be performed on them. Specific orders required them to frequent places and make friends with people to encourage the commission of perverse acts; each was to use his own judgement as to how far to go. "It is unfortunately necessary," the senators reported, "to state that in some cases the men used their 'judgment' and 'discretion' and allowed to be committed upon themselves the most vile and unnameable acts."

Second, victims had been identified by Hudson and Arnold, who claimed the ability "to recognize degenerates by the way they walk along the streets." Investigators concluded that certain individuals were indeed selected upon whom to focus attention, that they had been followed, and that operators had provided them ample opportunities "to commit lewd and immoral acts—in other words they were trapped within the police meaning of the word. . . ." Arnold had boasted to the Senators in language that paralleled what he had said to Bishop Perry of abilities to identify homosexuals by sight. Evidence also confirmed that members of Section A had received orders "to commit offenses . . . with the men selected for this persecution." Instructions had been given "officially" under "written confidential orders" from Roosevelt. Sailors had been told what to do on "duty sheets" they signed.

Rathom charged that both Roosevelt and Daniels knew of these methods for several months, had "been deaf to all appeals for the breaking up of such practices," and had ordered or at least permitted citations commending the operators for "their interest and zeal in their work." As evidence, the committee cited a letter addressed to Attorney General Palmer requesting legal services. Moreover, as Arnold had noted in his testimony, the Navy Department had endorsed the recommendations of the Foster court of inquiry that placed commendatory notations in the operators' personnel files. Attendance at several conferences where details of the investigation were discussed, the establishment of Section A within his office, and a referral of Hudson to government lawyers for advice demonstrated the degree of Roosevelt's participation. "In the opinion of the committee," reported the senators, "it was the grave doubt created even in the sound legal mind of Franklin D. Roosevelt, by virtue of the extraordinary and unusual methods" being used at Newport that led him to recommend obtaining expert legal advice from the Justice Department. Nor was there any doubt that following the complaints of Rev. Hughes, Mr. Webster, and Bishop Perry, Section A continued to exist and that Kent was prosecuted in the federal courts at Providence. Through these activities, the methods used by the anti-gay vice squad had been "given the stamp of approval, of commendation and approbation. . . ."

Fifth, boys "instructed in the details of a nameless vice" had been sent throughout Newport "to entrap certain degenerated individuals" despite complaints about this "iniquitous procedure" directly to Roosevelt and Daniels. The evidence, concluded Keyes and Ball, "will clearly substantiate the committee's belief that this charge is proved."

A sixth allegation accused the navy of using "third degree" methods to secure confessions from sailors and that a representative of Naval Intelligence "declined to enter into any details with regard to its power or its methods." Arnold's testimony showed conclusively that "third-degree" interrogations had been administered to some twenty men, the most prominent of whom was Harrison Rideout. Moreover, Arnold had refused to reveal anything about either the operations of Section A or its methods of interrogation. When interviewed by the Naval Affairs sub-committee, he had "developed a most convenient memory" in which his acts were "enveloped in a smokescreen of hesitancy and doubt." The committee judged the testimony of convicted sailors "more credible" than that of Arnold. "Third degree" methods that might be appropriate to civilian police operations had no place in naval discipline, and any officer who used them should be court martialed and either dismissed from the service or severely punished.

Finally, Rathom charged that servicemen arrested in April 1919 had been confined for months without trial. Protests from Captain Campbell, their friends, and relatives failed to speed up the processing of their cases. Absolutely true, reported the committee, resulting in "great injustice" and "inhuman" treatment for those involved.

This section of the report concluded that all the charges of the Newport clergy and the *Providence Journal* were "justified by the conditions that existed and have been proved." Both deserved "the thanks of the people at large," especially the parents of sailors, for bringing the matter to public attention and helping the Senate gather evidence. As a result, immoral conditions among enlisted personnel at Newport had been "largely eliminated."[36]

Following a list of navy men involved in anti-gay activities and descriptions of their activities, the committee surveyed the work of the Foster Court of Inquiry, traced the sleuthing of Section A, and noted the growth of concern among Newport residents. The committee carefully avoided conclusions related to the "guilt or innocence" of either sailors or civilians. "The committee was not appointed for that purpose," they explained. "It was named only to inquire into the alleged immoral practices of the enlisted personnel at Newport in their efforts to secure evidence against all alleged sexual perverts."

The senators' conclusions stretched to twenty-seven paragraphs filling over seven closely printed pages. They acknowledged the commission of "immoral and lewd" acts by sailors under "orders, instructions, or suggestions" from Arnold and Hudson. That any naval officer could have given such directions was "most reprehensible and beyond comprehension." Daniels and Roosevelt's sanction was a "most deplorable, disgraceful, and unnatural proceeding." Civilians heading the Navy Department had shown "an utter lack of moral perspective" in allowing sailors to testify in Providence "to the beastly acts that had been performed upon them." Any naval official, they concluded, who "should direct, permit, or suggest" that sailor detectives "allow their bodies to be used immorally" to collect evidence was "not a safe person to have charge of enlisted personnel in the Navy." "It is inconceivable that anyone in the Naval Establishment could countenance such proceedings as took place at Newport." Whether the men were told to be passive or not was immaterial; what mattered was that "the moral code of the American citizen" had been violated; ultimately, "the rights of every American boy who enlisted in the Navy to fight for his country" had been "utterly ignored." It was doubtful if "such an immoral condition" could be found anywhere in "the annals of the United States Navy."

Nearly every aspect of Section A's operation was found wanting. Leaders were wholly unqualified and inexperienced, "a totally unknown Navy doctor and an equally unknown petty officer." Arnold was "in no manner fitted to be in charge of men of any kind." Conceding that some of the youngsters who volunteered as operators were themselves homosexual, the committee preferred to believe that most were naive schoolboys "practically forced into this duty because of their ignorance of naval procedure and civil law and their mental perspective regarding the obedience of any order given them by their superior." Thus they, too, became victims, sent "forth into Newport . . . as a sacrifice to, and the prey of, every degenerate and sexual pervert" in the vicinity.

Once the investigation got under way, no one halted it or considered other means by which the same objectives could have been achieved. A better alternative, concluded the Senators, would have been "the arbitrary wholesale discharge of suspected perverts" from the navy. Similarly, "every suspected civilian pervert, male or female" could have been expelled from Newport. Such action would have been preferable to placing even one sailor "in the position of allowing his body to be polluted—a crime perpetrated upon him which he will remember and regret to his dying day."

The Republican lawmakers reserved their strongest condemnation for Roosevelt and Daniels. Any reasonable man attending one of several Navy Department conferences about the Newport investigation would have recognized the methods used to apprehend suspects. And even if they had not, Roosevelt's failure to inquire about the means to collect evidence constituted "derelic[tion] in the performance of his duty." Roosevelt's requests for legal advice from the Justice Department and orders that a communication to Admiral Niblack be kept "wholly secret" were especially incriminating.

While neither FDR nor Daniels might have been "officially informed" in writing of what occurred, undoubtedly they had knowledge through informal sources "as the ordinary layman has it."

The report concluded with specific charges against nearly everyone associated with the investigation. Hudson's actions as squad leader were "shameful and disgraceful;" he "showed an utter lack of moral responsibility from the beginning to the end of the entire investigation." Justice required that he be court-martialed and excluded from the service. Arnold was not only totally unqualified to command young men, but his morals were "entirely warped." A desire to become a "great detective," a modern Sherlock Holmes, led him to sacrifice the morals of his men and to blame others for his own shortcomings. "It is the sense of the committee," continued the report, "after hearing Arnold testify, that he is not the character of man which adds to the high standing of the personnel of the United States Navy. . . ." The service would be better off if "Ervin Arnold's name [were] stricken from the roster of the Navy."

Ensign Hyneman, who served as judge advocate during the Dunn inquiry, received severe criticism for attempts to prove the ministers' charges were "not technically accurate." These clergymen were not lawyers and had not prepared their letter to President Wilson so it could be "scrutinized with a judicial microscope." Indeed, the Newport clergymen were "public-spirited citizens" whose only objective was calling attention to objectionable conditions. Nevertheless, Hyneman had devoted days to "vigorous, searching, grueling cross-examination" with the singular objective of denigrating their charges and challenging their facts. All the while, transcripts from the Foster court in Dunn's possession "amply proved all the charges [the ministers had] made."

Such an approach inevitably precipitated contradictory conclusions in the Dunn court's report. On one hand, Arnold and Hudson had been cleared of claiming "the unusual power of detecting sexual degenerates on sight" while the very next finding lauded their ability to "form an opinion as to whether a man was a degenerate." "This is one of many instances of the judge advocate . . . straining to differentiate between tweedledee and tweedledum," noted the Senators. Furthermore, Hyneman and members of the Dunn court had utilized "petty red tape procedure" to defend navy men to avoid "real justice" while at other times "waving aside all recognized rules of evidence in order to admit something against" the complainants.

Still greater injustice had resulted from exceptional delays in transcribing reports of the Dunn inquiry and transmitting them through channels to Secretary Daniels. No civilian associated with the scandal remained in office; Hudson and Arnold had left the navy. The Senators made it clear that nothing in their report could "in any manner touch or affect the [current Republican] personnel of the department or the naval service as at present constituted" and emphasized that malfeasance extended to only a tiny proportion of all officers and men in the navy; none of those involved had undergone the "regular training" required of naval officers.

The report concluded with two major policy recommendations. In the first place, the treatment of sailors accused of homosexuality revealed serious deficiencies in the naval justice system. Regulations required men to be charged with specific crimes at the time of their arrest, yet sailors had been jailed for months without being charged, a situation the lawmakers labeled "outrageous and inhumane." Moreover, it was wrong for a man to be convicted without confronting and cross-examining those who testified against him. To right the wrongs already done, Page and Keyes recommended the release of everyone confined at Portsmouth. Furthermore, existing procedures made it impossible for reviewing authorities to conduct speedy, thorough analyses of each case. "Some change," the report suggested, "should be made in the procedure." Sailors appearing before courts of inquiry should have counsel to represent them instead of having to rely on the fairness of a judge advocate.

Last, Keyes and Ball favored a prohibition against ever using enlisted personnel to investigate perversion. A better approach would be the immediate, undesirable discharge of suspected gays. The senators modified this idea by noting that "perversion is not a crime on one sense, but a disease that should be properly treated in a hospital."[37]

The printed report made no mention of how Senator King's conclusions differed from those of his Democrat colleagues, but the day after release of the majority report, a document representing his views was submitted to the Senate and released to the press. Several days earlier, as soon as he had seen the majority manuscript, King realized he needed expert assistance in preparing a rebuttal. He sought out Roosevelt, but learned of his absence at Campobello. Ultimately it was FDR's assistant, Louis Howe who urged Roosevelt to come immediately to the capital. In the meantime, Roosevelt was to ask Hyneman to meet Howe and King in the latter's Senate office Friday at 10:00 a.m.[38] Roosevelt joined them as soon as he reached the capital. The minority report King signed came from a draft filled with corrections and amendments in Roosevelt's handwriting; the replacement of a "me" (referring to Roosevelt] with "him" strongly suggests that the document had been drafted by the former Assistant Secretary. The only known copy is in the Roosevelt Library. After reviewing the minority report, Daniels observed to Roosevelt that he "could see that you had furnished him some data." Moreover, much of FDR's correspondence during the week is on U.S. Senate stationery undoubtedly provided by King.[39]

King complained that "many particulars" in the majority report were "unjust and unfair." "Deductions are drawn," he continued,

> which are entirely unwarranted and conclusions permitted which find no real or substantial basis in the testimony. The report contains innuendoes and implications calculated to convey inaccurate and erroneous conclusions and, which will inevitably confuse the reader and compel unjust and false judgments with respect to the persons and the subject matter to which they refer. Important items of testimony are exaggerated and positive and unimpeachable testimony ignored. The result is that the majority report fails in my opinion to fully and fairly present the situation.

King's strongest disagreements came over the roles of Roosevelt and Daniels. The entire affair, he insisted, had been carried out "without the knowledge of either of the navy department chiefs." Those responsible were not the appointive civilian leaders in the department but the many senior officers whose "knowledge of conditions in Newport" exceeded that of Roosevelt and Daniels. "The inferences and statements and innuendoes that Mr. Roosevelt and Mr. Daniels knew of these methods," explained the Utah Mormon, "are wholly without justification and do a great injustice to the persons mentioned." He could not spare FDR all responsibility, however: "I believe that the officers referred to [Captain Leigh and the Judge Advocate General] erred in recommending or approving the use of enlisted personnel," he wrote, "and I also believe that Mr. Roosevelt erred in adopting and approving their recommendations." After citing numerous other examples where Daniels and Roosevelt's roles had been distorted or misrepresented, the minority report concluded that the majority's opinion was characterized by "a pronounced bias unwarranted by the evidence" against the pair. "Testimony favorable to them seems to be ignored," he argued, "and evidence which is so attenuated and innocuous as to be of no weight or importance . . . is clothed with a potency not warranted and treated as important if not controlling in reaching conclusions upon the vital issues in the case."[40]

V

Reaction to the Senate report was as intense as it was predictable. The issue of the *Providence Journal* for July 20 featured banner headlines across the entire front page: "SENATE NAVY COMMITTEE REPORT SUSTAINS CHARGES MADE BY PROVIDENCE JOURNAL BEFORE U.S. SENATE" Three pages summarized the majority report with segments condemning Roosevelt receiving major attention. A less detailed account issued by the Associated Press appeared on the front page of nearly every American newspaper.[41]

Roosevelt considered issuing a press release and prepared one dated the 18th from the Shoreham Hotel in Washington for release the following afternoon. He accused the committee of "breach of faith," and confessed that his testimony was of "no possible use" in changing the report. "All this shows a premeditated and unfair purpose," he concluded, "of seeking what they mistakenly believe to be a partisan political advance."

"None of this worries me," the prepared release continued, "nor does the report itself worry me personally. As an American," however, he deplored

> bad faith and a conscious perversion of facts on the part of any Senator. As an American, irrespective of party, one hates to see the United States Navy, an organization of the nation, not of party, used as a vehicle for cheap ward politics. It rather worries me to know that these Republican Senators consider me worth while attacking so maliciously and savagely. Perhaps they may later on learn what a boomerang is.[42]

Roosevelt also prepared a letter, dated at 11:00 a.m. on the 19th, to Senator Page, Chairman of the full Naval Affairs Committee reciting his grievances against the subcommittee. The report was unfair, he claimed, not only because he had been given inadequate opportunity to present his views but Senators Ball and Keyes had engaged in "deliberately improper practices" by securing assistance from Mr. "Fayerbrother" [Arthur Fairbrother], "the agent of the John R. Rathom who made the original charges to the Naval Affairs Committee." Just as soon as he could, Roosevelt intended to file a detailed reply to the committee report. In the meantime, he demanded that Page schedule a meeting of the committee "on which I may be heard in open meeting of the committee, not in a closed hearing."[43]

Roosevelt's strongest language, however, was reserved for Senator Keyes. On July 21, he drafted a letter announcing that after reading the committee report, he wanted to make certain that the Senator "not labor under any misapprehension of any opinion." "I have had the privilege of knowing many thousands of Harvard Graduates," he continued,

> Of the whole number, I did not personally know one whom I believed to be personally and willfully dishonorable. I regret because of your recent despicable action, I can no longer say that.
>
> My only hope is that you will live long enough to appreciate that you have violated decency and truth and that you will pray your Maker for forgiveness.[44]

Ultimately, however, Roosevelt recognized that however much these efforts might be solace for his own anger and frustration, it was impossible to overcome the damage that wide circulation of the Senate report would have to his reputation. ". . . it may seem best to drop the whole thing," he confessed to Eleanor, and do nothing but "file the complete brief and facts with the full Senate Committee and watch what if anything they will do."[45] In the end FDR decided not to mail the letter to Senator Keyes, but admitted his frustration by scribbling on the back of the envelope: "Not sent — what was the use? FDR."[46]

More revealing was a letter Roosevelt addressed to Daniels at the end of July. He had heard nothing from the committee except an acknowledgement of his request for a hearing and doubted that he would. "After all, what is the use of fooling any longer with a bunch who have made up their minds that they do not care for the truth and are willing to say anything which they think will help them politically and haunt their opponents," he observed, adding that Page was "a dear old man" but overly swayed by his partisan colleagues. In his most philosophical observation on the matter, FDR added that "in the long run neither you nor I have been hurt by this mudsling, and it is best to file the whole thing away."[47]

Josephus Daniels, who had retired to his North Carolina home at the end of the Wilson administration, issued no immediate public response. He wrote FDR to congratulate him on his "statesman [like] press statement, which he thought "most of the public" accepted. Only the "Newport crowd" and the "ultra-partisan papers" remained antagonistic. It looked as though the Senators were "firing at us as a target," he concluded, "and they missed every time."[48]

Daniels' autobiography published years later revealed both the depth of his anger and the faultiness of his memory. In a section headed, "Newport needed bitter medicine," he explained how his attempts to clean up the city's "festering places of ill-fame" became objectionable when "the only derelict chaplain of the Navy was found guilty [*sic*] of immoral conduct." (He must have forgotten the Newport and Providence trials.) Bishop Perry had refused to "believe that there was a Judas Iscariot in his church. He should have unfrocked him promptly." For exposing such "rottenness," Daniels conceded he was "not as popular as I desired to be with some laissez-faire officials, and some who wanted a wide-open town for pecuniary reward." He made no mention of the objectionable methods used by Section A and ignored the conclusions of both the Dunn inquiry and the Senate Committee on Naval Affairs.[49]

VI

Interest in the Newport anti-gay scandal subsided quickly, its place in the headlines of the nation supplanted by news of a declining economy and, by early 1922, of widespread corruption in the Harding administration. In fact, the Newport episode had been largely forgotten before any action could be taken to deal with the recommendations of the Naval Affairs Committee. Copies of the minority and majority reports had been sent to the new Secretary of the Navy, Edwin Denby, in late summer or early fall. He requested the Judge Advocate General, Admiral Latimer, to draft a reply to Senator Ball.[50] Not until December 24, 1921, did the Secretary prepare and sign a letter that terminated action regarding the affair.

The use of evidence from courts of inquiry at courts-martial, the secretary reported, was specifically authorized by law "provided oral testimony cannot be obtained." Changing this procedure was "beyond the authority of the department." Nevertheless, naval regulations would be modified so that henceforth defendants and interested parties before courts of inquiry would be warned that evidence presented there might be used against them and advised to obtain legal counsel. This procedure would assure that defendants' rights were "properly guarded." To rectify the wrong already done, on September 3, 1921, Denby ordered five men convicted entirely on the basis of evidence given before the Foster court released: Frank Dye, David Goldstein, Samuel G. Rogers, Harold J. Trubshaw, and Albert H. Viehl were freed with dishonorable discharges from the U.S. Navy a few days later.

The Navy Secretary also accepted the recommendation, rejected by his predecessor Daniels, that in the future enlisted men not be used to investigate immorality and issued an "emphatic order" to that effect. Exceptions applied only aboard ships where civilians obviously could not investigate. He hoped this decision would comply with the spirit of the recommendation and predicted that "no evil will result from continuing the present practice of policing ships of the navy."

The recommendation that sailors suspected of being gay receive immediate dishonorable discharges was not acceptable. Such a policy, as Denby explained it, would allow "innocent and valuable men" to be "ignominiously discharged . . . upon unfounded malicious reports" without the ability to exercise their rights. Moreover, mere discharge without further punishment was so lenient that the navy "would soon be[come] a refuge for perverts, who would have nothing to fear from apprehension."

Finally, the Senate committee had recommended that counsel be routinely provided for accused sailors unable to employ their own attorneys. Existing procedures required the convening authority to appoint counsel whenever requested according to Denby. Changes in naval regulations were ordered, however, so that defendants would be informed of their right to representation and warned that anything said without an attorney present could be used against them. Denby also reiterated the role of the judge advocate as guardian of a defendants' legal rights. This matter was under review, he admitted, and new procedures "which will insure a more certain administration of justice" could be adopted.[51]

Receipt of this letter by Senator Ball ended official proceedings regarding the investigation of homosexuality among the sailors and civilians of Newport.

Henry W. Keyes, Republican Senator from Vermont, headed the congressional investigation of the Newport scandal and earned the antipathy of Roosevelt and other Navy officials.
Credit: National Cyclopedia of American Biography.

The stateroom in the U.S.S. Constellation where sailor Fred Hoage told Senators he had been coerced into testifying against friends.
Credit: *Newport Recruit*, U.S. Naval Historical Center.

Democratic standard bearers James M. Cox (left), and Franklin D. Roosevelt on the campaign trail in 1920.
Credit: Roosevelt Library, Hyde Park.

Sevellon Brown, the *Providence Journal* representative in Washington. Later, as editor of the paper, he became known as the "conscience of New England."
Credit: *Providence Journal*.

ALLEGED IMMORAL CONDITIONS AT NEWPORT (R.I.) NAVAL TRAINING STATION

REPORT

OF THE

COMMITTEE ON NAVAL AFFAIRS
UNITED STATES SENATE

SIXTY-SEVENTH CONGRESS

FIRST SESSION

RELATIVE TO

ALLEGED IMMORAL CONDITIONS AND PRACTICES AT
THE NAVAL TRAINING STATION, NEWPORT, R. I.

Printed for the use of the Committee on Naval Affairs

WASHINGTON
GOVERNMENT PRINTING OFFICE
1921

The U.S. Senate report on the Newport scandal is still the standard source of information.
Credit: Author's collection.

53 WALL STREET
July 21st 1921

Senator Keyes:
Washington. D.C.

Sir: I have had the privilege
of knowing many thousands
of Harvard Graduates. Of
the whole number I did
not personally know one
whom I believed to be
personally and wilfully
dishonorable. I regret that
because of your recent
despicable action I
can no longer say that.

My only hope is that
you will live long enough
to appreciate that you
have violated decency and
truth and that you
will pray your Maker
for forgiveness.

Very truly yours,
Franklin D. Roosevelt

Franklin Roosevelt's anger at the U.S. Senate committee erupted in this angry letter to Vermont Senator Henry Keyes. "I have had the privilege of knowing many thousands of Harvard graduates," wrote Roosevelt. "Of the whole number I did not personally know one whom I believed to be personally and wilfully dishonorable. I regret because of your recent despicable action, I can no longer say that."

"My only hope," he concluded, "is that you will live long enough to appreciate that you have violated decency and truth and that you will pray your Maker for forgiveness."

Ultimately Roosevelt thought better of his actions and never mailed the letter.

Credit: Roosevelt Library, Hyde Park.

The day following release of the Senate's report condemning the Navy for the Newport affair, the *Providence Journal* trumpeted its triumph in a story that covered most of the first page and continued at length inside the paper.

Credit: *Providence Journal* copy from UMI

Edwin Denby, Daniels' successor as Secretary of the Navy, freed many of those convicted at Newport.
Credit: World's Work.

CHAPTER 13

Legacies

We now know as much as can probably ever be known about the U.S. Navy's campaign against homosexuals at Newport. As often happens in complex and controversial historical incidents such as this, even with massive documentation available, differences in perception, personal or professional prejudice, faulty memory, and intentional or inadvertent misstatements cloud reality. Moreover, the lenses through which we observe these past events lack sufficient perspective to place them in precisely the correct context. Nevertheless, the impact of the scandal on those who participated in it can be measured; most important, the Newport anti-gay campaign provides perspectives on the emergence of a self-conscious gay community in the United States and on the persecution of gay men in America, especially, in the U.S. Navy.

I

A considerable number of sailors and civilians in Newport during World War I were homosexuals who sought the company of others like themselves. This is not surprising to those who have assumed that some proportion of the population in all societies during every era has been attracted to their own sex. The Newport case may be startling, however, to individuals who date the emergence of homosexuality-identifying men to more recent periods or who associate homosexuality with recent alterations in traditional sexual values.[1] Moreover, the gay population of Newport spanned classes, occupations, races, and geographic origins, representing a cross-section of American males.

Of greater importance, among both sailors and civilians, homosexual men had begun to develop the trappings of a distinctive so-

cial group. They shared similar dress, used a distinctive vocabu-
lary, and joined together for social activities, not all of which were
explicitly sexual. They identified with one another not merely as
sailor-buddies or friends but as individuals whose sexual orientation
set them apart from others in society. The Newport scandal thus
provides the first detailed documentary evidence in America of a
distinctive homosexual community; from these small beginnings
one of the most important social rights movements of the twentieth
century—the gay rights struggle—may trace its origins.[2]

The Newport scandal poses an historical dilemma, for the rich,
complex gay society described by navy operators and accused sailors seems to spring full-born without antecedents. The language,
customs, dress, and other social characteristics revealed among gay
men in Newport had to have developed gradually over the previous
decades, yet almost nothing is known about gay life in America
before Newport.[3] Although the process of tracing and explaining the
evolution of homosexual activities and a gay consciousness that emerged publicly in Newport during World War I has just begun, a
number of explanations are possible.

Several students of gay American history have suggested that
service in the military provided a unique opportunity for homosexuals, especially those from conservative and rural areas, to meet
others who shared their orientation and to begin enjoying the pleasures of gay life.[4] These men seldom returned to their rural homes;
following discharge, they moved to a large city where extensive
homosexual communities developed. While most studies have focused on World War II in bringing together groups of gay men,[5]
much the same phenomena—perhaps to a lesser degree—may have
occurred in America, as it did in Europe, during World War I. Thus
far efforts to document similar occurrences during the U.S. Civil
War or the Spanish American War have been unsuccessful.[6]

Other historians have emphasized the gradual emergence during
the late 19th century of a body of medical and psychological literature describing, categorizing, and analyzing homosexual behavior.[7]
Such studies were initiated in Europe, but by the 1880s and 1890s
appeared in American professional journals with increasing fre-
quency. Through them, a generation of physicians began to view
homosexuality as an illness to be "treated" according to established medical practices. Moreover, individuals who recognized

their own characteristics in these descriptions began to identify themselves as gay and to seek the company of like-minded "deviants."[8]

Because many publications existed by World War I, medical literature could reasonably have been cited during the Newport case. In truth, however, such was not the case; the physician most closely involved with the anti-gay campaign, Dr. Erastus Hudson, seemed largely unfamiliar with this body of literature.[9] One is tempted to conclude, therefore, that while such treatises appeared in the professional literature, they had relatively little impact on popular opinion, even among physicians.

Further research and analysis is necessary for a full understanding of the origins of Newport's gay community. Three leads are suggested from the Newport case. First, the zeal with which Arnold pursued gays seems to have evolved from the "purity crusade" that aimed at sweeping nearly every major American city clean of gambling, prostitution, and liquor sales around the turn of the century. Public officials and police forces were pressured to make the pursuit of sin a major priority.[10] The elimination of homosexuality was not a prominent goal in most anti-vice campaigns, but having largely achieved their initial objectives by World War I, moralistic energies may well have been diverted to "perverts." This is certainly a topic requiring further historical investigation.

Second, several sailors arrested at Newport confessed that their initiation into gay life had occurred through connections with the theatre, especially productions in which men played female roles. In Newport itself, a direct connection existed between sailors' transvestite shows and the gay subculture discovered by Arnold's operators. No significant historical work has focused on the development of the "drag" show as a gay institution,[11] but it is tantalizing to suggest that men with a homosexual orientation might have been drawn to such performances and that they might have become a beacon around which homosexuals first congregated.

Third, popular literature from the mid-19th century to World War I included increasingly frequent and frank mentions of homosexuality, usually in a derogatory context. Several witnesses during the Newport hearings who admitted having "heard" about men who enjoyed sex with other males prior to entering the Navy were probably referring to this popular genre. And such writings, widely distributed in cheaply printed editions, may well have had significantly more impact on popular thought than the medical literature distributed through small printings only to physicians.[12]

The Newport scandal reveals the degree to which the arbitrary, irrational hatred of homosexuals known among psychologists as homophobia had become entrenched in American society.[13] Many people then as now believed that because homosexuals constituted a menace to society, the democratic principles and rights common to all Americans should exclude those whose sexual orientation differed from their own. No one in the navy seriously questioned the validity of whatever sinister means seemed necessary to identify "perverts." Entrapment, false promises of endearment and fidelity, the use of mental and physical torture to extract confessions, surveillance of mail and telephone messages, thievery, solitary confinement, and extended jail sentences seemed appropriate for individuals accused of nothing more than sexual intimacy with other, consenting men. Senators who considered themselves liberal justified arbitrarily expelling suspected gays from the armed services or prohibiting their residence in particular towns without so much as a hearing. The most humane observers preferred confinement in mental hospitals which defined drugs, surgery, electric shocks, and even sexual mutilation as "treatment."[14] No one suggested that an individual's sexual orientation was a private manner over which society should exercise no control.

Attitudes toward homosexuals varied considerably in intensity and sophistication. No one was more homophobic than Ervin Arnold, whose crusade against gays became so intense that one is tempted to speculate that some deep-seated inadequacy in his own sex life generated such hatred. Arnold equated gays with murderers, robbers, rapists, drug addicts, and other "fiends." All were criminals whose very existence threatened the purity as well as the future survival of American society! Anyone whose demeanor even hinted at femininity should, therefore, be trailed, entrapped, arrested, confined, and, ultimately, excluded from society.

No less homophobic but more polished was Dr. Erastus Hudson. The majority of individuals, exemplified by Campbell, Drury, Daniels, and Roosevelt, shared a latent revulsion toward homosexuality, though they had never thought seriously about the matter and were unfamiliar with literature exploring the subject. They might even be willing to tolerate gays who kept their sex lives private. In later years FDR had a number of friends or associates who were homosexuals, notably Sumner Welles, and at least once President

Roosevelt restrained himself from using charges of homosexuality against a political adversary.[15]

The attitudes of the New England clergy toward gays gain significance because of the on-going controversy over the compatibility of Christianity and homosexuality. Bishop Perry, Rev. Hughes, and other Newport ministers defended Chaplain Kent because the navy had used execrable methods to entice him into sexual acts. Possibly the operators had lied about having sex with him at all. None of the Biblical references used by contemporary conservative Christians to condemn gays ever came up during their testimony, however, and most reflected a significant level of tolerance, especially toward private sexual activities. Humanity, in their view, required fair-minded, compassionate treatment of all people; entrapment, "third degree" interrogation, or solitary confinement were immoral when used against anyone, even a homosexual.

Nevertheless, nearly every clergyman argued that sex between men was immoral and inevitably polluted the moral character of anyone who partook of such activities. Their sympathies were especially strong, therefore, for operators whose first sexual experiences could well have been with Newport homosexuals. Never, however, did the ministers suggest how society should deal with homosexuals except that counseling might persuade gays to alter their sexual orientation. Nor were they willing to tolerate a gay clergyman: they refused to consider Kent as director of the Seamen's Institute when they heard rumors about his behavior; once the Dunn inquiry ended, Kent never again occupied an Episcopal pastorate.

A more elaborate interpretation has been suggested by a young gay historian, George Chauncey, Jr. He contends that Rhode Island clergy became so intensely interested in the Newport case because the charges against Kent and Green challenged the legitimacy of the "Christian brotherhood" that each of them practiced. "When the Navy charged that Kent's and Green's behavior and motives were perverted," Chauncey argues,

> many ministers feared that they could also be accused of perversion, and, more broadly that the inquiry had questioned the ideology of nonsexual Christian brotherhood that had heretofore explained their devotion to other men. The confrontation between the two groups represented fundamentally a dispute over the norms for masculine gender behavior and over the

boundaries between homosociality and homosexuality in the relations of men.[16]

As stimulating and provocative as such an explanation seems, its acceptance requires further investigation and more evidence than can be derived from the Newport testimony. Additional research regarding the concept of "Christian brotherhood" as it related to masculine roles, bonding among males, and differences between "homosocial" and homosexual behavior will undoubtedly provide the information needed to broaden and clarify Chauncey's thesis.

II

Apart from the significance of the Newport scandal for gay Americans, it reveals important characteristics of U.S. society after World War I. The military has generally been viewed as an authoritarian institution in which decisions made at the top filter down through chains of command for routine implementation at operational levels.[17] Yet exactly the opposite occurred at Newport. As the senators correctly described it, "a totally unknown doctor and an equally unknown petty officer" conceived of an anti-gay campaign, moved upward through the military bureaucracy seeking approval, and carried out their sleuthing activities under the sponsorship of senior navy officials. That a plan developed at this level could have been implemented at all is surprising. It also became clear in the aftermath of events, however, that lines of authority and accountability became so blurred that ultimately no one bore responsibility for what had happened. This made it impossible to place blame or mete out punishment for malfeasance.

Moreover, the investigation following the sex-hunt dramatized the ability of a bureaucracy to protect itself from outside scrutiny. Clergymen who exercised the fundamental constitutional right of petitioning the U.S. President found themselves accused of disloyalty, challenged to justify every word they had written, forced to reveal their private conversations, and threatened with trial and imprisonment for their actions. Government officials transformed those who questioned them into defendants. On the other hand, the navy itself hid secrets behind complex legal machinations; officers and enlisted men refused to answer questions, obfuscated in their testimony, or suffered convenient lapses of memory to avoid revealing embarrassing information. Ultimately, officials charged with malfeasance reviewed recommendations regarding their own behavior. Ordinary citizens seemed helpless in seeing that the truth was fully revealed. Only active involvement by another branch of government, the U.S. Senate, stimulated partially by partisan political considerations, broke through the protective shield in which they navy enshrouded itself.

Developments during the scandal also highlighted the press's important role in defining and publicizing major issues. John R. Rathom had obviously been influenced by the "yellow journalism" of the late nineteenth and early twentieth century. Like newspaper magnates Joseph Pulitzer and William Randolph Hearst, he knew that a good story including drama, personality clashes, and, if possible, sex and intrigue sold newspapers while bringing significant questions to public prominence.[18] The Newport scandal, like the sinking of the battleship *Maine* in Havana harbor, might never have become widely known had stories about it not appeared day after day, month after month, in the *Providence Journal*. No evidence suggests, however, that Rathom fabricated or significantly embellished stories about the anti-gay campaign or, as Roosevelt partisans have sometimes alleged, that the scandal existed only in Rathom's mind.

Events at Newport and the controversy evolving from them reveal how resistant social institutions are to change. True, some individuals may have given greater thought to the rights of homosexuals after learning how they had been persecuted by the government, but nothing which resulted spared gays from continued hatred and persecution. Even the obvious injustices of the naval court system were only slightly modified as a result of Senate recommendations. Navy Secretary Edwin Denby may have been motivated as much by a desire to discredit the previous administration as to make naval procedures more just. As a result, conditions for gay Americans changed little as a result of the controversial sex hunt.

III

The impact of these events on individuals taking part in them can be partially measured. Attempts to locate sailors arrested at Newport or operators who entrapped them have been largely unsuccessful. In all likelihood, none is alive today. They never achieved sufficient prominence to have been listed in standard biographical references or to have had their deaths noted in indexed newspapers.

Most undoubtedly retreated into anonymity either in their home towns or in larger cities where size or the presence of other gays made their lives more tolerable. The two operators about whom information has been found are, perhaps, typical. Harry Smith, a personnel clerk who did no actual investigating, returned to his rural Minnesota home at Brown's Valley where he lived until his death in 1932. "We have pictures of his funeral & coffin being drawn by horses," recalls a relative, " — the biggest military funeral this small [town] (1000 people) had."[19]

Charles B. Zipf, one of the most active operators, testified against Kent and before the Dunn inquiry. He resumed studies at the University of Michigan after the war. He graduated with an M.D. degree in 1924, interned at St. Luke's Hospital in Chicago, and practiced medicine in nearby Freeport, Illinois, until his retirement in 1958. His marriage to Nellie Jones produced one child, Theodore, who practices medicine in Canada. If Zipf spoke of his activities with Section A before his death, neither his son nor second wife, Edna, seem aware of them.[20] Nothing is known of Ervin Arnold's post-war life.

Dr. Erastus Hudson achieved some notoriety after the anti-gay scandal. Following release from naval service, he practiced medicine in New York City while pursuing detective work as a hobby. Development of a technique by which police could take fingerprints from uneven surfaces earned him a post as consultant to the city police department after 1935.[21] Hudson's greatest fame came during the trial of Bruno Hauptman on charges of kidnapping the son of aviator Charles Lindbergh. Hudson testified that his examination of a ladder rail revealed only one nail hole; later, when confronted by a photograph of himself holding a board containing four holes, he admitted his error.[22] Appointment to the medical advisory board of the Federal Trade Commission took Hudson, his wife, and daughter to Washington, D.C., where he died September 17, 1943, at age 55. He is buried in Arlington National Cemetery.[23]

Several who complained about the navy's Newport activities attained added prominence. As rector of Trinity Episcopal Church, Rev. Stanley C. Hughes remained a pillar of Newport through World War II. He was the last individual buried in the Trinity churchyard overlooking Newport harbor.[24] Hamilton Fish Webster continued to be active in civic affairs until his death at age 77 in

1939. His wife, Lina Post Webster, achieved notoriety in 1947 when she legally adopted retired Brigadier General Ralph C. Tobin, whom she had met at Newport during the war. She died in 1951.[25]

Bishop Perry's leadership in Episcopal affairs culminated with election as Presiding Bishop in 1930. During the next decade, he and his wife frequently traveled overseas, especially to study missions. Criticism of a Rockefeller-sponsored report generated considerable controversy within the church. He represented American Anglicans at several conferences in England and, at an international meeting in Switzerland, advocated greater interdenominational cooperation. Perry retired as Bishop of Rhode Island in 1945 and died March 20, 1947. Vindication by the Senate marked the virtual end of John R. Rathom's journalistic career; he underwent surgery for cancer in August of 1922 and lived in virtual seclusion until his death December 11, 1923. Bishop Perry conducted his funeral.[26]

Of all those men victimized by the government's anti-gay crusade, none was more grievously injured than Chaplain Samuel Neal Kent. Following his first arrest and acquittal at Newport, Kent had been temporarily assigned by his mentor, Bishop Phillip Rhinelander, to St. Mary's Parish Church in the village of Warwick, Pennsylvania. From February 7, 1920, until December 17 of that year, he conducted burials, baptisms, and marriages, as well, presumably, as conducting Sunday services. As late as December 19, 1921, he participated in a wedding in the diocesan headquarters at Philadelphia.[27]

Even though Bishops Perry and Rhinelander as well as other Newport clergymen defended Kent publicly, they must have been sufficiently convinced of his homosexuality to disqualify him from future service in the church. From 1921 to 1930 he found employment directing the Chautauqua Association in the Philadelphia suburb of Swarthmore, Pennsylvania.[28] Thereafter, he worked in the New York office of the English Speaking Union of the United States, an organization that encouraged Anglo-American cooperation. He headed a committee promoting relations between American and British towns with the same names, served as assistant editor of the organization's *Common Speech* magazine, and presented talks about various aspects of English life and culture.[29] Kent traveled abroad frequently and following retirement from the Union because of ill-health, served as chaplain and educational director aboard cruise ships, including the S.S. *Belgenland*. He died November 1, 1943, at Daytona Beach, Florida. A church obituary, making no mention of the Newport scandal, identified Kent as "a Mason and unmarried."[30]

Of the most famous participant in the anti-gay episode, Franklin D. Roosevelt, little need be said. The crippling effects of polio proved only a temporary setback, for in 1928 FDR was elected governor of New York. Four years later he captured the Presidency of the United States from Herbert Hoover. His activities over the next twelve years in reshaping the American economy, altering relations between the government and its citizens, and guiding the country through World War II require no detailed discussion, except to note that many of the same administrative skills and deficiencies revealed in his handling of the Newport affairs became evident. He occasionally relied excessively on subordinates, routinely signed papers without reading them, and spoke mistruths when political expediency necessitated. Equally noteworthy, as psychologist C. A. Tripp has pointed out, President Roosevelt "repeatedly went out of his way" to protect homosexuals from discovery and disgrace. Any homophobia manifested in the navy department, according to Tripp, "is sharply at variance with his later attitudes and actions."[31] Roosevelt partisans succeeded for generations in minimizing the significance of the Newport scandal; early biographers seldom mention the incident and accept FDR's explanations. Only in recent years has the incident received prominence among the major episodes in Roosevelt's life.[32]

IV

However much Roosevelt's personal attitudes toward homosexuality may have changed, a hatred of gays remained strong within American society as a whole, especially in the military. Civilians who happened to prefer their own sex lived in constant fear of arrest, public disgrace, imprisonment, or commitment to mental hospitals. The philosophy that no man with homosexual tendencies could be allowed in the military not only persisted but found its way into an increasing number of military regulations. Nevertheless, policies and practices did gradually change. In 1919 Navy Secretary Josephus Daniels had justified the lengthy imprisonment of men convicted of homosexual offences, presumably for punitive rather than rehabilitative reasons. His successor, Edwin Denby, rejected the Senate suggestion that suspected gays be dishonorably discharged on grounds that such "leniency" would encourage homosexual enlistees. Although exact historical details are unknown, sometime over the next two decades, military regulations were modified so that less-than-honorable discharges rather than imprisonment became the norm.[33]

The impact of these changes became evident during World War II. The need for massive, rapid mobilization of men (and women) after Pearl Harbor had much the same impact it had at Newport a quarter century earlier. Many who volunteered or were drafted felt a natural attraction to their own sex, and service in the armed forces provided a convenient opportunity to manifest their preferences. "Servicemen openly cruised each other in the anonymity of crowded bus and train stations, city parks, restrooms, YMCAs, beaches and streets," reports historian Alan Berube. "They doubled up in hotel beds," he continues, "slept on the floor in movie theatres, and went home with strangers when there was no place to sleep."[34]

Treatment differed considerably from what had occurred during World War I. Despite regulations prohibiting the retention of known gays, the Surgeon General's office issued a circular suggesting that homosexual relations be tolerated "as long as they were private, consensual, and didn't disrupt the unit." Witch hunts such as that at Newport were actively discouraged, and officers received warnings against spreading unfounded rumors. Nonetheless, individuals whose sexual desires became too obvious, who were caught in sexual liaisons, or who sought release on grounds they were gay could be given a "discharge without honor," commonly known as a "blue discharge" because of the colored paper on which they were printed.[35] Of 20,620 persons discharged as "constitutional psychopaths" in 1943, only 1,625 were "of the homosexual type." Given estimates that as many as one million gays served in the war, these numbers are remarkable for their smallness. Imprisonment was rarer yet. Many who discovered their gayness during the war later sought refuge in large cities, contributing to the growth of predominantly homosexual communities.[36]

More humane treatment of gay sailors focused renewed attention on procedural issues raised during the World War I scandal but never satisfactorily resolved. Discharges, whether honorable or otherwise, were issued by boards of officers comparable to the courts of inquiry headed by Lt. Commander Foster and Admiral Dunn. As had been the case at Newport, during board hearings the testimony of accusers was not always subject to cross-examination; witnesses did not necessarily have to appear in person. Furthermore, while all branches of the armed services gave accused parties the right to counsel, such a person need not be a lawyer. A Congressional investigation accused the navy of bringing men before administrative boards rather than courts-martial because of the greater likelihood of conviction. As a result of these limitations, Colin Williams and Martin Weinberg have concluded in phrases as applicable today as sixty years ago, "the person accused of homosexual acts or tendencies who appears before such boards can expect small help from them in the face of the way they routinely operate and the prejudice against homosexuals in the armed forces."[37]

At least two incidents reminiscent of the Newport scandal occurred during World War II, and there were likely others which have not yet been chronicled. In one case, the Federal Bureau of Investigation established a house of male prostitution in Greenwich Village, New York, which was staffed by "young, handsome, multilingual, adequately trained homosexual agents." In marked contrast with the Rhode Island investigation, the government's objective was not to entrap gays; instead, foreign sailors entertained in the house provided shipping information of value to American intelligence agencies.[38]

During 1942 Navy Intelligence discovered, placed under surveillance, and later raided what was characterized as a "house of degradation" on Pacific Street in Brooklyn. It had been operated by a middle-aged immigrant named Gustave Beekman and was allegedly frequented by American sailors, local civilians, and foreigners suspected of espionage. The incident gained national attention when the *New York Post*, utilizing journalistic techniques far more sensational that those of Rathom's *Providence Journal*, reported that a prominent U.S. Senator frequented the place. After several days of tantalizing references to "Senator X," the paper identified him as Democrat Thomas I. Walsh of Massachusetts, chairman of the Naval Affairs Committee. Coincidentally, Walsh had served on the committee during its investigation of the Newport affairs and had written the Navy Department on behalf of imprisoned sailor Wade Stewart Hervey.[39] An FBI report raised the possibility that a New England physician who frequented the house could have been mistaken for Walsh. Senator Alben Barkley distorted these conclusions in a speech claiming that Walsh had been exonerated that he read on the floor of the U.S. Senate May 20, 1942. Later publicity blamed the exposé on liberal politicians and journalists eager to blemish the reputation of an isolationist conservative.[40]

A lessened need for fighting men coupled with greater societal pressures toward conformity stimulated a resurgence of virulent homophobia in the military after World War II. In 1946 a War Department circular more liberal than any before allowed homosexuals who had not committed sexual offences in the service to receive honorable discharges. Three years later, however, spurred by claims that gays constituted serious security risks in the government, the military promulgated a harsher policy classifying homosexuals according to what "offences" they had committed and further restricting access to honorable discharges. The navy maintained itself as the most aggressively homophobic branches of the military. Between 1950 and 1965, 17,392 sailors received undesirable discharges because of their sexual preference; this number accounted for nearly forty percent of all less-than-honorable discharges and was significantly higher than in any other service.[41]

Explaining the navy's persistent discomfort with homosexuality is difficult. Maritime traditions often associated close confinement of men aboard ships for long periods with homosexuality; indeed, aboard Spanish galleons, English naval vessels, and Caribbean pirate ships, same-sex intimacies were common. Myths even circulated that ships bouncing about at sea aroused the sexual passion of sailors and stimulated approaches to shipmates.[42]

Publicity given episodes like that at Newport only increased the navy's obsession with rooting out gays. As a result, detailed regulations prevented situations where men would come into close proximity with one another, and naval police devoted considerable energy to tracking down suspects. When someone is identified as gay, according to C. A. Tripp, "it is not unusual for him to be treated as a real criminal and dealt with in shabby and illegal ways." Moreover, the navy consistently acts against enlisted men and even officers on the basis of nothing more than idle gossip.[43]

The iniquity of navy procedures in our own day is demonstrated by the case of Ensign Vernon E. Berg III. A naval academy graduate with a perfect performance record and an attractive personality, he was stationed at a U.S. Navy base in Italy during the mid-1970s when rumors of his relationship with a civilian teacher reached senior officers. With almost no concrete evidence to support his accusations, the ship's executive officer demanded Berg's resignation and ordered him off the ship within fifteen minutes' notice. "There's no place in the navy for people like you," he shouted.

Thereafter, as at Newport, the government martialed its resources and manipulated procedures against Berg. When he chose to withdraw his forced resignation and demand reinstatement, a board of officers remarkably similar in composition and prejudice to those at Newport half a century earlier heard the case. Denied adequate time to prepare and forced to depend on a civilian attorney unfamiliar with navy procedures, Berg faced a navy lawyer every bit as antagonistic as Ensign Hyneman. Moreover, accusers provided testimony in writing so they could not be cross-examined, and the navy refused to bring character or defense witnesses from overseas stations to the hearings. Much evidence came from an anonymous informant.

The one difference between Berg's case and those in Newport was that he admitted being homosexual. He denied, however, specific acts with which he was charged and argued that because of an outstanding performance record, he should be allowed to remain in the service. Given the tradition of homophobia within the navy, the board's recommendation could hardly have been surprising: Ensign Berg was "separated from the naval service . . . under other than honorable conditions." He subsequently lost all military benefits and was denied eligibility for unemployment compensation. Only the fear that Berg's suit in federal court would prove successful, perhaps forcing the navy to retain homosexuals on a routine basis, persuaded senior Washington officials to award Berg an honorable discharge in mid-1977. The upgrade "undoes some injustice," noted a *New York Times* editorial; "the central question, whether the armed forces are wise to exclude homosexuals, remains unaddressed."[44]

V

While the treatment of gay soldiers and sailors improved gradually during this century, civilians continue to be fair prey for the kind of entrapment practiced by Arnold's operators. Police routinely frequent locations where gays can be found, make friends, and wherever possible accept invitations to engage in sexual activities. Arrest follows, sometimes after the investigator has enjoyed intimacy with his victim. Where entrapment involves a single individual, questions about the truthfulness of the arresting officer inevitably arise.[45]

Twentieth century American history is replete with examples of widespread campaigns against gays. Soon after World War II, the FBI staked out bars frequented by gays across the country and compiled massive lists of persons frequenting them. Such establishments were often raided, those present arrested, and the place closed for minor violations of liquor laws. Under pressure from Wisconsin Senator Joseph R. McCarthy (himself suspected of being homosexual), hundreds of alleged homosexuals were fired from positions in the federal government. In Boise, Idaho, efforts by local politicians to embarrass reformist city officials stimulated an anti-gay witch-hunt in 1955. Under the direction of an outside investigator, police enticed men into sexual situations; individuals were promised leniency if they cooperated by naming others. Local newspapers fanned the fires of hatred, emphasizing age differences among those arrested and speculating that an organized "ring" of "perverts" existed. As hundred of individuals were rounded up and interrogated about their sex lives, every gay who could left town. Some were pursued across the country, arrested, and returned for trial. Evidence against many was so weak that police and court officials agreed to light sentences in exchange for guilty pleas. Nonetheless, publicity surrounding their arrests devastated the lives of numerous individuals.[46]

New England was the venue for at least two major campaigns. The arrest of several Smith College professors in 1960 on charges of possessing pornography precipitated a series of widely publicized events, including the arrest of additional suspects. Newspaper articles suggested that "rings" of gays preyed on children. Ultimately, even though the convictions of several men were overturned on appeal, numerous careers were destroyed.[47] As recently as 1978, Boston officials conducted a witch-hunt that included raids in search of pornography and accusations that men engaged in sex with boys; more than a hundred individuals were entrapped by police in the Boston Public Library. Few cases ever went to trial, for most of the accused pleaded guilty to lesser charges and paid fines or were placed on probation. Rather than flee the city or denounce their friends, the city's homosexual community actively supported those arrested and publicized the injustice perpetrated by officials.[48]

How comforting it would be to view the Newport scandals of 1918-21 as a relic of history, reflecting a particularly dark period in the American past but irrelevant to the present. Unfortunately, however, to do so would be dangerously naive. Homophobia is so deeply ingrained in American society that the persecution of gays continues to be the rule rather than the exception. Within both military and civilian life, homosexuals have repeatedly suffered from harassment and entrapment. And while it would be nice to imagine that our society has become sufficiently enlightened that greater tolerance can be expected in the future, such is unlikely to be the case. Panic related to the spread of Acquired Immune Deficiency Syndrome (AIDS) among homosexuals has stimulated "queer bashing" incidents across the country, along with increasing discrimination in employment, housing, insurance, and health care. As much as we might like to pretend otherwise, in recent years self-righteous Christian zealots have exhibited a homophobia as harsh and unreasoning as that of Ervin Arnold. As such groups gain influence in the country, gays rightly fear a resurgence of persecution.

VI

In Newport, much has changed in the seventy years since the great homosexual scandal. The presence of the navy greatly diminished after closure of the Naval Training Station in the 1960s left only the Naval War College and the naval hospital operating. Sailors no longer crowd seaside docks in search of entertainment, and most businesses that catered to them have closed. In their place, a myriad of restaurants, condominiums, and hotels serve affluent visitors from Boston or New York. Along Belleview Avenue, the mansions that made Newport famous retain their stately grandeur, although many are maintained only through the sale of admissions tickets to tourists. The highly publicized trial of Klaus Von Bulow once again focused national attention on America's most historic luxury resort. Newport remains a city of churches: the spire of Trinity Episcopal Church dominates the skyline; and most other churches utilize the same buildings as in 1920. On Washington Square, the court house where Samuel Neal Kent stood trial has been restored as a museum; records of his case now reside in the vault of the newer county building nearby. Across the street, the Army and Navy Y.M.C.A. is still open. Most facilities available during World War I have closed, however; few visitors occupy the sleeping rooms; and much of the building has been leased to social service agencies.

Gays still find Newport seductive. Some enjoy evenings along Cliff Walk, cruise the city beaches, or make contacts in Touro or Washington Parks. Others saunter up Prospect Hill where less than five minutes' walk from the spot where Arnold's operators once plotted entrapment, at number 28, one of the city's best known gay bar bids them welcome. Here the cultural descendants of Section A's victims gather: servants from Belleview Avenue, clerks and waiters in local businesses, hospital professionals, executives and artists, students and tourists. Haircuts identify some as sailors or soldiers. They are old and young and in-between, tall and short, thin and thick, black, white, occasionally Hispanic or Asian. In this warm setting old friends exchange news or report on their latest conquests. Newcomers eager to make acquaintances blend into the crowd. As an evening wears on, those present begin to pair off. Some drift onto the shadowy patio in search of privacy; others depart to spend a night or a lifetime together.

Ask anyone at 28 Prospect Hill about the history of gays in Newport, however, and you will discover that few remember that it was here nearly three quarters of a century ago where the United States government conducted the most extensive systematic persecution of gays in American history. Perhaps this generation is better off not realizing how their government treated those gay sailors and civilians. Or maybe the hazards of forgetting are greater than the pains of knowing.

While most Americans imagined that life in the Navy during world War I was, literally, as traditionally American as motherhood and apple pie, the activities of gay sailors and the interest of the government in entrapping them suggest profound changes in American society. Credit: *Leslie's Illustrated Weekly Magazine.*

As Presiding Bishop of the Episcopal Church in America, James DeWolfe Perry became one of the nation's best-known clergymen.
Credit: Copy by the author of a portrait in the offices of the Episcopal Diocese of Rhode Island, Providence.

The Army and Navy Y.M.C.A. in Newport is still a landmark on Washington Square, although much of the space has been rented to social service agencies, the upstairs rooms are seldom occupied, and the once-busy lobby stands vacant.

Credit: Photo by the author.

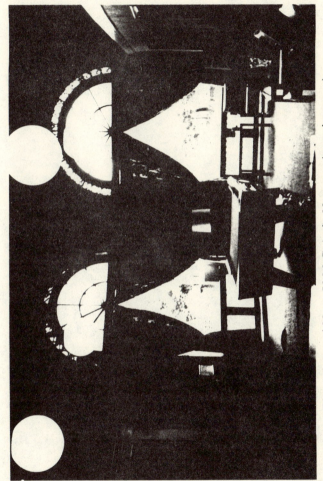

The Army and Navy Y.M.C.A. in Newport (upstairs room).
Credit: Photo by the author.

Notes

CHAPTER 1: "HALF THE WORLD IS QUEER"

1. William G. McLoughlin, *Rhode Island: A Bicentennial History* (New York: W. W. Norton & Company, 1978), 169-75. For photographs of the finest Newport mansions, see Henry-Russell Hitchcock, *Rhode Island Architecture* (New York: Da Capo Press, 1968), plates 56-63.
2. Thomas J. Williams, *Coasters Harbor Island and Newport Naval Training Station* (Newport: privately printed, 1937), 1-18. A copy is in the Rhode Island Historical Society, Providence; the ms. is in the Naval Historical Collection, Naval War College, Newport.
3. Cushing Stetson, "A School for Tars," *Harper's Weekly* 55: 1868 (December 9, 1911), 9.
4. *Providence Journal*, September 9, 1926. U.S. Senate, Committee on Naval Affairs, *Naval Investigation*, 66 Cong., 2d sess. (1921), II, 267-74. Williams, *Coasters Harbor Island*, 19-26.
5. W. G. Cassard, "The Churches and Welfare Societies of Newport," *Newport Recruit* 7: 1(February, 1919), 29-31. *Newport News*, October 24, 1918.
6. *Men of Our Navy in the Making* ([Newport: Y.M.C.A.], n.d.), 6 pp. *Y.M.C.A. for the Army and Navy in Newport R.I.* ([Newport: Y.M.C.A., 1916 (?)]), 11 pp; and *Safe Guarded: Men of Our Army and Navy at Home in Newport, R.I.* ([Newport: Y.M.C.A.], n.d.), 8 pp. Copies of these pamphlets are in the Rhode Island Historical Society, Providence. Also, Cassard, "Churches and Welfare Societies," 31.
7. *Providence Journal*, August 15, 16, 1919.
8. Cassard, "Churches and Welfare Societies," 31.
9. Josephus Daniels to Chief of the Bureau of Navigation, March 3, 1921, file 2628-32591:36, Daniels Papers, Library of Congress. For Daniels' crusade against alcohol consumption in the

navy, see his, *The Wilson Era: Years of Peace, 1910-1917* (Chapel Hill: University of North Carolina Press, 1944), 386-403.

10. Louis Glaser, "We Sail the Ocean Blue," *Newport Recruit* 6: 1 (August, 1918), 9-11; "Jack and the Beanstalk," *ibid*. 7: 5 (June, 1919), 17; Alfred Johnson, "Jack and the Beanstalk," *ibid*. 7: 6 (July, 1919), 17-22; and *Providence Journal*, May 26, 27, 1919.

11. Daniels to Chief of the Bureau of Navigation, March 3, 1921, file 2628-32591:36, Daniels papers.

12. *The Reservist* (Newport), March 20, 1918, 1; *Newport Mercury*, March 9, 23, 1918.

13. *Providence Journal*, November 22, 1918; April 22, 1919.

14. *Ibid*., November 24, December 1, 1918.

15. *Ibid*., March 5, 1920.

16. Transcript, *U.S. vs Samuel Neal Kent*, U.S. District Court, Providence, [hereinafter cited as U.S. vs Kent], R.G. 125, National Archives, 501-9, 519, 530. U.S. Senate, Committee on Naval Affairs, *Alleged Immoral Conditions at Newport (R.I.) Naval Training Station*, 67 Cong., 1 sess. (1921) [hereinafter cited as U.S. Senate, *Alleged Immoral Conditions*], 8, 15.

17. Arnold testimony, Transcript, Court of Inquiry presided over by Commander Murphy J. Foster [hereinafter cited as Transcript, Foster Inquiry], R. G. 125, National Archives, 2-38; Walter Smith testimony, 168. *Providence Journal*, March 5, April 17, 1920.

18. Transcript, Foster Inquiry, 3435.

19. *Ibid*., 2628, 3238.

20. U. S. Senate, *Alleged Immoral Conditions*, 15.

21. *Providence Journal*, March 14, April 2, 1920.

22. *Ibid*., April 1, 1920.

23. Wood to Foster, March 15, 1919, filed with Transcript, Foster Inquiry.

24. Transcript, Foster Inquiry, March 18, 20, 1919.

25. Foster to Commandant, First Naval District [Wood], March 20, 1919, appended to Transcript, Foster Inquiry.

26. *Providence Journal*, March 18, 20, May 21, 1920.

27. Roosevelt to Palmer, March 22, 1919, printed in *Providence Journal*, March 19, 1920.

28. Robert Murray, *Red Scare* (Minneapolis: University of Minnesota Press, 1955).

29. *Providence Journal*, March 5, 18, 1920.

CHAPTER 2: CLEANING UP THE NAVY

1. Transcript, Court of Inquiry Presided Over by Admiral Herbert O. Dunn, R.G. 125, National Archives [hereinafter cited as Transcript, Dunn Inquiry], 1400-02.

2. *Ibid.*, 1412-13.

3. *Ibid.*, 1401.

4. Transcript, U.S. vs. Kent, 3-4.

5. Commandant, First Naval District, to Arnold, March 18, 1919, Exhibit 80, Court of Inquiry Presided Over by Admiral Herbert O. Dunn, R. G. 125, National Archives, 772 [hereinafter cited in the form Dunn Inquiry, Ex. 80/772].

6. Dunn Inquiry, Exs. 165/1390, 171/1437.

7. *Ibid.*, Ex. 186/1564.

8. *Ibid.*, Ex. 167/1411.

9. *Ibid.*, Ex. 171/1488-9.

10. Transcript, Dunn Inquiry, 1411, 1517-8.

11. Dunn INquiry, Ex. 80/72.

12. *Ibid.*, Exs. 128-32/1291-5.

13. Arnold to Haynes (and all other operators), "Duties," *Ibid.*, Ex. 244/1308-9.

14. Transcript, Dunn Inquiry, 1519-20; oaths taken by men comprise Dunn Inquiry, Exs, 133-42/1296-1306.

15. Arnold testimony, Transcript, Dunn Inquiry 1428-9.

16. Dunn Inquiry, Exs. 163/1354, 191/1620.

17. *Ibid.*, 179/1508.

18. *Ibid.*, Ex. 187/1604.

19. Arnold to "President, Board of Investigation" (Foster, 20 March 1919, *Ibid.*, Ex. 160/1342.

20. *Ibid.*, Ex. 173/1461.

21. *Ibid.*, Ex. 165/1395.

22. *Ibid.*, Ex. 185/1551.

23. *Ibid.*, Ex. 168/1424.

24. Transcript, Dunn Inquiry, 1418, 1430, 1524.

25. *Ibid.*, 1525.

26. *Ibid.*, 1431-2.

27. Dunn Inquiry, Exs. 185/1553, 180/1518.

28. *Ibid.*, Ex. 177/1483-4.

29. *Ibid.*, Exs. 191/1623, 1616; 186/1567.

30. *Ibid.*, Ex. 174/1468.

31. *Ibid.*, Ex. 179-1512-3.
32. *Ibid.*, Ex. 173/1464-5.
33. *Ibid.*, Ex. 174/1469-70.
34. *Ibid.* Ex. 191/1639, 1632.
35. *Ibid.*, Ex. 185/1555-8.
36. *Ibid.*, Ex. 185/1557, 1559-60.
37. *Ibid.*, Ex. 168/1425.
38. *Ibid.*, Ex. 184/1550.
39. *Ibid.*, Ex. 165/1397.
40. *Ibid.*, Ex. 164/1368.
41. *Ibid.*, Ex. 164/1371.
42. Transcript, Foster Inquiry, 266-7.
43. Dunn Inquiry, Ex. 179/1515.

CHAPTER 3: NAVY JUSTICE

1. Transcript, Foster Inquiry, 2-6.
2. *Ibid.*, 7-16.
3. Dunn Inquiry, Ex. 167/1414.
4. *Ibid.*, Ex. 185/1562.
5. Transcript, Foster Inquiry, 17-21.
6. *Ibid.*, 21-31.
7. *Ibid.*, 32.
8. Dunn Inquiry, Ex. 171/1449.
9. Transcript, Foster Inquiry, 32-7.
10. *Ibid.*, 38-64.
11. *Ibid.*, 66-100.   •
12. Transcript, Dunn Inquiry, 1495, 1530.
13. Arrest dates are in Commanding Officer, Naval Training Station, to Commandant, First Naval District, July 10, R.G. 125, National Archives, Also see U.S. Senate, *Alleged Immoral Conditions*, 36-37.
14. Dunn Inquiry, 1530-31.
15. Transcript, Foster Inquiry, 105-122.
16. *Ibid.*, 122-27.
17. *Ibid.*, 127-67.
18. *Ibid.*, 173-82.
19. *Ibid.*, 182-237.
20. *Ibid.*, 239-41.
21. *Ibid.*, 242-68.
22. *Ibid.*, 268-324.

23. *Ibid.*, 324-34.
24. *Ibid.*, 335-61.
25. *Ibid.*, 361-7.
26. *Ibid.*, 367-74.
27. *Ibid.*, 375-81.
28. *Ibid.* 382-4.
29. *Ibid.*, 385-91.
30. *Ibid.*, 391-7.
31. *Ibid.*, 398-400.
32. *Ibid.*, 401-5.
33. *Ibid.*, 406-14.

34. Commanding Officer, Naval Training Station, Newport, R.I. [Campbell] to Commandant, First Naval District, Boston, Mass. [Dunn] July 21, 1919, and Commandant, First Naval District [Dunn] to Secretary of the Navy, July 23, 1919, File 26283-2591:3, Josephus Daniels Papers, Library of Congress [hereinafter cited in the form 26283-2591:3, Daniels Papers].

35. Commanding Officer, Naval Training Station, Newport R.I. [Campbell] to Commandant, First Naval District [Dunn], August 1, 1919, and Commandant, First Naval District [Dunn] to Secretary of the Navy, August 5, 1919, 26283-2591:4, Daniels Papers.

36. Secretary of the Navy to Chief of the Bureau of Navigation, August 21, 1919, 26283-2591:5, Daniels Papers.

37. Commanding Officer, Naval Training Station, Newport, R.I. [Campbell] to Secretary of the Navy (Judge Advocate General), October 7, 1919, 26283-2591:7, Daniels Papers.

38. Walsh to Bureau of Navigation (Attn. W. E. Barber), October 3, 1919, 26283-2591:6, Daniels Papers. Augusta Kreisberg to Calder, July 10, 1919, 26283-2591:2, Daniels Papers.

39. Thos. Washington to Judge Advocate General, October 22, 1919; Judge Advocate General to Chief of the Bureau of Navigation, November 6, 1919; Bureau of Navigation to Judge Advocate General, November 14, 1919; and Secretary of the Navy to Chief of the Bureau of Navigation, November 19, 1919, 26283-2591: 8-9, Daniels Papers.

40. "Memorandum for the Judge Advocate General Concerning the Newport Cases," June 14, 1921, 26283-2591: 55, Daniels Papers.

41. U.S. Senate *Alleged Immoral Conditions*, 36, 37.

CHAPTER 4: SECTION A., O.A.S.N.

1. Transcript, Dunn Inquiry, 2309.
2. *Ibid.*, 2309-10.
3. *Ibid.*, 1533, 1540, 1694, 2311.
4. *Ibid.*, 1534-5, 2311-2.
5. *Ibid.*, 1540-1, 2181, 1311-3.
6. Roosevelt to Chief of Naval Intelligence, May 5, 1919, Memo N-14 CBM, recorded in Transcript, Dunn Inquiry, 2257-8.
7. *Ibid.*, 2258-73.
8. *Ibid.*, 1623.
9. Rowe to Director of Naval Intelligence, May 19, 1919, Dunn Inquiry, Ex. 236/2163-9.
10. Transcript, Dunn Inquiry, 1632-3.
11. *Ibid.*, 1633-4.
12. *Ibid.*, 2319.
13. *Ibid.*, 1633-5.
14. Secretary of the Navy [F.D. Roosevelt, Acting] to Hudson, June 11, 1919, Dunn Inquiry, Ex. 206/2130.
15. Roosevelt "to whom it may concern," May 15, 1919, *Ibid.*, Ex. 201/2124. A similar letter for Arnold is Ex. 217/2143. Also Transcript, Dunn Inquiry, 2321.
16. *Ibid.*, 1637-8, 1699-1700.
17. Acting Secretary of the Navy [Roosevelt], to Bureau of Navigation, June 6, 1919, Dunn Inquiry, Ex. 200/2123; Roosevelt to Bureau of Navigation, June 20, October 13, 1919, Exs. 209/2133 and 213/2137.
18. Transcript, Dunn Inquiry, 1650-1.
19. *Ibid.*, 1645-7. Williams to "Dear Admiral" [Niblack], June 15, 1919, Dunn Inquiry, Ex. 237/2172.
20. "SecNav" to Hudson [telegram], June 14, 1919, *Ibid.*, Ex. 204/2127; Josephus Daniels to Secretary of the Treasury, Ex. 205/2128. Transcript, Dunn Inquiry, 1646-7.
21. Transcript, Dunn INquiry, 1656.
22. Dunn Inquiry, Ex. 191/1639.
23. *Ibid.*, Ex. 191/1643.
24. *Ibid.*, Ex. 191/1645-6.
25. *Ibid.*, Ex. 191/1651.
26. *Ibid.*, Ex. 191/1662.
27. *Ibid.*, Ex. 191/1689, 1691-3.
28. *Ibid.*, Ex. 186/1573-5.

29. *Ibid.*, Ex. 186/1579.
30. *Ibid.*, Ex. 186/1581.
31. *Ibid.*, Ex. 186/1584.
32. *Ibid.*, Ex. 178/1499.
33. Reports were read into Paul's testimony, Transcript, Dunn Inquiry, 1844.
34. *Ibid.*, 1846-7.
35. *Ibid.*, 1847-8.
36. *Ibid.*, 1848-9.
37. *Ibid.*, 1849.
38. Reports were read into McKinney's testimony, Transcript, Dunn Inquiry, 1951-2.
39. *Ibid.*, 1952.
40. *Ibid.*, 1953.
41. *Ibid.*, 1953-4.
42. Transcript, Dunn Inquiry, 1806-8.
43. *Ibid.*, 1808-10.
44. The report was read into Phillips' testimony, Transcript, Dunn Inquiry, 1828.
45. The report is in Minnick's testimony, *ibid.*, 1913.
46. *Ibid.*, 1914.
47. *Ibid.*, 1929-30.
48. The report was read into Scanland's testimony, Transcript, Dunn Inquiry, 1874-5.
49. *Ibid.*, 1875-6.
50. *Ibid.*, 1831.
51. *Ibid.*, 1735-7.
52. The report was read into Crawford's testimony, Transcript, Dunn Inquiry, 2005.
53. *Ibid.*, 2006.
54. *Ibid.*, 2007.
55. *Ibid.*, 2008-09.
56. Testimony of Rudy, *ibid.*, 1765-8 and Arnold, 1704-06.
57. Dunn Inquiry, Ex. 191/1694-1718.

CHAPTER 5: ON TRIAL IN NEWPORT AND WASHINGTON

1. Transcript, Dunn Inquiry, 1769.
2. Transcript, U.S. vs. Kent, 262, 288-9, 317-23, 361-2, 384.

3. *Ibid.*, 144-51.
4. *Ibid.*, 134-43, 283-6.
5. *Ibid.*, 293-6, 391.
6. *Ibid.*, 365-7, 392-9.
7. *Ibid.* 338-40, 345-8, 351-3, 400-5.
8. Dunn Inquiry, Ex. 191/1918-20.
9. Transcript, Dunn Inquiry, 348-66, 1708-9.
10. *Ibid.*, 1658-60, 1706-8, 2333.
11. *Ibid.*, 1665.
12. *Ibid.*, 1707-8.
13. *Ibid.*, 1659-62, 1706-7.
14. *Ibid.*, 2117.
15. *Ibid.*, 1928-71.
16. *Ibid.*, 1658.
17. *Newport News*, August 21, 25, 1919. Records, cases 28790 and 28794, District Court, Court House vault, Newport, R.I.
18. Transcript, Dunn Inquiry, 2333-4.
19. *Ibid.* 2358-9.
20. *Ibid.* 1542-4, 2360.
21. *Ibid.*, 866-84, 1554-6, 2367-9.
22. *Ibid.*, 1004, 1661-2.
23. *Ibid.*, 1662-5, 1711-3.
24. *Ibid.*, 2276-9; 2410-2.
25. *Ibid.*, 2284-6.
26. *Ibid.*, 1598-9, 2287-8, 2411-1, 1414-6.
27. *Ibid.*, 808-13, 1074-5.
28. Stewart to Cawley, September 25, 1919, Dunn Inquiry, Ex. 232/2160.
29. Section 13, U.S. Act of May 18, 1917, Transcript, U.S. vs. Kent, 535.
30. Transcript, Dunn Inquiry, 808.
31. *Ibid.*, 1715. Dunn Inquiry, Ex. 191/1932.
32. Dunn Inquiry, Ex. 191/1769-72.
33. *Ibid.*, Ex. 191/1787-8.
34. *Ibid.*
35. *Ibid.*, Ex. 191/1799-1801.
36. *Ibid.*, Ex. 191/1951, 1801.
37. *Ibid.*, Ex. 191/1799-1801.
38. *Ibid.*, Ex. 191/1808-11.
39. Transcript, Dunn Inquiry, 1811.

9. Transcript, Dunn Inquiry, 2426-48.

10. *Ibid.*, 2471-2506.

11. Because no copy of the court's final report has been located, other documents summarizing them provide the only available sources. In particular, see "Memorandum for the Judge Advocate General. Being a Brief resume of the Newport Courts of Inquiry," May 6, 1921. File 26283-2591:36, Daniels papers. U.S. Senate, *Alleged Immoral Conditions*, 33-4.

12. Judge Advocate, Newport Court of Inquiry [Hyneman] to Judge Advocate General, September 20, 1920, 26283-2591-33, Daniels papers; Hudson to Daniels, December 13, 1920, enclosed with Daniels to Roosevelt, December 24, 1920, Papers Pertaining to Family, Business and Personal Affairs, 1882-1945, Box 80, R. G. 14, Roosevelt Library, Hyde Park, NY [hereinafter cited in the form RFP, Box 80].

13. Hudson to Daniels, December 13, 1920, RFP, Box 80.

14. Daniels to Roosevelt, December 24, 1920, RFP, Box 80.

15. Roosevelt to Daniels, January 5, 1921, RFP, Box 80. Despite his recommendation that the resignation be rejected, FDR wrote Hudson, January 5, 1921, that he hoped "that some action will be taken on the resignation." *Ibid.*

16. Daniels to Roosevelt, January 7, 1921, RFP, Box 80.

17. Roosevelt to Daniels, January 15, 1921, RFP, Box 80.

18. Roosevelt to Daniels, January 21, 1921, RFP, Box 80.

19. Daniels to Roosevelt, January 22, 1921, RFP, Box 80.

20. Roosevelt to Daniels, February 2, 1921, RFP, Box 80.

21. Daniels to Roosevelt, February 12, 1921, RFP, Box 80.

22. Judge Advocate General to Chief, Bureau of Navigation, February 25, 1921, 26283-2591:36, Daniels papers.

23. Roosevelt to Daniels, March 1, 1921, RFP, Box 80.

24. Palmer to Daniels, March 3, 1921, RFP, Box 80.

25. Daniels to Roosevelt, March 4, 1921, RFP, Box 80.

26. "The Whole History," undated typescript with corrections in FDR's hand, "Navy Papers, Newport" folder, Louis M. Howe papers, Box 20, Roosevelt Library.

27. Daniels to Chief, Bureau of Navigation, March 3, 1921, 26283-2591:36, Daniels papers. U.S. Senate, *Alleged Immoral Conditions*, 34.

28. Press Release, Navy News Bureau, March 3, 1921, How Papers, Box 20, FDR Library.

CHAPTER 7: A NATIONAL GAY SCANDAL

1. Garrett D. Byrnes and Charles H. Spilman, *The Providence Journal: 150 Years* (Providence: The Providence Journal Company, 1981), 261-2.
2. *Ibid.*, 262-94.
3. Kenneth S. Davis, *F.D.R.: The Beckoning of Destiny, a History* (New York: G. P. Putnam's Sons, 1972), 597-601. Also Frank Friedel, *Franklin D. Roosevelt: The Ordeal* (Boston: Little Brown and Company, 1954), 46-7; and Ted Morgan, *FDR: A Biography* (New York: Simon and Schuster, 1985), 216-17.
4. Byrnes and Spilman, *Providence Journal,* 295. Donald Schewe to the author, February 3, 1981.
5. *Providence Journal*, January 9, 1920.
6. *Ibid.*
7. *Ibid.*, January 10, 1920.
8. *Ibid.*, January 11, 1920.
9. Cawley to Daniels, January 12, 1920, enclosed with Hudson to Daniels, January 22, 1920, 26283-2591:11, Daniels papers.
10. William Safford Jones et al. to Woodrow Wilson, January 10, 1920, 26283-2591:11, Daniels papers.
11. *Ibid.*; D. L. Dumond, *America in Our Time, 1896-1946* (New York: Henry Holt and Company, 1947), 273-4.
12. *Providence Journal* and *New York Times*, January 14, 1920. The latter dated the AP story the 13th.
13. Secretary of the Navy [Daniels] to Perry, January 17, 1920, file 26283-2591:11, Daniels papers.
14. *Providence Journal*, January 15, 1920.
15. Friedel, *Roosevelt*, 45. *New York Times*, February 14, 1939.
16. *Providence Journal*, January 21, 1920.
17. Printed in U.S. Senate, *Alleged Immoral Conditions*, 5, 7-13. *New York Times*, January 23, 1920.
18. *Providence Journal*, January 22, 1920. *New York Times*, January 23, 1920.
19. *Providence Journal* and *New York Times*, January 23, 1920.
20. *Ibid.*, January 21, 1920.
21. *National Cyclopedia of American Biography* (New York: James T. White Company, 1898-), 47: 466-77. *Providence Journal*, January 22, 25, 1920.
22. *Ibid.*, January 23, 1920.

23. *Ibid.*
24. *Ibid.*
25. *Ibid.*
26. *Ibid.*
27. *Ibid.*, January 25, 1920.

CHAPTER 8: DEFENDING THE RIGHT OF PETITION

1. Daniels to Dunn, Transcript, Dunn Inquiry, 1.
2. *Ibid.*, 1-3.
3. *Ibid.*, 4-11.
4. *Ibid.*, 12-55, *Providence Journal*, January 24, 25, 1920.
5. Transcript, Dunn Inquiry, 56-68. *Providence Journal*, January 27, 1920.
6. *Providence Journal*, February 4, 5, 1920. Transcript, Dunn Inquiry, 132-96.
7. *Ibid.*, 197-227.
8. *Ibid.*, 228-95.
9. *Ibid.*, 295-8.
10. *Ibid.*, 327-47.

CHAPTER 9: RHODE ISLAND VERSUS THE U.S. NAVY

1. Allan Nevins, *Hamilton Fish* (New York: Dodd Mead & Co., 1937), 82, 94. *Who Was Who in America: Vol. One, 1897-1942* (Chicago: A. N. Marquis, 1943), 1314. *New York Times*, May 11, 1951.
2. Minutes, Executive Committee, Newport Red Cross Chapter, November 2, 1917, Red Cross Office, Newport. *New York Times*, May 11, 1951.
3. Transcript, Dunn Inquiry, 367-464. *Providence Journal*, February 15, 1920.
4. *New York Times*, March 21, 1947.
5. Transcript, Dunn Inquiry, 465-547.
6. *Ibid.*, 561-688. *Providence Journal*, March 3, 4, 1920.
7. Transcript, Dunn Inquiry, 713-56; *Providence Journal*, March 5, 1920.
8. Transcript, Dunn Inquiry, 820-65. *Providence Journal*, March 12, 13, 1920.

CHAPTER 10: SECTION A ON TRIAL

1. Transcript, Dunn Inquiry, 866-94.
2. *Ibid.*, 895-921. *Providence Journal*, March 18, 1920.
3. Transcript, Dunn Inquiry, 1045-88.
4. *Ibid.*, 1121, 1237-42.
5. *Ibid.*, 1093-1109, 1122-48, 1201-36, 1248-56.
6. *Ibid.*, 1160-98, 1243-6. *Providence Journal*, March 30, 1920.
7. Transcript, Dunn Inquiry, 1345-72.
8. *Ibid.*, 1372-87. *Providence Journal*, April 7, 1920.
9. Transcript, Dunn Inquiry, 1388-1501. *Providence Journal*, April 8, 9, 1920.
10. *New York Times*, September 18, 1943.
11. Transcript, Dunn Inquiry, 1508-38, 1617-76. *Providence Journal*, April 10, 17, 18, 1920.
12. Transcript, Dunn Inquiry, 1691-4.
13. *Ibid.*, 1721-44, 1782-1804.
14. *Ibid.*, 1761-71.
15. *Ibid.*, 1805-34. *Providence Journal*, April 21, 1920.
16. Transcript, Dunn Inquiry, 1835-60.
17. *Ibid.*, 1892-1903.
18. *Ibid.*, 1928-71.
19. *Ibid.*, 1972-91.
20. *Ibid.*, 2109-38. *Providence Journal*, May 9, 1920.

CHAPTER 11: DEFENDING THE U.S. NAVY

1. Transcript, Dunn Inquiry, 2180-96, 2209-41.
2. *Ibid.*, 2256-85.
3. *Ibid.*, 2285-6.
4. *Ibid.*, 2286-98.
5. *Ibid.*, 2298-2301.
6. Davis, *F.D.R: The Beckoning of Destiny, passim.* Also Joseph P. Lash, *Eleanor and Franklin* (New York: W. W. Norton, 1971) and James Roosevelt, *My Parents: A Differing View* (Chicago: Playboy Press, 1976), 96-110. The best account of Roosevelt's role in the anti-gay scandal including this testimony is in Morgan, *FDR*, 234 ff.
7. Transcript, Dunn Inquiry, 2302-2407.
8. *Ibid.*, 2407-25. *Providence Journal*, May 23, 1920.

9. Transcript, Dunn Inquiry, 2426-48.

10. *Ibid.*, 2471-2506.

11. Because no copy of the court's final report has been located, other documents summarizing them provide the only available sources. In particular, see "Memorandum for the Judge Advocate General. Being a Brief resume of the Newport Courts of Inquiry," May 6, 1921. File 26283-2591:36, Daniels papers. U.S. Senate, *Alleged Immoral Conditions*, 33-4.

12. Judge Advocate, Newport Court of Inquiry [Hyneman] to Judge Advocate General, September 20, 1920, 26283-2591-33, Daniels papers; Hudson to Daniels, December 13, 1920, enclosed with Daniels to Roosevelt, December 24, 1920, Papers Pertaining to Family, Business and Personal Affairs, 1882-1945, Box 80, R. G. 14, Roosevelt Library, Hyde Park, NY [hereinafter cited in the form RFP, Box 80].

13. Hudson to Daniels, December 13, 1920, RFP, Box 80.

14. Daniels to Roosevelt, December 24, 1920, RFP, Box 80.

15. Roosevelt to Daniels, January 5, 1921, RFP, Box 80. Despite his recommendation that the resignation be rejected, FDR wrote Hudson, January 5, 1921, that he hoped "that some action will be taken on the resignation." *Ibid.*

16. Daniels to Roosevelt, January 7, 1921, RFP, Box 80.

17. Roosevelt to Daniels, January 15, 1921, RFP, Box 80.

18. Roosevelt to Daniels, January 21, 1921, RFP, Box 80.

19. Daniels to Roosevelt, January 22, 1921, RFP, Box 80.

20. Roosevelt to Daniels, February 2, 1921, RFP, Box 80.

21. Daniels to Roosevelt, February 12, 1921, RFP, Box 80.

22. Judge Advocate General to Chief, Bureau of Navigation, February 25, 1921, 26283-2591:36, Daniels papers.

23. Roosevelt to Daniels, March 1, 1921, RFP, Box 80.

24. Palmer to Daniels, March 3, 1921, RFP, Box 80.

25. Daniels to Roosevelt, March 4, 1921, RFP, Box 80.

26. "The Whole History," undated typescript with corrections in FDR's hand, "Navy Papers, Newport" folder, Louis M. Howe papers, Box 20, Roosevelt Library.

27. Daniels to Chief, Bureau of Navigation, March 3, 1921, 26283-2591:36, Daniels papers. U.S. Senate, *Alleged Immoral Conditions*, 34.

28. Press Release, Navy News Bureau, March 3, 1921, How Papers, Box 20, FDR Library.

29. Hyneman to Judge Advocate General, August 6, 1921, 26283-2591:53, Daniels papers.

CHAPTER 12: BEFORE THE SENATE OF THE UNITED STATES

1. *Providence Journal*, January 25, 26, 1920.
2. Roosevelt to Page, July 19, 1921, RFP, Box 80.
3. *Providence Journal*, March 3, 1920.
4. *Ibid.*, April 14, 1920.
5. *Ibid.*, August 7, 10, 11, 12, 13, 1920.
6. *Ibid.*, April 14, August 15, 1920.
7. *Ibid.*, August 17, 18, 1920.
8. *Ibid.*, August 12, 1920.
9. Byrnes and Spilman, *Providence Journal*, 295-6.
10. Roosevelt to Caffey, October 24, 1920, RFP, Box 81.
11. Caffey to Roosevelt, October 25, November 5, 1920, RFP, Box 81.
12. Roosevelt, "Notice to Editors," October 24, 1920, RFP, Box 81.
13. Krock to Roosevelt, December 22, 1920, RFP, Box 81.
14. *Providence Journal*, October 27, 28, 29, 1920. A copy of the suit is in RFP, Box 81.
15. *Providence Journal*, October 29, 30, 1920.
16. U.S. Bureau of the Census, *Historical Statistics of the United States, Colonial Times to 1957* (Washington, D.C.: Government Printing Office, 1960), 687.
17. Roosevelt to McCarthy, February 10, 1921, RFP, Box 81.
18. Copies of legal documents are in RFP, Box 81. Also see Supreme Court County of New York. Franklin D. Roosevelt, Plaintiff, against John R. Rathom, Scott C. Bone and Edward B. Clark. Defendants. *Answer of Defendant John R. Rathom*. New York: n.p., [1921], a copy of which is in RFP, Box 82.
19. Krock to Roosevelt, December 22, 1920, and Roosevelt to Krock, January 7, 1921, RFP, Box 81.
20. Roosevelt to Shearn, March 11, 1921, RFP, Box 81.
21. McCarthy to Roosevelt, March 7, April 16, April 20, 1921, RFP, Box 81.
22. Morgan, *FDR*, 219.
23. Quotes from official records are in McCarthy to Roosevelt, April 20, 1921, RFP, Box 81.

24. *Ibid.*

25. Byrnes and Spilman, *Providence Journal*, 298.

26. McCarthy to Roosevelt, April 20, 1921, RFP, Box 81.

27. *Providence Journal*, February 21, 1921.

28. Howe to Roosevelt (telegram), July 13-14, 1921, RFP, Box 80.

29. Daniels to Roosevelt (telegram), July 12 13 [*sic*], 1921, July 14, 16, 1921; Daniels to Britton, July 14, 1921; Roosevelt to Daniels, July 14, 1921, all RFP, Box 80.

30. Ball to Roosevelt, July 14, 1921; King to Roosevelt, July 15, 1921, RFP, Box 80.

31. Roosevelt to Page, July 19, 1921, RFP, Box 80.

32. *Ibid.*

33. Elliott Roosevelt, ed. *F.D.R.: His Personal Letters* (New York: Duell, Sloan, and Pearce, 1948), 517-8.

34. [Roosevelt], manuscript notes for U.S. Senate subcommittee presentation, n.d., RFP, Box 80.

35. U.S. Senate, *Alleged Immoral Conditions*, 1-7.

36. *Ibid.*, 7-14.

37. *Ibid.*, 14-36.

38. Howe to Roosevelt, July 13-14, 1921, RFP, Box 80.

39. "Statement and Preliminary Minority Report," and Daniels to Roosevelt, July 27, 1921, RFP, Box 80.

40. "Statement and Preliminary Minority Report," RFP, Box 80.

41. See, for example, *The Washington Post, New York Times*, and *Chicago Tribune*, July 20, 21, 1921.

42. *Providence Journal*, July 20, 1921. Roosevelt's statement is also reprinted in E. Roosevelt, *F.D.R.: His Personal Letters*, 519-22.

43. Roosevelt to Page, July 19, 1921, RFP, Box 80.

44. Roosevelt to Keyes, July 21, 1921, RFP, Box 80. The letter is also quoted in Morgan, *FDR*, 245.

45. E. Roosevelt, *F.D.R.*, 523 ff.

46. The copy provided me by the Roosevelt Library did not include the envelope. It is quoted in Morgan, *FDR*, 245.

47. Roosevelt to Daniels, July 29, 1921, RFP, Box 80.

48. Daniels to Roosevelt, July 27, 1921, RFP, Box 80.

49. Daniels, *The Wilson Era*, 199-200.

50. J. A. Carey to Latimer, September 30, 1921, 26283-2591:52, Daniels papers, Library of Congress.

51. Denby to Ball, December 24, 1921, 26283-2591:52, Daniels papers.

CHAPTER 13: LEGACIES

1. Vern L. Bullough, *Homosexuality: A History* (New York: New American Library, 1979) summarizes existing historical knowledge and concludes that homosexuality "does exist, and as far as history can tell us, it has always existed."(2)

2. John D'Emlio, *Sexual Politics, Sexual Communities: The Making of a Homosexual Minority in the United States, 1940-1970* (Chicago: University of Chicago Press, 1983), esp. 11-12.

3. A singular autobiographical document is Edward I. P. Stevenson's *The Intersexes: A History of Similisexualism as a Problem in Social Life* published in Rome, Italy, in 1908 under the pseudonym Xavier Mayne. It is available in reprint form from New York: Arno Press, 1975. Vern L. Bullough, *Sexual Variance in Society and History* (Chicago: University of Chicago Press, 1967), 587 ff. provides an outline of nineteenth-century gay life in America. Readers may also anticipate a detailed exploration of the growth of a gay consciousness in New York City through the forthcoming work of George Chauncey, Jr. Peter Gay's on-going study of nineteenth century sexuality in the western world may also prove helpful, although the first volume (*The Bourgeois Experience, Victoria to Freud. Volume I. Education of the Senses.* New York: Oxford University Press, 1984) focuses entirely on heterosexuality and the second (*The Tender Passion.* New York: Oxford University Press, 1986) deals with homosexuality among "problematic attachments." For a European-based study that might be emulated by American historians, see Louis Crompton, *Byron and Greek Love: Homophobia in 19th Century England* (Berkeley: University of California Press, 1985).

4. Gregory Sprague, "The Historical Transformation of the Urban Gay Subcultures into an American Gay Culture," paper delivered at Discovery '82/GAU 8 Conference, Chicago, Illinois, October 9, 1982. Also see Sprague's "Male Homosexuality in Western Culture: The Dilemma of Identity and Subculture in Historical Research," *Journal of Homosexuality*, 10:3/4 (Winter 1984), 29-44. Less well developed are John Alan Lee, "The Gay Connection," *Urban Life* 8 (July 1979): 175-98, and G. Edward Stephen and Douglas R. McMullen, "Tolerance of Sexual Conformity: City

Size as a Situational and Early Learning Determinant," *American Sociological Review* 47 (June 1982): 411-15.

5. D'Emilio, *Sexual Politics*, 23-40. Alan Berube, "Coming Out Under Fire," *Mother Jones*, February-March 1983, 24-49, 45.

6. Lawrence R. Murphy, "The Enemy Among Us: Venereal Disease Among Union Soldiers in the Far West, 1861-1865," *Civil War History*, 31:3 (September 1985), 257-69 resulted when my own attempts to uncover homosexual behavior during the Civil War revealed the extent to which venereal disease plagued Union troops in the West.

7. Vern L. Bullough, "Homosexuality and the Medical Model," reprinted in Vern L. Bullough, *Sex, Society and History* (New York: Science History Publications, 1976), 161-72.

8. For convenient excerpts, see Johnathan Katz, *Gay American History: Lesbians and Gay Men in the U.S.A.* (New York: Thomas Y. Crowell Company, 1976), and Katz', *Gay/Lesbian Almanac: A New Documentary* (New York: Harper and Row, 1983). Examples of contemporary thinking are A. A. Brill, "The Conception of Homosexuality," *Journal of the American Medical Association*, 61 (1913): 335-40, and J. A. Gilbert, "Homosexuality and Its Treatment," *Journal of Nervous and Mental Diseases* 52 (1920); 297-332.

9. Transcript, Dunn Inquiry, 1508-38, 1617-56.

10. David J. Pivar, *Purity Crusade: Sexual Morality and Social Control, 1868-1900* (Westport, Connecticut: Greenwood Press, 1973). Also Allan M. Brandt, *No Magic Bullet: A Social History of Venereal Disease in the United States Since 1880* (New York: Oxford University Press, 1985).

11. For further insight, see Earl Lind, *Autobiography of an Androgyne* (New York: The Medico-Legal Journal, 1918).

12. No comprehensive analysis of the attitudes of nineteenth-century sex manuals toward homosexuality exists, although my own collection of materials aims toward such a study. In the meantime, John S. Haller and Robin M. Heller, *The Physician and Sexuality in Victorian America* (Urbana: University of Illinois Press, 1974), G. J. Barker-Benfield, *The Horrors of the Half-Known Life: Male Attitudes Toward Women and Sexuality in Nineteenth Century America* (New York: Harper and Row, 1976), and Phillip A. Gibbs, "Self Control and Male Sexuality in the Advice Literature of Nineteenth Century America, 1830-1860," *Journal of American*

Culture, 9:2 (Summer 1986), 37-41 suggest the important role of this literature in influencing popular attitudes.

13. John P. De Cecco, *Homophobia: An Overview* (New York: The Haworth Press, 1984) collects recent thoughts on the subject.

14. Katz, *Gay American History* and *Gay/Lesbian Almanac* reprints excerpts from many articles prescribing "treatment."

15. C. A. Tripp, *The Homosexual Matrix* (New York: McGraw Hill Book Company, 1975), 215-6. James MacGregor Burns, *Roosevelt: The Soldier of Freedom* (New York: Harcourt Brace Jovanovich, Inc., 1970), 350. C. A. Tripp to the author, October 4, 1982.

16. George Chauncey, Jr., "Christian Brotherhood or Sexual Perversion? Homosexual Identities and the Construction of Sexual Boundaries in the World War One Era," *Journal of Social History*, 19 (Winter 1985), 189-211. The quotation is from 199.

17. See, for example, Edward M. Coffman, *The Old Army; A Portrait of the American in Peacetime, 1784-1898* (New York: Oxford University Press, 1986).

18. Daniel Boorstin, *The Americans: The Democratic Experience*. (New York: Random House, 1973), 402 ff.

19. Elaine A. Smith to the author, November 10, 1981.

20. Martha C. Zipf to the author, July 28, 1982.

21. *New York Times*, September 18, 1943.

22. George Walter, *Kidnap: The Story of the Lindbergh Case* (New York: The Dial Press, 1961), 452-3.

23. *New York Times*, September 18, 1943.

24. Visit by the author to Trinity Episcopal Church, Newport, August, 1982.

25. *New York Times*, September 27, 1939; May 11, 1951.

26. *New York Times*, March 21, 1947.

27. The Rev. John F. Maher, Jr., Rector, St. Mary's Episcopal Church, to the author, November 4, 1982.

28. *The Living Church*, November 28, 1943, 21-2.

29. *Ibid.*; "Travel Talks," *Common Speech* 4, no. 1 (March-April 1932); 4-5; "Namesake Towns Development," *ibid.* 4, no. 2 (May-June 1932): 6; "Review and Advance," *ibid.* 5, no. 4 (Fourth Quarter, 1933): 12.

30. *The Living Church*, November 28, 1942, 21-22; *Stowe's Clerical Directory of the Protestant Episcopal Church in the United States of America, 1941* (New York: Church Hymnal Corp., 1941), 155.

31. Tripp to the author, October 4, 1982.

32. Morgan, *FDR* broke with the long-standing tradition of downplaying the Newport incident by devoting an entire chapter to the subject.

33. William C. Menninger, *Psychiatry in a Troubled World: Yesterday's War and Today's Challenge* (New York: Macmillan, 1948), 225-30.

34. Alan Berube, "Lesbian and Gay GIs in World War II," *The Advocate*, 328 (October 15, 1981): 20-1; also see his, "Coming Out Under Fire," *Mother Jones*, February-March 1983, 24-9, 45; and John Costello, *Virtue Under Fire: How World War II Changed Our Social and Sexual Attitudes* (Boston: Little, Brown and Company, 1985).

35. Berube, "Coming Out," Colin J. Williams and Martin S. Weinberg, *Homosexuals and the Military* (New York: Harper & Row, 1971), 26.

36. Menninger, *Psychiatry*, 225. Berube, "Lesbian and Gay GIs," 21-4; D'Emilio, *Sexual Politics*, 31-33.

37. Williams and Weinberg, *Homosexuals*, 32-3.

38. Tripp, *Homosexual Matrix*, 217.

39. Walsh to Bureau of Navigation, Navy Department, October 3, 1929, 26283-2591: 53, Daniels papers.

40. Lawrence R. Murphy, "The House on Pacific Street," *Journal of Homosexuality*, 12: 1 (Fall 1985), 27-50.

41. Williams and Weinberg, *Homosexuals*, 27, 48-9.

42. Tripp, *Homosexual Matrix*, 222-3. Also Arthur H. Gilbert, "Buggery and the British Navy, 1700-1861," *Journal of Social History* 10 (Fall 1976): 72-98, and "The 'Africaine' Courts-Martial: A Study of Buggery in the Royal Navy," *Journal of Homosexuality* (1974): 111-32; B. R. Burg, *Sodomy and the Perception of Evil: English Sea Rovers in the Seventeenth-Century Caribbean.* (New York: New York University Press, 1983); and Walter L. Williams, *The Spirit and the Flesh: Sexual Diversity in American Indian Culture.* (Boston: Beacon Press, 1986), 152 ff.

43. Tripp, *Homosexual Matrix*, 223.

44. E. Lawrence Gibson, *Get Off My Ship: Ensign Berg vs. The U.S. Navy* (New York: Avon Books, 1978).

45. For an impassioned defense by a man arrested under such circumstances, see Edward Eugene Baskett, *Entrapped: An Accused Homosexual Looks at American Justice* (Westport, Conn.: Lawrence Hill & Company, 1976).

46. John Gerasi, *The Boys of Boise* (New York: Collier, 1968), is a detailed analysis. Also see Tripp, *Homosexual Matrix*, 204-7, and Katz, *Gay American History*, 109-19.

47. *Ibid.*, 582-3.

48. "Mitzel," *The Boston Sex Scandal* (Boston: Glad Day Books, 1980).

Bibliography

Manuscript Materials

Daniels, Josephus, papers. Container 464, file 2628-32591. Library of Congress.

Howe, Louis M., papers. "Navy Papers, Newport" folder, Franklin D. Roosevelt Library, Hyde Park, N.Y.

Maher, Rev. John F., Jr., Letter to the author, November 4, 1982. Author's collection.

Newport District Court, Records, cases 28790 and 28794, Court House, Newport, Rhode Island.

Newport Red Cross chapter, Minutes, Executive Committee, Red Cross office, Newport, Rhode Island.

Roosevelt, Franklin D. Papers Pertaining to Family, Business, and Personal Affairs, 1882-1945. R. G. 14. Franklin D. Roosevelt Library, Hyde Park, N.Y.

Schewe, Donald B. Letter to the author, February 3, 1981. Author's collection.

Smith, Elaine A. Letter to the author, November 10, 1981. Author's collection.

Sprague, Gregory. "The Historical Transformation of the Urban Gay Subcultures into an American Gay Culture." Paper delivered at Discovery '82/GAU 8 Conference, Chicago, Illinois, October 9, 1982.

Transcript and Exhibits, Court of Inquiry Presided over by Admiral Herbert O. Dunn, R. G. 125, National Archives, Washington, D.C.

Transcript, Court of Inquiry Presided over by Commander Murphy J. Foster, R. G. 125, National Archives, Washington, D.C.

Transcript, *U.S. versus Samuel Neal Kent*, R.G. 125, National Archives, Washington, D.C.

Tripp, C. A. Letter to the author, October 4, 1982. Author's collection.

Zipf, Martha C. Letter to the author, July 28, 1982. Author's collection.

Newspapers

Chicago Tribune, 1919-21.
Newport Herald, 1917-20.
Newport Mercury, 1918-21.
Newport News, 1918-20.
New York Times, 1918-51.
Providence Journal, 1917-26.
The Reservist (Newport), 1918-19.
The Washington Post, 1920-21.

Government Documents

Library of Congress, Manuscript Division, Research Department. *Josephus Daniels: A Register of His Papers in the Library of Congress*. Washington, D.C.: Library of Congress, 1976.
U.S. Bureau of the Census. *Historical Statistics of the United States, Colonial Times to 1957*. Washington, D.C.: Government Printing Office, 1960.
U.S. Senate, Committee on Naval Affairs. *Alleged Immoral Conditions at Newport (R.I.) Naval Training Station*. 67 Cong., 1 sess., 1921.
U.S. Senate, Committee on Naval Affairs. *Naval Investigation*. 2 vols., 66 Cong., 2d sess., 1921.

Articles

Berube, Alan. "Coming Out Under Fire," *Mother Jones* February-March 1983, 24-9, 45.
_____. "Lesbian and Gay GIs in World War II," *The Advocate* No. 328 (October 15, 1981): 20-1.
Brill, A. A. "The Conception of Homosexuality," *Journal of the American Medical Association* 61 (1913): 335-40.
Cassard, W. G. "The Churches and Welfare Societies of Newport," *Newport Recruit* 7 (February, 1919): 29-31.
Chauncey, George, Jr. "Christian Brotherhood or Sexual Perver-

sion? Homosexual Identities and the Construction of Sexual Boundaries in the World War One Era," *Journal of Social History*, 19 (Winter 1985): 189-211.

"Deaths," *The Living Church*, November 28, 1942, 21-22.

Gibbs, Phillip A. "Self-Control and Male Sexuality in the Advice Literature of Nineteenth Century America, 1830-1860," *Journal of American Culture*, 9 (Summer 1986): 37-41.

Gilbert, Arthur H. "Buggery in the British Navy, 1700-1861," *Journal of Social History* 10 (1976): 72-98.

_____ "The 'Africaine' Courts-Martial: A Study of Buggery in the Royal Navy," *Journal of Homosexuality* 1 (1974): 111-32.

Gilbert, J. A. "Homosexuality and Its Treatment," *Journal of Nervous and Mental Diseases* 52 (1920): 297-332.

Glaser, Louis, "We Sail the Ocean Blue," *Newport Recruit* 6 (August, 1918): 9-11.

"Jack and the Beanstalk," *Newport Recruit* 7 (June, 1919): 17.

Johnson, Alfred. "Jack And the Beanstalk," *Newport Recruit* 7 (July, 1919): 17-22.

Lee, John Alan. "The Gay Connection," *Urban Life* 8 (1979): 175-98.

Murphy, Lawrence R. "The House on Pacific Street," *Journal of Homosexuality*, 12 (Fall 1985): 27-50.

_____. "The Enemy Among Us: Venereal Disease Among Union Soldiers in the Far West, 1861-1865," *Civil War History*, 31 (September 1985): 257-69.

"Namesake Towns Development," *Common Speech* 4 7(May-June, 1932): 6.

"Review and Advance," *Common Speech* 5 (1933): 12-3.

Sprague, Gregory. "Male Homosexuality in Western Culture: The Dilemma of Identity and Subculture in Historical Research," *Journal of Homosexuality*, 10 (Winter 1984): 29-44.

Stephen, G. Edward and McMullen, Douglas R. "Tolerance of Sexual Conformity: City Size as a Situational and Early Learning Determinant," *American Sociological Review* 47 (1982): 164-80.

Stetson, Cushing. "A School for Tars," *Harper's Weekly* 55 (December 9, 1911): 9.

"The Torpedo Station and the War," *Newport Recruit* 7 (May, 1919): 5-9.

"Travel Talks," *Common Speech*, 4 (March-April 1932): 4-5.

Books and Pamphlets

Barker-Benfield, G. J. *The Horrors of the Half-Known Life: Male Attitudes Toward Women and Sexuality in Nineteenth Century America.* New York: Harper and Row, 1976.

Baskett, Edward Eugene. *Entrapped: An Accused Homosexual Looks at American Justice.* Westport, Conn.: Lawrence Hill & Company, 1976.

Boorstin, Daniel. *The Americans: The Democratic Experience.* New York: Random House, 1973.

Brandt, Allan M. *No Magic Bullet: A Social History of Venereal Disease in the United States Since 1880.* New York: Oxford University Press, 1985.

Bullough, Vern L. *Homosexuality: A History.* New York: New American Library, 1979.

———. *Sex, Society and History.* New York: Science History Publications, 1976.

———. *Sexual Variance in Society and History.* Chicago: University of Chicago Press, 1967.

Burg, B. R. *Sodomy and the Perception of Evil: English Sea Rovers in the Seventeenth-Century Caribbean.* New York: New York University Press, 1983.

Burns, James MacGregor. *Roosevelt: The Soldier of Freedom.* New York: Harcourt Brace Jovanovich, Inc., 1970.

Byrnes, Garrett D. and Spilman, Charles H. *The Providence Journal: 150 Years.* Providence: The Providence Journal Company, 1981.

Coffman, Edward M. *The Old Army: A Portrait of the American Army in Peacetime, 1784-1898.* New York: Oxford University Press, 1986.

Costello, John. *Virtue Under Fire: How World War II Changed our Social and Sexual Attitudes.* Boston: Little, Brown and Company, 1985.

Crompton, Louis. *Byron and Greek Love: Homophobia in 19th Century England.* Berkeley: University of California Press, 1985.

Cronon, E. David, ed. *The Cabinet Diaries of Josephus Daniels, 1913-1921.* Lincoln: University of Nebraska Press, 1963.

Daniels, Josephus. *The Wilson Era: Years of Peace, 1910-1917.* Chapel Hill: University of North Carolina Press, 1944.

Davis, Kenneth S. *F.D.R.: The Beckoning of Destiny, A History.* New York: G. P. Putnam's Sons, 1972.

De Cecco, John, Ed. *Homophobia: An Overview*. New York: The Haworth Press, 1984.

D'Emilio, John. *Sexual Politics, Sexual Communities: The Making of a Homosexual Minority in the United States, 1940-1970*. Chicago: University of Chicago Press, 1983.

Dumond, Dwight L. *America in Our Time, 1896-1946*. New York: Henry Holt and Company, 1947.

Friedel, Frank. *Franklin D. Roosevelt: The Ordeal*. Boston: Little Brown and Company, 1954.

Gay, Peter. *The Bourgeois Experience, Victoria to Freud. Volume I. Education of the Senses*. New York: Oxford University Press, 1984.

_____. *The Bourgeois Experience, Victoria to Freud. Volume II. The Tender Passion*. New York: Oxford University Press, 1986.

Gerasi, John. *The Boys of Boise*. New York: Collier, 1968.

Gibson, E. Lawrence. *Get Off My Ship: Ensign Berg vs. The U.S. Navy*. New York: Avon Books, 1978.

Heller, John S. and Robin M. Heller. *The Physician and Sexuality in Victorian America*. Urbana: University of Illinois Press, 1974.

History of the Emmanuel Church. [Newport, R.I.: Emmanuel Church, n.d.].

Hitchcock, Henry Russell. *Rhode Island Architecture*. New York: Da Capo Press, 1968.

Katz, Johnathan. *Gay American History: Lesbians and Gay Men in the U.S.A.* New York: Thomas Y. Crowell Company, 1976.

_____. *Gay/Lesbian Almanac: A New Documentary*. New York: Harper and Row, 1983.

Lash, Joseph P. *Eleanor and Franklin*. New York: W. W. Norton, 1971.

Lind, Earl. *Autobiography of an Androgyne*. New York: The Medico-Legal Journal, 1918.

McLoughlin, William G. *Rhode Island: A Bicentennial History*. New York: W. W. Norton & Company, 1978.

Menninger, William C. *Psychiatry in a Troubled World: Yesterday's War and Today's Challenge*. New York: Macmillan, 1948.

Men of Our Navy in the Making. [Newport: Y.M.C.A., n.d.].

"Mitzel." *The Boston Sex Scandal*. Boston: Glad Day Books, 1980.

Morgan, Ted. *FDR: A Biography*. New York: Simon and Schuster, 1985.

Murray, Robert. *Red Scare*. Minneapolis: University of Minnesota Press, 1955.

National Cyclopedia of American Biography. New York: James T. White Company, 1898- .

Nevins, Allan. *Hamilton Fish*. New York: Dodd Mead & Co., 1937.

Pivar, David J. *Purity Crusade: Sexual Morality and Social Control, 1868-1900*. Westport, Connecticut: Greenwood Press, 1973.

Roosevelt, Elliott and Brough, James. *An Untold Story: The Roosevelts of Hyde Park*. New York: G. P. Putnam's Sons, 1973.

Roosevelt, Elliott, Ed. *F.D.R.: His Personal Letters*. New York: Duell, Sloan, and Pearce, 1948.

Roosevelt, James. *My Parents: A Differing View*. Chicago: Playboy Press, 1976.

Safe Guarded: Men of Our Army and Navy at Home in Newport, R.I., [Newport: Y.M.C.A., n.d.].

Stevenson, Edward I. P. [pseud. Xavier Mayne]. *The Intersexes: A History of Similisexualism as a Problem in Social Life*. Rome, Italy: n.p., 1908; repr. New York: Arno Press, 1973.

Supreme Court of New York. Franklin D. Roosevelt, Plaintiff, against John R. Rathom, Scott C. Bone and Edward B. Clark, Defendants. *Answer of Defendant John R. Rathom*. New York: n.p., [1921].

Tripp, C. A. *The Homosexual Matrix*. New York: McGraw Hill Book Company, 1975.

Stowe's Clerical Directory, 1941.

Weisberg, Elizabeth. *A Historical Sketch of the Newport County Chapter American Red Cross*. Newport: American Red Cross, 1981.

Williams, Colin J. and Weinberg, Martin S. *Homosexuals and the Military*. New York: Harper & Row, 1971.

Williams, Thomas J. *Coasters Harbor Island and Newport Naval Training Station*. Newport: privately printed, 1937.

Williams, Walter L. *The Spirit and the Flesh: Sexual Diversity in American Indian Culture*. Boston: Beacon Press, 1986.

Who Was Who in America: Vol. One, 1897-1942. Chicago: A. N. Marquis, 1943.

Y.M.C.A. for the Army and Navy in Newport R.I. [Newport: Y.M.C.A., 1917(?)].

Index

Acquired immune deficiency syndrome
(AIDS) 298
Administrative boards 293-294
Alcohol use, by naval personnel 8,11
Navy's control of 9
Navy's investigation of 82,84-85,219
Ames, Marion 115
Andrews, Edwin 138
Anti-homosexual investigation by U.S.
Navy
alcohol use investigation 82,84-85,219
arrest of suspects 46-47
civilian detectives 72-73
of civilians 69-71,81-84,85-91,220,221
clergy's condemnation of 104,106-108,
116,117,138,145,156-159,160-162,
170-183,190-193,199,268
courts of inquiry regarding. *See* Dunn
Court of Inquiry; Foster Court of
Inquiry
drug use investigation 25-26,27,28,30,
31-32,35,43
expansion of 69-91
goals 24-25
historical context of 283-289
initial stages 10-14
Office of Naval Intelligence involvement
71-72,73,74. *See also* Section A
offices 29-30
official authorization of 14,16
revocation of 47,66,202,203-207,
212-213,252
operators 13
code numbers 26
duties 24-26,105-106
legal status 30
proposed prosecution of 242,243,245,
246-247
qualifications 21-22
recruitment 21-22,24
reimbursement 30

reports 24-25
rules regarding 24-26
organization 105
Senate investigation regarding. *See*
Senate Naval Affairs Committee
Anti-vice campaigns 285
Army and Navy Journal 255
Arnold, Ervin
as anti-homosexual investigation operator
21-36,70,75,76,89,90,97
arrests of suspects 46,47,194-195
criticism of 72
anti-homosexual squad creation by 10-14
attitudes towards homosexuals 10,286
Dunn Court of Inquiry and 206
testimony before 209-210
testimony regarding 202,203,204,206,
207,227-228,229,233
evidence withheld by 17
Foster Court of Inquiry and 15
Court's recommendation of 61
testimony before 40,42,43,48,55,
56-57
identification of homosexuals by 10,160,
180
Samuel Neal Kent and 106,107
arrest of Kent 111,112,113-114,115,
116
testimony regarding 123,124,128,129,
134,135,136,138,146,148,149
letter of censure regarding 246,249
Naval Intelligence oath taken by 75
Senate Naval Affairs Committee and
criticism by 263,265-266,268
testimony 253,254
Art Association, Newport, Rhode Island 7,
45,48
Assistant Secretary of the Navy. *See*
Roosevelt, Franklin D.

Baker, Darius 138,143,175,234
Baker, Harvey 155,156